ROADSIDE- ONE MAN'S LOOK AT THE AFTERLIFE

ROADSIDE- ONE MAN'S LOOK AT THE AFTERLIFE

SCOTT MOSS

swm publishing

Contents

To my beautiful wife Eileen

I

Roadside

Roadside
by
Scott Moss
Dedication
I would like to dedicate this book to my
Strength in life
My wife Eileen

Edited by
Pamela Borvan
All Rights Reserved

By Scott Moss
Chapter 1

At this moment I'm not sure why I'm writing all of this down. I'm pretty sure no one in their right mind, or even not-so-right mind, will believe anything I say. This so-called adventure, or nightmare, depending on how you look at it, it began on December 4th, 1999.

I have worked for the Illinois Department of Transportation for 22 years. Not much of a job, but it pays the bills. Slowly working my way up the ladder, I became a supervisor in 1996. My crew is responsible for general maintenance and street illumination (a fancy word the CEO made up for lights). We use cherry pickers to change light bulbs, replace light poles that have been trashed in the latest drunk driving incident, and occasionally help with installation. I know what you're thinking: How can he handle all that excitement? Most days are, at best, boring.

Waking up on December 4th of 1999 was no different than any other day. The routine was the same: shave, shower, brush the choppers, you know the basics. My bride and I have been married for 17 years, and every morning I spend a couple of moments just staring at her.

Eileen still is a beautiful girl. She's all of 5'2" and 110 pounds. Her brown hair is shorter than the day I met her and even though it's the same color it was then, I know she has a little help maintaining that shade. Eileen has become the poster child for aging with grace. She still gets looks from guys 15 years her junior. Although this should bother me, I actually get a kick out of it. After all, I get to go home with her. Her quick wit and laugh are what convinced me that a lifetime with her was the best gift I could get.

Eileen and I have 3 kids: John, Casey, and Dana. John is 14, Casey is 10, and Dana is 7. To make the Norman Rockwell picture complete, we also have a dog, a cat I rarely see, and a goldfish named Lincoln. Why Lincoln? That's what happens when you let a 6-year-old name the fish. Lincoln and I don't talk much. So, we'll leave it at that.

I have wonderful children, a fantastic wife who I love dearly, and a job I can barely tolerate. That's not a complaint. It's just how things worked out.

That morning was hectic, as usual. Getting everyone out of the house and to their respective schools is a challenge, as it is for every parent. No one wants to go, including me. Eileen is a morning person. I hate that. I can barely maintain consciousness in the morning. It's been a fight for me all my life. If I was left to get myself up in the morning, I'm sure by now I'd be standing in the unemployment line. Eileen has to practically shake me to get me to wake up, and then I lay there like a 4th grader who has a math test and didn't study. I whine and complain, trying to remember some of the stellar excuses I was able to manufacture those mornings I didn't want to go to school. My mom wouldn't buy them then, and Eileen isn't buying them now. Eventually the nudge becomes more of a punch, and I drag my sorry ass into the shower in hopes that life will again enter my body.

I remember very little after breakfast that day. I do remember that Dana was flipping out because she couldn't find her library book and she was sure the penalty for a late library book was death. If there was some way to convince the library staff to avoid scaring the hell out of the kids, I'd be all over that. We did find the library book, under a pile of clothes in her bedroom. This was followed by lecture #23, regarding the neatness of her room. In the next few years, I should be able to just shout out a number that refers to the lecture needed at that moment. The child it is aimed at should know automatically what that lecture is and respond accordingly. Unfortunately, the lectures change rather rapidly. They go from "clean up your room" to "put your dishes in the dishwasher." They respond accordingly, with the standard roll of the eyes.

It sounds goofy, but I remember having an eerie feeling as I was starting my car that day. Not a premonition, but more of a feeling that change was coming. I had been considering going back to school to become a teacher. I love history. Always have. Dreaming about a career change was a pretty common thought as of late, due to my boredom with my current job. I had applied for entry into a college program and had been waiting to get a reply outlining how I would go about completing the program.

So, the thought that things were going to change was not a new one. But this feeling was different. I remember sitting in the car and feeling almost disconnected with the world around me. The radio was on, but I couldn't understand what they were saying. The car seemed to be moving, but not in a forward and reverse type of motion. More like an up-and-down, side-to-side movement. I started wondering if I was getting dizzy or sick, but the feeling disappeared as quickly as it came. When I backed out of the garage, I noticed something out of the corner of my eye. It was in and out of view in a split second but had a startling effect on me. It looked like a person walking around the side of the garage. I remember seeing gray hair and suspenders, in almost a fog, moving without a walking motion, more of a floating movement. I stopped the car, got out and slowly moved to the side of the garage to confirm what I had seen. Nothing. The side of the garage was filled with the normal sights. Bikes, big wheels, broken hockey nets, but definitely no floating old people. I spotted my wife as I was walking back to my car, and she seemed amused by my sudden trip to the side of the garage. She had been watching me through the screen door the whole time this was happening. Deciding to inquire about my sudden insanity, she asked if I had hit my head or was having a flashback from my "touring rock band days."

"You sat in the car for 5 minutes before you pulled out," she said. "I thought you were on the phone until I found this on the counter." She handed me my phone, something that had become a part of me right after they made me a supervisor. It's like someone sewed it to my body and no matter how hard I try; I can't get away from it. For me to forget my phone was way out of the ordinary. Eileen asked, "Why the sudden sprint to the side of the garage?" I figured she had already convinced herself that I was losing it and attributed my actions to my usual morning fog.

"I thought I saw someone walking towards the side of the garage," I said, still wondering what the hell was going on.

Eileen handed me my phone, gave me a kiss, and said "I'll call Tinley Park and see if your room is ready." Tinley Park Mental Institution was a nearby respite for people who see elderly floating men on the side of the garage. At that moment Tinley Park sounded appealing. I was thinking a nice long rest might be good for me.

The last thing I remember was laughing as I pulled out of the driveway as my wife did her best impression of a floating elderly woman heading towards the side of the garage.

From this point out, I only have bits and pieces of my memory of that day. I vaguely remember getting an assignment from my administrative director regarding the annual Christmas decorations to be placed down Route 30 on the light poles. I also remember trying to get the cherry picker stable enough to put a man up there to start the decorating. I wish I could remember the annual laugh fest we usually have as all of us put on our store-bought Santa suits and proceed to put up the decorations. We still wore our neon vests over the suits, but it was always good for a laugh as the motorists went by. That was the part we all loved. Some little kid pointing out the window of the standard issue minivan yelling "Mommy, Santa's putting up the decorations!" Kids and Christmas are two of my favorite things. I heard we were quite the hit that day. The local newspaper even came out to take some photos of us in our Santa suits. Most of us don't need a pillow in our costume belly; the beer has made that unnecessary. When we started dressing like Santa years ago, we all needed a pillow to fill out the costume. My crew had been together now for 15 years, so we've had time to develop our own Santa bellies.

From what they told me in the hospital, things were going as planned without any difficulties until a semi-truck driver going down Route 30 had a massive heart attack while driving. The truck veered toward our trucks, and being the lucky fellow I am, I was three stories above ground in the cherry picker when the truck lost control. All of the crew members were able to get out of the way except for Sully, who slipped during his attempt to escape. The back end of the semi ran over his right foot, breaking his ankle in several places. His leg was still in the grass when the truck ran it over. The doc told him if he had been on the pavement, he would have lost his lower leg. The coroner later found out that the truck driver was probably dead before he hit us.

I (from what I was told) did my best impression of Santa flying without his sleigh as the semi completely destroyed the cherry picker. My left leg was severely broken, probably before I hit the ground. I caught it on the control panel on the way out which sent me into a spin as I was being launched. I cleared all the wreckage and other vehicles we had brought to the job that day. My buddies started kidding me about it when they were sure I would make a full recovery. Sully, even on crutches, said I would have had a perfect 10 for my dismount from the basket but the French judge gave me a 9.5 because my legs came apart on the landing. Funny bastards. Jackson was the first to find me. He's about a 6'5" 275-pound African American teddy bear. He thinks it's funny to make us uncomfortable around the supervisors. He refers to himself as "Spot" because he's the only black guy on the crew. He'll say things like "Pickin' up the tools here, boss" or he'll start singing "Jump down, turn around pick a bale of cotton! Jump down, turn around, pick a bale of hay!" Then he watches us squirm as the administrators start looking at their cell phone contacts to see if they still have their lawyers' numbers somewhere on the speed dial.

Jackson tells me I was semi-conscious when he found me. I was saying something very bizarre, which at first, made no sense to me or anyone else. I kept say "Grandpa's here, he's by the side!" I guess I said it multiple times and Jackson said later that I seemed to be looking right through him while I was yelling. Not long after that I passed out.

Jackson dragged me out of the water-filled ditch I was lying in and was able to cover me with a rain slicker he had in the truck. Several ambulances and fire rescue trucks arrived, and Jackson helped them load me and Sully into different ambulances. He then tried to get in the driver's seat to assist the fire department with their duties. Now, I've been trying to picture this scene for quite some time. Imagine the chaos of a multi-vehicle accident with fatalities and critical injuries, and to top it all off, a near 300-pound black Santa trying to get behind the wheel of an ambulance to get his buddies to the hospital. You couldn't make this shit up if you wanted to.

As it turns out, Jackson found out later that he had a 2-inch piece of glass in his leg and the sock and boot on his left foot were soaked with blood. The adrenaline of the situation masked the pain until things settled down. He ended up with12 stitches. Sully gave him a Mickey Mouse sticker that he stole from the pediatric section of the supply cart at the hospital.

CHAPTER 2

I've heard my trip to the hospital was pretty eventful. They worked on trying to stabilize me in the ambulance with little to no luck. I woke up once, told the two paramedics they were blocking the light, and quickly passed out again. I was later told my blood pressure bottomed out as we were pulling into the emergency room at the hospital. I coded just inside the emergency room. Jackson told me later that they were beatin' the hell out of my chest, and he was sure I wasn't going to make it. He said for some reason, I seemed ok with that because of the (and these are Jacksons' words) … "Shit kickin' grin on my face." It appears that wherever I was going at that minute wasn't bad at all. I wish I could say I remember a pearly gate, or an old man dressed in a flowing white robe with a long beard holding a sign that said "Welcome to Heaven! Please exit the cloud and file off to the right where Saint Peter will give you your red Ferrari, supermodel, and a bag full of gold. We will discuss your sins tomorrow at 7:00 am. Purgatory will begin at 8:00. Until then enjoy yourself!"

The truth is it's all blank to me. The next two weeks are completely gone. I didn't even get to enjoy the helicopter ride to the Rush Presbyterian-St. Luke's Hospital in nearby Chicago. It was something I always wanted to do; take a ride over the Chicago skyline in a helicopter. I could never talk my bride into it. I could have gone it alone, but it would have been a lot more fun with her by my side holding on to me with a death grip. As it turns out, the paramedics in the air transport helicopter were doing that to me. I coded in the air too. I seemed to be pretty good at this coding thing. All told, I did it four times. Can't believe I came back every time. I figured I probably had four Ferrari's, four super models, and four bags of gold waiting for me. I'm sure God and Saint Peter were whispering back and forth "I wish he'd make up his mind!"

They figured out in the first emergency room that I definitely had a closed head injury. I was bleeding into the space around the brain. My wife later told me she wasn't worried about that because I had a lot of free space up there. I quickly told her about the supermodels, and she quit with the comedy routine. As bad as that was, along with the broken bones, the real problem was a torn aorta. When I hit the ground, I tore the upper part of my aorta near the heart and I was bleeding pretty severely. The tear wasn't big enough to kill me immediately, but it was trying hard to finish the job. They were waiting for me at Rush University Medical Center on the helipad and took me right into surgery. I coded there right after they put me under. They quickly got me on the bypass machine and fixed my aorta as quickly as possible. I made it through the surgery for the aorta but got to make a return trip to the operating room for a subdural hematoma. In the hospital I quickly found out that anything that ends in "oma" is not good at all. Hematoma, Coma, Myeloma, they all suck. Two weeks later they started taking me out of my drug-induced coma. I had some experience with drug-induced comas during my college years, though they were all self-inflicted. This was the mother of all comas though. It seemed to take forever to come out of the fog I was in. I was healing well, but the pain I had was excruciating. A cough of any kind was a new experience in pain. My chest had been cut open the same way they open up a deer after a kill. My head hurt like hell. I experienced the most pain after a sneeze. I grabbed my chest and head and wished I had another hand to grab my leg. I was ready to give it all up at that point. Fortunately for me, that was also the first day I saw the kids after the accident. They had been there off and on for the first two weeks, but I wasn't aware of their presence. Seeing those beautiful faces brought the good kind of tears to my eyes. My wife joined me in a good cry, and I knew from that point I was going to be alright.

The rehab in the hospital for the broken leg and fractured collar bone was nasty. The leg was a mess. The doctor told me at one point they considered amputating it because of the damage. There was a good chance I would need a follow up surgery to further repair the damage and scarring around the lower part of the leg. The collar bone break was just painful. They didn't find that until someone noticed every time, I tried to move my left arm I would moan or make a face. Whenever I tried to pull myself up in bed it hurt. Holding on to the walker while trying to balance the cast and navigate the hallways of the hospital was a bitch. It started off slow. I'd walk with the physical therapist and my friend Silver (not many people name their walker, but being we were becoming such close friends...). With time I progressed to a high speed of approximately 1 mph, dragging my leg in its designer cast (a red and white checkerboard pattern) and enough metal in my lower leg to set off detectors at the airport. Some of the metal could come out at a later date, but I'll probably leave it there just to enjoy future frisking's at all TSA security checkpoints.

I knew the recovery would be long and hard with plenty of setbacks and a whole hell of a lot of anger. I would also be visited by every other emotion you can probably think of.

I did have this sense of being given a second chance. Right at that moment I wouldn't go as far as calling it a gift. But I guess in the long run it was. I don't know why the sense was so strong, or why it lingered with every emotion I experienced. It was like the neon sign that never went off. You know the one, it's in the bar window and no matter what time of day it is, it's flashing. That's how this thought kept creeping into my head. One bright flash at a time.

Eileen and I decided that as soon as the ok was given, I would return home and continue my physical therapy there. The physical therapist would come to my house, which made a great deal of sense to me. I would need to learn how to walk up and down my stairs, not the cold stairwells at the hospital. There were no toys or sporting equipment to navigate around in the hospital like there were at home. I'm sure the kids would set up some fine slalom courses for me. After all, rehab starts at home...or something like that.

The discharge date was in sight at this point. My staples had been removed. That is one thing you don't see coming when you wake up from a traumatic injury. They don't use stitches to sew up large wounds or surgical incisions anymore. They staple them closed. Now when I woke up from all this and saw the staples in my head and in my chest, I couldn't help but wonder what the stapler looked like. Was it shaped the same as the one on my desk? Did the same thing that happens to me every time I reach for the stapler on my desk also happen to the surgeon? You know, you put the first staple in and then nothing. You spend the next 5 minutes rummaging around your desk to find the box of staples, and when you finally locate them there's nothing, but those tiny little pieces of staple rows left. You try to drop them in the stapler, and they fall in two or three different directions. I could envision him dropping a couple of extra staple refills in my chest cavity. Great, now my lungs are stapled to my liver and my spleen is stapled to my pancreas. I believe this is how people are affected by anesthesia long term. You find yourself going off on these long thought excursions that lead to nowhere. It could also just be related to being bored out of my mind sitting on my ass for the last three weeks here in the hospital.

I had also become so sick of daytime TV. I was just hours away from pulling an Elvis Presley and shooting the TV. Jerry, the judge shows, soap operas, and yes, even Oprah. Although I must say, Oprah's show was by far the most tolerable. At least she would occasionally put together a show that a guy could watch. Jerry Springer's show makes you realize that no matter how crazy you think your family is, there is always one on Jerry's show that makes your family look like the Brady Bunch. After a while I couldn't watch it anymore. Just a little hint to anyone out there who's interested...if Jerry Springer ever calls your house and asks to speak to you, just assume that nothing good will come of it and hang up. No matter how tempting it is, you'll end up seeing or hearing something you don't want. An example of this is the wife I saw on Springer finding out that her husband was a transvestite and was stealing her clothes and selling them to his cross-dressing friends. Time to change your name and move out of state.

Day to day we waited for the magic word. Finally, they told me I could go home on Saturday. The only words I had ever heard more beautiful than, "We're discharging you," in my life were "Yes I'll marry you," and "Congratulations, you're going to be a dad!" Both very special, these words were on the same level. Hearing those words started the tears flowing. My own bed, my own clothes, my own food. I had lost 22 pounds during my stay. I had needed to lose some weight, but I surely don't recommend the "tear your aorta diet." Keep the extra weight. In the long run it will be less painful than the diet. My muscles had atrophied so much that everything was a chore. Getting out of bed, walking with the walker, physical therapy's weightlifting program, it all hurt. It's not that I didn't want to do it, it just seemed like everything sucked the life out of me. I was sleeping so much I was making the elderly people in the hospital jealous. When you hear an 85-year-old say, "That guy sure sleeps a lot!" you know it's making an impression on everyone. This is what you do though with a head injury. You sleep. That's the body's way of healing you and you just have to go with it.

CHAPTER 3

As Saturday approached my excitement was uncontainable. I was dressed at 8:00 am waiting for the discharge papers to be delivered to me on a ceremonial silver platter. Eileen showed up at 9:00 and told me to settle down. "You've waited this long, one more hour won't matter," she sternly told me. At that point the daggers I shot her from across the room hit their mark and she treaded lightly about waiting from that point on.

My doctor showed up at about 9:30 and went over the standard things with me regarding my discharge. You know, don't go water skiing, sky diving, or play tackle football. I agreed and laughed at the bad jokes he was spilling out in hopes it would get me out of there sooner. He said I would be off work for some time. I asked if he could give me a rough idea how long that would be. He explained that I had eight more weeks with the leg cast, and at the six-week mark they'd remove the external hardware and see how I was doing. He had some words of wisdom for me. "After the leg is healed, it's up to you. The faster you progress in physical therapy, the quicker you'll get back to work. The main thing is not to rush it and do any extra damage. It will take time to heal, so let it."

I don't know why I was anxious to get back to work. The truck driver's insurance company was paying for everything in hopes I would not sue them. They were paying my salary, expenses, and hospital costs. They had offered me a generous settlement if I promised not to pursue a lawsuit. I felt bad enough for the poor truck driver and his family; I don't think I could put them through a trial. I would get over my injuries as long as they took care of the medical expenses. I'd probably take the settlement they offered me, just in case I had significant problems later on that prevented me from working. I figured I'd stash that away for our retirement, just in case.

By 10:00 am, I had signed all the discharge papers. I was sitting in my exit ride wheelchair giving out hugs to the fantastic nurses who get none of the credit and yet do all of the work. They called me the miracle man and also had constantly checked on me as if they expected that any moment could be my last. What's amazing is the way they cheered me on, and once they knew I was on my way to recovery they encouraged me all the time. Fantastic people. No other way to describe them.

I got a round of applause from everyone at the front desk which was surrounded by employees from the ER, ICU, 3rd floor and several of the doctors who had worked on me. I stood up slowly and offered my true thanks to them. I meant every word of it. Without these people, I'd be worm food by now.

As the power sliding doors opened and the sunlight hit me, the tears started again. Not a major crying fit, just "happy to be the hell out of there" tears. After a near-death experience, I noticed that one of the only things that continues to work, no matter what, are the tear ducts. Strong emotions about my experience were not going to die easy and neither would I. The sun had struck me as a victory tape at a marathon. Having the warm sun hit me had been everything I thought it would be. I may not have won the race...but I finished.

Although the warmth of the sunshine felt good, it hurt my head at the same time. I realized that my eyes had not been exposed to the sun in quite some time. The brightness of the sun was almost painful. I still had an annoying headache, which should not have been that surprising, knowing that I had a subdural hematoma and surgery on my brain to remove it. I guess I was entitled to a headache. I found that if I looked through the windshield, even with the visor and the sunglasses, it was still difficult. I decided that it was easier to keep my head turned to the side and look out the side window for the ride home. The ride home took about 40 minutes. It was uneventful until we reached the area where there is a forest preserve, some old farmhouses, a kind of country setting that people wanted to sustain. I often thought that maybe a family owned the area years ago and never sold it, who knows? I had been past the area so many times that I never really gave it a second thought. What really drew my attention to the area was a guy standing on the side of the road. He had a blank stare and was looking down at a roadside memorial. I've become familiar with roadside memorials over the years because of my job. The memorials are often near the light poles that we have to pick up off the ground and put back up or replace completely. The memorials are very heartfelt; you see a picture of the person, the date, and how badly they are missed. God, I can't tell you how many teddy bears I have picked up over the years. It's sad, but it is more of a healing factor for the family than anything else. It is an attempt to let the world know that this is where their loved one left this earth. I also feel like even though the city wants them removed, I sometimes just leave them there. I figure when the memorial is worn out and doesn't look like it has been attended to, then maybe it will be ok to take it apart. I like to give the family a little more time than most people would.

The gentleman that was looking at the memorial looked a little disheveled and out of place. I turned to my beautiful bride and said "Boy, that guy looked kind of out of it, no car near him. Do you think he walked all the way to that memorial area?"

She quickly responded "What guy? What are you talking about?" I pointed to the side of the road.

"That guy standing right over there by the cross."

She said "There wasn't a guy by the cross. Are you sure that's what you saw?"

"That's what I thought I saw," I responded slowly. "Maybe my head is playing tricks on me. Maybe the sunlight is too bright for me, I don't know."

My wife kind of blew it off as being part of my recovery process. She didn't pay much attention as she was just glad, I could walk and talk and wasn't in some kind of vegetative state. I didn't give it too much thought after that. I just attributed it to my being on too many medications like morphine and the other fun things they put you on after such trauma. Maybe I was just spacing out, or even seeing things.

Before I knew it, I was home in my own bed, surrounded by fluffy pillows. I had an unofficial prescription for milk shakes whenever I wanted them, which is the next best thing to heaven, I think. There's nothing better than having your beautiful wife bring you a milk shake and having your children around you. The kids were just as thrilled to have me home as I was to be there with them. I realized something else I'd missed greatly, and that was my remote control. It was easy to use and there were plenty of channels. Let's face it guys, there's nothing better than your own remote. I turned on the television and was fast asleep in about 15 minutes.

I started thinking back to the day of the accident and something kept popping into my head. I didn't understand why, but I couldn't shake it. I went back to when I was backing out of the garage onto the driveway and saw that shadow that I swore was an old man. I'm still confused as to why he was there. I know that if this was truly an old man who was confused and walking around the house, by the time I got out of the car he wouldn't have been gone. The guy looked like he was 104 and wasn't going to be moving very fast. I started thinking that maybe I was just seeing something. They say there are little angels around, guardians that keep an eye on us, and maybe he was one of those. Or maybe he was in the vicinity because he knew what was going to happen to me.

I had the most bizarre dream during my two-hour nap. Bizarre dreams are common while under the influence of morphine, but this one was very vivid. My mind replayed the incident when I backed out of the garage on the day of my accident and saw the old man standing next to the driveway. During the dream, the man's face was not quite as foggy, and I could have sworn it was my Grandpa Bill. I hopped out of the car and very quickly turned the corner, and I caught his figure turning the corner and fading away. I called his name and got no response. As I turned the other way to head back to the car, he was standing in front of me. This startled me in the dream, and although I was having trouble focusing, I knew this was my grandpa.

Grandpa Bill died when I was 18. When Grandpa Bill came over it was a celebration. He was one of those down-to-earth guys. He was a meat packer by trade and was tough as nails. He wasn't always the greatest father in the world but seemed to be a decent guy when he got around his grandchildren. I missed him; I hadn't seen him for so many years. The first thing I wanted to do was to ask him how things were. That seems silly, but in a dream, anything is possible. I said, "Grandpa Bill, how are you? I haven't seen you in so many years!"

He looked at me and said "Scott, you need to know something. I'm giving you a gift. Your gift will allow you to help people. It will be frightening at first, but then it will become something you can do a world of good with. Do not deny your feelings; do not deny your abilities. Do you understand me, my son?" With that I woke up.

When you wake up in kind of a startled state and you've just gotten out of the hospital after major surgery, you can't just spring out of bed without major shocking pain. I let out a roaring scream when I attempted to sit up in bed. My wife and kids came running up the stairs when they heard me scream but were comforted to know that I had just had an astonishing dream. With that, I decided that another milk shake was in order, because that's what you do when you're sick.

CHAPTER 4

Back at work, Jackson took over supervising the crew in my absence, and from what I heard was doing a great job. Funny how those things happen; you kind of step into something and you realize that you can handle it, and Jackson did just that. Unfortunately, I'm sure I won't have him much longer, because when I get back, they'll probably transfer Jackson to another crew where he'll be the supervisor, but I'm sure he'll be a damn good one and that's all that matters.

I was nowhere near being ready to think about work. My leg throbbed all the frickin time. If I got up it would throb, if I sat down it would throb, if I looked at it funny it would throb. It was a new experience for me. Most of my life I'd spent with very little pain. I would rarely even get a headache. I felt good all the time. Every now and then I'd get the little things; you know a cold or the flu. And I, like most men, am a big wimp when it comes to getting sick. I play it for everything I can. Thank God I have an understanding wife, or I'd still be lying in the fetal position from something as severe as a sinus infection.

The pain was all a part of the healing process. Pain is there for a reason. It tells you something is wrong, or you're pushing yourself too hard. During physical therapy, I had a tendency to do that. I figured the harder I pushed myself the faster I would heal. Wrong. The physical therapists know exactly how hard you should push yourself and they can see the pain in your eyes. They know when it's time to take a break. I tried to listen to them, but like most man-child lugs, I'm a little on the stubborn side.

After a couple of weeks of therapy at home, it was time to graduate to the physical therapy department at the medical center. They have many more torture devices there and know how to use them with expertise. I found myself on balance balls the size of a Volkswagen, walking with crutches instead of my old faithful Silver, and working quite a bit on my balance which had suffered due to the head injury. My chest had healed up nicely and only hurt when I sneezed or coughed really hard. It's hard to avoid a sneeze, although I tried everything possible to do so. Whatever you do, if you feel one coming on, don't look up at the lights. You'll be swearing up a storm after the sneeze works its way out of you.

They worked hard on strengthening my good leg to help support my body while the other leg healed. The cast was coming off in a week and I would be wearing a soft cast with metal supports in it for the next four weeks or so. For now, I was on crutches and had non-weight bearing physical therapy. I knew when the cast came off the pain during these lovely trips to Hades would increase. Physical therapy can be 45 minutes of pure hell. I couldn't imagine how it was going to be once they got a hold of that beat-up leg. Just getting to the point of bending it again was going to take weeks.

I still was reliant on Eileen to get me to and from places. Because it was my right leg that was injured, I was unable to drive. I hoped that as soon as I got the soft cast, I would be able to drive myself to and from physical therapy. My collar bone was still pretty sore and sometimes I had trouble getting out of the car. So until I was stronger, Eileen would have to be my limo driver. And by limo, I mean a 1996 Chevy Impala with just enough dents in it to make it easy to find in the parking lot.

You get kind of angry watching your wife do all the work and all the running around in the house. She had to take all the kids to their specific activities and was also constantly trying to make sure I was comfortable. She never complained. She was sometimes a drill sergeant, like when it came to getting the kids to do the extra chores, she had assigned them. I was good for one thing, folding clothes. She would set the basket in front of me and say with a smile, "Earn your keep." I became the best folder of clothes this side of the Mississippi. I'm sure after all this was over, I could get a job at Nordstrom's as their supervisor of clothes-folding. A job wanted by so many, but only a few are chosen.

The kids were an inspiration to me. They stepped right up and really helped Mom and did more than their fair share of the work around the house. I felt bad that I wasn't much help, but I also felt good that people were there to make things happen. That way I could concentrate on the physical therapy and not worry about the little things that needed to be done around the house. And there were so many little things that needed to be taken care of; things you take for granted like fixing a leaky faucet. One that makes enough noise just to keep you awake at night and you want so bad to get at it and fix it but are not quite strong enough to do so. Thank God for my neighbor Bob. He was kind of a handyman and could come over and fix things while I was recuperating.

Bob even changed a flat tire that my wife had one morning before going to work. I came down to thank him and he proceeded to yell at me. He told me to go back to bed, that he wasn't going to be able to do this forever. He joked, "You need to get better so I can call in all these favors I've been doing for you." I like Bob; he's got a great sense of humor and has been a fantastic neighbor.

A few weeks passed, and my collar bone was finally healed enough, and I could drive with the soft cast on my leg. I felt like I could get myself to physical therapy. My wife went with me the first time just to make sure I could do it, which I thought was brave on her part. I made it there with no problem. I had just a little bit of pain, and maybe a little more pain on the way back. But as for concentrating and being able to do everything I needed to do in the car, it wasn't a problem. As long as I had my trusty crutches with me, I was now able to be a little more self-sufficient. I became an expert at going up and down the stairs, something that was taught to me by the physical therapists. This meant that I could have dinner with the kids and Mom on a regular basis again. In the beginning, it was so hard to get up and down the stairs that I ate most of my meals up in the bedroom. Now that I was feeling better it was important to eat together as a family and talk about the events of the day. I didn't talk much, I just listened. No one wanted to hear about my physical therapy trip, or about how I sat there watching TV, or maybe reading a book. The kids were doing well in school, and things seemed pretty much back to normal. John had decided he wanted to play baseball in the spring for the freshman team at his high school. This gave me even more incentive to work hard in physical therapy because I wanted to be there for his games. Sitting through a nine-inning game was not going to be easy, especially on cold bleachers, but I wanted to give it my best shot.

During this time, I was still getting headaches, but they weren't as frequent as they were before. They were kind of annoying. I felt that there was a kind of aura around my head as the pain set in. I don't know how else to explain it. It just felt weird. It felt kind of like someone had lowered a fog over my head and glazed everything over. What was weird was that my thinking always seemed to be very clear during these times and I was even more sensitive to the sounds and sights outside my window. I usually got these spells later in the evening or early in the morning. They seemed to occur right after the children and left for school and my wife left for work. Sometimes I would get them again when I lay down at night. The fog never scared me; I just felt that it was part of the healing process. The doctors did tiptoe through my brain, so I guess there might be some long-lasting effects that would take time to heal. I was happy that there didn't seem to be any permanent brain damage, although my wife might disagree. She was convinced that I was goofier than ever. I guess without the stress of work every day I learned to relax and become a little bit more lighthearted. I think this also made my healing process a little bit more effective. Without all the stress of worrying about money, my job, and everything else that would normally go along with the huge accident like I had, I must say I felt pretty lucky.

On my way to physical therapy one day, I noticed one of these auras coming over me, and the headache started. It wasn't bad, just more annoying than anything. The so-called aura didn't seem to affect my driving and all, nor did it deter me from reaching my destination. The headache stuck with me through the physical therapy session, which made it a little bit more difficult than usual. I explained to the physical therapist that I felt a little different today because of the headache and wasn't sure if I would be able to perform all the tasks. She told me to do the best that I could, and that the headaches would be expected after brain surgery. I believed her. She had gotten me this far. As usual, when I left physical therapy, my collar bone, leg, and chest were all hurting like hell. It takes time for the sternum to heal up and it seemed like that's what was bothering me the most. They'd had me doing some mild weightlifting in hopes of getting the muscles built up in that area, in an effort to alleviate some of the pain.

After I finished my session, I decided I felt well enough to take the scenic route home. I wanted to go through the forest preserve area that I enjoyed seeing so much during my trip home from the hospital. I also must say I was still curious about the man I had seen at the side of the road that my wife obviously did not see. I still believed it was my imagination coupled with the morphine that caused this vision, or whatever you want to call it, to pop into my head. I took the scenic route from Route 30 to Gougar Road, and made a right on Francis Avenue. About 100 yards up the road I saw him again. He was standing in nearly the exact position that he was on the day I came home from the hospital. He looked disheveled and confused and seemed to be so out of place that I had to slow the car down to get a good look at him. He suddenly looked up at me, almost staring me down. Then he turned and waved as if he wanted me to stop. I didn't understand why this stranger was waving me down, so I kept on going. In my rearview mirror I could see him staring down at the roadside memorial just like the day I came home from the hospital. This whole scene kind of freaked me out and I quickly retreated to my home and back up to the safety of my bedroom. As soon as I lay down, the headache and the aura I felt around my head seemed to lift. The physical therapy took quite a bit out of me, and it wasn't long before I fell asleep.

I awoke about an hour later recalling a dream that seemed more than real. I awakened somewhat startled but not in a panic. In this dream, the same scenario played over in my head about seeing my grandfather the day of the accident, including the words that he had spoken to me in the previous dream. He spoke about being given a gift, a gift to help heal. I still had no idea what this meant, but the dream was as real as I could imagine. This was the first time I'd sat down and tried to analyze the dream and figure out what my grandfather was trying to tell me. The only thing I could come up with was that maybe it was time for a change of careers and he wanted me to go into the health care industry so I could help people. Maybe he wanted me to help people who had been through the same trauma that I had been through. But to tell the truth, I've never had the guts for the medical field. The sight of blood makes me sick to my stomach. I can't even watch some shows on TV because of the way they make me feel. So, the scenario seemed strange to me. I couldn't see myself in the medical field. So, what did grandpa mean by saying he was giving me a great gift and it would help heal people? No matter what I did, I couldn't see the route he wanted me to take.

CHAPTER 5

I received physical therapy every day during the week, so the next day I was off to visit my torture chamber once again. On this day, there was no headache or aura. Just the usual pain I've become so used to that it's become the second part of me. The therapist had me doing exercises and stretching to help get some of the flexibility back in my leg and shoulder. The therapy sessions usually took between 1 – 1 ½ hours and by the time they were over, I was pretty much spent. The only stop I would make on the way home would be at the video store to try to find a movie I hadn't seen already. After a recovery period this long, I had pretty much seen every video in the store. I guess I'm dating myself by saying video when I mean DVD. It seems that certain words just stick in your head, and video is one of them. What would I choose today? Some sort of shoot-em-up or maybe a western? My favorite actors included Jimmy Stewart and John Wayne, and I think I had seen every Jimmy Stewart movie out there. I also liked the comedy stuff, especially standup comedy. I would rent several of them at a time to keep my spirits up. I would even venture into the learning section of the video store and pick up something related to history. I've always liked history, so I liked anything about wars and presidential assassinations. Learning about the Lincoln and Kennedy assassinations was one of my favorite things to do. I had seen almost every show on every assassination from Julius Caesar to the attempt on Ronald Reagan. It always amazed me that someone as crazy as Oswald or John Wilkes Booth would have such access to the president to actually get away with killing him. Anyhow, it kept me from going stir crazy, so I stopped at the video store almost every day to pick up a video. I said it again, I mean DVD. The DVDs kept me sane.

As I was browsing through the DVDs, I noticed the headache coming on again. It wasn't severe, but the fogginess or aura seemed a little more intense. I quickly grabbed a couple of my DVDs and proceeded to the check out. By this time, the employees knew me by name, and I was out the door quickly.

On my way home I noticed a young woman standing by the side of the road near a cross. She was crying. She wore what looked like a prom dress, high heels, and flowers in her hair. She was very close to the road, and I was worried about her safety. As I drove by her, she crouched down and picked up a small teddy bear that was lying near the cross. This all seemed so surreal to me, mainly because she was wearing a prom dress. The other thing that was strange was that she seemed unaffected by the traffic that was so close to her. As I drove by, I gently honked the horn to make sure she was paying attention. The sound did not seem to affect her at all. She calmly stood up and started walking towards the field that was adjacent to the cross. I was starting to doubt my own senses at this point. I was starting to realize that every time I got one of these headaches with the aura, I seemed to see one of these people by a roadside memorial. When the headaches and weren't there, I saw no one.

I began to wake up earlier each morning and was able to see the kids off to school and even to help with breakfast. I hobbled around on one crutch using the counters of the kitchen to help me move along. My helping with breakfast was great for the kids; they would get pancakes or eggs or waffles just about every day. Despite all this wonderful food, Dana still loved her Lucky Charms. I could rarely talk her out of them. Every once in a while, she would go for a waffle, but it wasn't too often. Although my wife loved to help in the kitchen, I would always try to make her breakfast too. This gave me a sense of worth as I was recuperating. At least I was doing something other than sitting in my room watching DVDs.

I set up my physical therapy appointments so that they immediately followed getting all the kids on the bus and my wife off to work. That way I could get the pain over with and have the rest of the day to recuperate. I was now lifting weights on a machine that I was sure was from the Dark Ages and used by the Spanish Inquisition. It was for the quadriceps on my bad leg to help strengthen them. But this contraption had the most unique ability to make me swear under my breath. The damn thing was killing me. Three reps of 10 and then a 10-minute rest. Then I would go do some balance work on one of those huge bouncy balls followed by another 10 minutes on the Spanish Inquisition contraption. My clavicle had healed up pretty well and now all I was doing was strengthening the shoulder muscles. This work had gotten somewhat mundane. I didn't feel as if I needed to do these exercises anymore, but I wasn't about to doubt the physical therapist whose expertise had gotten me through all this. Her name was Amanda and she had been on my case since I started my physical therapy. She was tough, but never mean. I don't do mean. I can't stand mean people. I always felt like if you needed to be that mean you ought to step in front of a train and get it over with. I like Amanda. She pushes me in a funny sort of way, never lets me whine, and keeps me smiling even during my time on the Spanish Inquisition machine.

For Christmas this year my son got the X box 360. I hadn't played it; I just opted to use it to watch movies during my recovery. But now I was out of movies to watch, or at least couldn't think of any more to watch, and decided it was time to take up the Xbox. I could rent the games at the same DVD store and play them for as many days as I wanted or return them immediately if they were beyond my age bracket. And by that, I mean they were far too complex for an old guy like me to figure out. I did like the war games and some of the sports games. This got me out of my bedroom and onto the couch downstairs which I also felt was more progress. I would yell and scream at the TV like a 12-year-old every time I got shot. Every time I failed to win a tennis match, I would be tempted to throw the controller across the room. I realized this was more frustrating than it was worth, and decided the Xbox was better left to the teenagers.

I wasn't sleeping as much as I had been over the last couple months and was almost ready to have the pins removed from my leg. This would allow me a little more freedom of movement, and also the ability to bear weight on the leg. This was something that I had dreamed of for the last 2 ½ months. I knew it would hurt like hell at first to bear weight on it, but I had been kind of trying it out anyway. I knew this was against the doctor's orders, but sometimes you've just got to be the rebel. The surgery was scheduled in two weeks on a Friday so Eileen would have the weekend off to take care of me.

John was starting to practice baseball with the team after school. I hoped that I would be ready to sit and watch John practice without too much pain. The bleachers weren't comfort friendly, if you know what I mean, and I knew it would be a long practice. I figured if things got rough, I could go sit in the car. I hobbled over to the bleachers on my crutches and took a seat on the lower level. I was a little nervous every time someone walked by me, thinking they were going to kick my leg, but everybody was kind enough to see it and walk around it.

The practice went as long as I thought it would go, and before I knew it John and I were in the car heading home. It still hurt to rest my foot on the floor of the car while driving, so I couldn't drive any distance. A short hop to the baseball field wasn't a problem. I also had managed to make my way to most of my doctor's appointments by my-self, taking some of the heat off of my wife. This long-term care is for the birds. But I knew the worst of it was over and things would really get better from this point out.

As John and I left the ball field, I wondered if we could stop and get some ice cream. I had become quite the ice cream connoisseur since the accident, and fortunately John also thought it was a good idea. The ice cream place was on the way home, so it wasn't like we were going out of our way to get there. John stood in line and came back with a hot fudge sundae for me and a chocolate dipped cone for him. Everyone knows that major league baseball players all finish practice with a chocolate dipped ice cream. It's the only way to become a pro.

We enjoyed our treats in the car and then started off for home. The ice cream shop was only a mile and a half from our house, and it was the same familiar route I remembered so vividly the day I came home from the hospital. I couldn't believe it. As I turned onto Francis Road, that guy was standing there again. He was in the same place, by the roadside memorial, with the same confused look on his face and was pacing slowly back and forth in front of the small cross.

I said to John, "There's that guy again. He really can't seem to shake this tragedy in his life, whatever it may be." John had the same response that Eileen had when I asked her if she saw the man.

"What guy dad?"

"Don't tell me you don't see that guy on the side of the road standing right there by the roadside memorial with the cross sticking up out of the ground! You don't see him?" I asked.

"No, Dad, I don't. Do you mean by the building?" John asked.

"No, standing right there by the cross that's next to the road. Do you see the cross?" I asked.

John replied, "Yes, I see the cross, but there's no one standing by it."

"John, this is the third time I've seen this guy and mom said she couldn't see him either. Who knows, maybe I'm seeing ghosts," I said laughingly.

But deep down inside I wasn't laughing and was scared out of my mind. If I was having hallucinations I probably should talk to the doctor and see if this was related to the brain surgery. They did tiptoe through my brain so I guess there could be after-effects. But I sure as hell didn't want this to be one of them. Hallucinations are usually reserved for the significantly mentally ill. I didn't feel mentally ill. In fact, through this entire ordeal, I had even managed not to be depressed. So, the idea of a hallucination didn't sit well with me. John was concerned.

"Maybe coming to watch my practice was just a little too much for you, Dad," he said cautiously.

I turned to him and said, "Maybe you're right."

When we arrived at home, I hobbled into the house and sat down at the kitchen table. Eileen was sitting at the table when I arrived. I mentioned to her that I had seen that same guy by that roadside cross that I saw the day I came home from the hospital. She had a genuine look of concern in her eyes and wondered if I had overdone it for the day.

"You push yourself too hard," she said. "I think maybe you're just having a visual disturbance of some sort that your brain just can't quite process. It might be making you think you're seeing people, but it may only be a form of a migraine headache." Although this seemed like a logical explanation, it still didn't make much sense because this didn't look like an optical illusion. This looked like a full-sized human walking back and forth in front of a roadside cross. I could describe him in perfect detail, from the clothes on his back, to the color of his hair, to the look on his face. The first time this happened, I brushed it off as just the trauma I had been through. It might seem easy to forget, but this time it was sticking with me. I tried to go on with the day and forget about the experience. Maybe Eileen was right. Maybe this was just an effect of the brain surgery and would fade as time went on.

As we prepared for bed that night, I was somewhat silent and still having trouble shaking the bizarre feelings I was having. It was like something was calling me back to that spot, just to see if I could reproduce the hallucination. The feeling was eating at me pretty badly and I tried to distract myself by watching a movie. Nothing like a Disney movie to distract you from everything in the world, being that everything is perfect in a Disney movie.

CHAPTER 6

The next day was a school day for the kids and a workday for my wife, so I was going to be alone for most of the day. I was counting down the days till I got the pins out of my leg and could start to bear weight and possibly lose these crutches. I was so sick of them I could've thrown them out the window. I was still trying to shake the feeling that I had the night before, so I decided to pick up a book and try to read. I was never a big reader before the accident, but when you're bored and sick of TV, reading becomes a serious option. I'd grown to like a few select authors and had read most of their books. Today as I picked up one of my favorites by Nicholas Sparks, I found myself reading a whole chapter without comprehending anything. My mind was so preoccupied that I couldn't seem to concentrate. I tried a little TV. If you've ever been stuck watching daytime TV, you know how quickly you can get bored or even annoyed with it. I couldn't take it anymore and had to get in the car. My heart was racing as I slowly drove to the roadside memorial area. It was about 11 o'clock in the morning and there was very little traffic on the road, so I felt like I could slow down and take close look if I needed to. To be honest with you I was hoping I wouldn't need to. I had hoped to see nothing. Just a cross in a plot of grass. As I approached the site, I noticed the same man standing by the cross. It looked like he had never left. The suit he wore hadn't changed; even his tie was the same. He still paced slowly and kept looking down at the cross. I slowed down to almost a crawl and decided to stop the car. I was parked on the shoulder of the road at kind of a funny angle.

I rolled down the window and yelled to the guy "Are you okay sir?" I got no response. It was as if I was non-existent to him. I knew I was yelling loud enough for him to hear me and there was no other traffic on the road, so I was confused by his lack of a response. As much as I knew that it was a bad idea, I opened the car door and got out. I hobbled with my crutches across the street, looking both ways several times. God knows I didn't want to end up in the hospital again. I slowly approached the man and as I got closer to him, I felt a sensation of warmth in my body, like the pins and needles you feel when your arm goes to sleep. Except this was all over my body. When I got within 5 feet of him, I felt a surge of what almost felt like electricity go through my body, and suddenly I was standing in front of him.

He looked up at me and without hesitation simply asked, "What happened?"

I was more than confused by this point because he hadn't responded when I talked to him from the side of the road. Suddenly he was talking to me eye to eye.

"I don't know what you mean," I said. "I've seen you standing here two or three times as I passed by, and no one else seems to see you but me. What's your name?"

He looked up at me and said, "John Patterson, who are you?"

At this point I was a little nervous about giving him my name. So, I gave my first name. "My name is Scott."

"Pleasure to meet you Scott," he replied. He didn't offer his hand, so I didn't offer mine.

"I have to ask you John, did you lose someone you loved here? Because I see you here quite a bit."

"I don't know," he replied. "I just can't seem to leave." He looked puzzled by my questions and confused by his own thought process. Without a doubt this was a man in distress. I asked him if I could give him a ride somewhere and he seemed to think for a second. "I have nowhere to go. Besides, with all this fog, I wouldn't feel safe driving anywhere. In fact," he said to me, "you kind of startled me when you walk out of the fog."

Now I was really confused because this was one of the clearest days we'd had in months. The sun was shining and there wasn't a cloud in the sky. When I asked John where the fog started, he said "I can't see anything past you. I keep trying to walk out of this fog in hopes of finding my way home. The fog distorts my sense of direction and I always seem to end up back here."

He was looking down at the cross. For the first time I got a close-up look at the cross. It just said 'Dad' on it, and it looked like it had been there a while. At this point I had lost most of my fear and had a real feeling of passion for this man's pain. I asked again about the fog.

"John has the fog been here since you've gotten here?" I asked. He replied yes. "How long have you been here?" I asked, seeming confused. John said he didn't know how long, but it'd been some time. He remembered that it had been cold when he first found himself at the spot and that there was snow on the ground. It was May now, so I knew he had been there for quite some time. Now I was sure that this was either an elaborate hallucination or I was having some sort of a psychic experience. This was something I had never believed in until the day I was sure I had seen my grandfather walk behind my garage. He'd said I would be given a great gift, and I thought I was starting to figure out what this gift was. I was sure John was dead. The cross that said

'Dad' on it was meant for him. And he was lost between two worlds. I questioned him further.

"John, do you remember this corner?" Because John couldn't see far out of the fog, he had to think hard as to the last thing he remembered.

"I remember taking this corner too fast, my wheels slipping, and then sliding off the road. It all seemed to go in slow motion. That's all I remember." he replied.

"John, do you know why you're still here?" I asked.

"I'm not sure, but I know I have to get home because my daughter has her recital tonight and I can't miss it. She worked so hard on her little dance routine. She practiced it for my wife and I over the last two months so she could get it right. Now I can't seem to get out of this fog and make it home in time to see her recital." I noticed John had a watch on and I asked him what time the watch said. "Six-thirty," he said, looking at the watch. "The recital starts at 7:30 and I'm still 30 minutes from home. I have to change out of my suit and pick up my wife so we can get to the recital and get a good seat.

At this moment I looked at my watch which said 11:30. It seems as if time has stood still since John slid off the road. I questioned him some more. "John, are you standing in the snow?"

He looked at me in disbelief and said, "You're standing in it too, you should know!" My heart was racing about 120 beats a minute because I knew I was talking to a ghost. I told John that I had to go and get some information that may help him. John said "You're the first person who stopped to talk to me. I really don't want you to go."

"I know, John," I said, "but I think the information may help you. And I promise I'll come back as soon as I get the information."

John said okay. He asked if I would call his wife and tell her to come get him because he had slid off the road and his car wasn't drivable. I said I could try, and he gave me the phone number. I put it in my cell phone and said goodbye to him. For some reason, I felt the need to back out of the fog that John described. I guess I was a little paranoid about turning around and having my back towards him. Too many ghost stories as a kid, I guess. As soon as I got about 5 feet away from him, he yelled, "Don't forget to come back!"

I felt that same shocking feeling as I passed through this barrier that surrounded John. The pins and needles feeling was back and I was light-headed. As I kept backing up I could still see him but it was obvious he couldn't see me. He began to focus downward on the cross again and started pacing. I hobbled across the street and got into my car. I drove off with my heart still racing and was feeling that either I was going insane, or the so-called gift was obvious now.

As I headed home, I checked my watch and noticed that only five minutes had passed since I had parked the car. So, it appeared that during the time I was with him, time had pretty much stood still. I must've talked to him for 20 minutes and only five minutes had passed. So there was definitely a slowing of time.

Making my way home, I looked up at the road ahead of me just to make sure there was no fog. Still one of the clearest days I had seen months. This fog John described was only in his world, not in mine. As I pulled into the driveway, I almost ran the car into the side of the garage because my mind was so preoccupied with what I had just experienced. I've never seen such a sad situation and wanted to do everything I could to help John figure out what happened, even though I really hadn't figured out what had happened to him.

My first instinct was to get on the computer, something I wasn't very good at, to see if I could find an obituary with John's name in it. Unfortunately, John Patterson was a pretty popular name. After some searching, I was able to find an obituary for a John Patterson that lived in the next town over from us. That town would be about half an hour from the spot where I had my conversation with John. The obituary was pretty standard. It read, "John Patterson, beloved husband of Mary, devoted father of Alexis and William..." and it went on from there. I knew immediately that Alexis was his little girl who was having the recital on the night that John was killed. But I needed more details about the accident or about the circumstances of his death. Some people have a heart attack and drift off the side of the road. It's not always an accident like hitting a tree or another vehicle. I had seen this many times in my days at work where we would find a car with someone in it who was either having a heart attack or who had already died from the heart attack. That's exactly what happened to the truck driver that hit me.

My next step was to go to the library and see if I could find an article in an older newspaper regarding John's death. I was told that they no longer scan each paper and put them on microfiche for further reference, so this option was out.

The only other thing I could think of doing, other than the obvious, which would be to call his wife, was to approach the police department and see if they could give me any information on the accident site. I talked to a very nice, very polite police officer who basically told me that due to the new laws regarding confidentiality they were no longer able to give non-family members information about traffic accidents unless a subpoena was involved.

Unfortunately, this left one option, an option I was having trouble wrapping my head around. By no means was I a counselor or any kind of a psychologist. Calling John's wife scared the hell out of me. She would obviously think I was crazy, and probably would call the police.

The day went on as I contemplated how I was going to approach this. The kids came home from school, my wife came home from work, and before I knew it dinner was on the table. I was obviously in a different world. Eileen asked me if I was feeling okay and I told her I had a small headache. I figured this would account for my quietness. The truth was that my head was spinning. I had no way of knowing why this was happening to me. Even though my grandpa said I would be given a gift I never could've imagined that it would be a gift such as this.

The next day I realized that maybe I hadn't researched the accident hard enough. I went to the local newspaper publisher and asked if they might have a copy of the papers dated right around the time of the obituary. When I was about sixteen, I worked in a print shop, and I remember everything being handset and large plates being used to print newspapers. We had to run every article through a waxing machine that allowed the article to stick to the cardboard layout sheet that would eventually become the printing plate. But now, like everything else in the world, it was all done by computer. So, I knew that there was a chance that if I could find John Patterson's name in an article, I might find out the circumstances of his death.

The newspaper people were very helpful when I made up a story saying John Patterson was an old friend of mine and I hadn't found out about his death until recently. They were able to do a search for his name and come up with an article on his death. It read as follows:

A car driven by John Patterson 38, of Mokena, Illinois was driving southbound on Francis Road during bad weather when he lost control of his vehicle and crashed into a tree. Mr. Patterson was declared dead at the scene. He leaves behind two children and a wife. Funeral services for Mr. Patterson will be held on Friday, January 21 at 10 a.m. at St. Mary's Church in Mokena Illinois.

So now I knew what happened to John and even though I dreaded it, I felt obligated to go back and explain to him the circumstances that led him to the point he was at now.

It had been three days since I had met with him, and I hadn't been past the site since then. I didn't know what would happen when I informed John of the circumstances leading up to his death, but something told me I had to do it. I was also trying to hide this new aspect of my life from my wife and children. They had noticed that I had been very quiet the past three days and wondered if maybe I was having more trouble with the headaches than I was telling them. I kept reassuring them that I was fine and that the headaches were mild they just kind of slowed me down and I felt a little foggy. I thought foggy was a pretty ironic word being that I'd just been sent through a fog that no one I knew had experienced.

My wife had to leave early for work the next day, so it was my responsibility to get the kids off to school. I waited out at the bus stop with my crutches, making sure they got on the bus, and then hobbled back inside. I finished cleaning up the breakfast mess and knew it was time to go back to John's spot. I didn't know if he would still be there, and part of me wished that he would be gone. I got into the car, crutches and all, and headed out towards the roadside memorial where John had been. As I approached, I could see him still pacing back and forth but at a higher speed than he was before. He now seemed anxious and nervous, at least from a distance. I parked the car in the same area, tried to hold the door open while I got myself out, and hobbled across the road with my crutches. Again, this time of day the road was pretty open. I was lucky last time that in the five minutes that I'd spent talking to John no cars had passed by. This area wasn't far from my house, and I worried that someone I knew would see me stopping on the side of the road. The last thing I wanted was someone asking me what I was doing. As I got closer to John I felt the pins and needles feeling start to gather in my body and the lightheadedness that I had experienced before. As I broke through the layer of fog I got the shock feeling. John looked up from the cross and straight into my eyes. His eyes were now nervously darting back and forth, and I felt his level of stress filling the air. John said, "Something's wrong, I don't know what it is but I feel that something is really wrong." It was almost a cue for me to start explaining to John what happened to him.

"John," I said, "the reason you're stuck in this area behind the fog is because you're dead. Do you know that you're dead, John?"

John looked up at me and said, "I had a feeling and was just hoping I was wrong." I continued my explanation.

"I did some research at the library, the police station, and with the local newspaper. Your car slid off the road right here at this point and you hit that tree."

"What tree?" John asked. I realized that John could not see a tree beyond the five-foot range he had in his little world.

I said, "John, just behind the fog there is an old tree that is about 150 years old. Your car hit it at a pretty high rate of speed. Do remember going fast as you tried to make the turn?"

John said, "I was in such a hurry to make it to the recital. I guess I was speeding."

I continued with the explanation. "You were killed instantly."

John looked at me and started to cry. He wasn't sobbing, he just had tears. He looked up at me and said, "Not only am I going to miss the recital, but I'm also going to miss their whole lives." I tried to reassure John that there was something else out there and that he would be able to watch over his children from that point. John started to mention his wife Mary, wondering how she was going to handle raising two kids on her own. I tried to comfort him.

"John, people go through this all the time and somehow find a way to go on living."

John said, "I sense that you have gone through great amount of pain recently. What happened to you that makes you able to communicate with me when I'm supposedly dead?"

I explained my story to John. I told him that I had died several times in the ambulance and on the surgical table. I'd had to have brain surgery, had many broken bones, and a torn aorta. I was not given more than a 10% chance to live. I also told him about the visit from my grandfather and how he had said I would be given a great gift.

"Well now know what that gift is," John said.

"Yes, I guess I do, but I'm not too sure what to do with it."

He said, "You've already done something with it. Now I know where I'm at." He looked at me with a glimmer of excitement and said, "Scott, this fog is lifting, I can see the tree. I can even see the bark that's missing off the tree from where my car hit it. I'm starting to see the road now too. Scott, I can't tell you how glad I am to watch this fog lift. I'm feeling my confusion is also lifting and I know what I have to do. Scott, I need a favor from you. I need you to call my wife say you're an old friend from high school and you want to talk to me. When she tells you that I've gone, ask her how she's doing and how the kids are dealing with this mess. If you make this phone call for me and come back and tell me how it went, I think I can move on."

I felt very uncomfortable with his request. "John, you're asking me to do something very uncomfortable. I don't even know your wife. What if she breaks down on the phone? What am I supposed to do if that happens? I don't know if I can handle it."

But John pleaded with me. "If I get the satisfaction of knowing that they're okay, I can be at peace. Please Scott, just this one favor, and I'm pretty sure I can move on." I reluctantly agreed. As I slowly walked backward, I noticed that the shocking feeling was less than it had been as I entered the area to see John. John was now leaning against the tree that he had hit putting his hand on the bark that had been removed by his front bumper. His sadness still resonated as I was getting in my car. I went back home and looked hard at my cell phone and the number John had given me. I needed to get John to a better place. I wasn't sure how this happened. I had read things about bright light, in fact during my recovery there were several times where I felt close to death where the lights in the room had seemed brighter and more comforting than any light bulb could generate. I think this was my glance at the afterlife, but it was obvious I was not ready to go. Not that I had a choice. Somebody had bigger plans for me.

It was only 11 a.m. when I looked at my cell phone again. I decided I was better off getting this over with and not putting it off any longer. I dialed the number and then quickly hung up. I had no idea what I was going to say. I knew that John had given me the perfect start by saying I was an old high school friend, but I still felt that I didn't know where I would go from there. I dialed the number again. This time I let it ring. The phone was picked up by a little girl. I assumed this was Alexis. I asked if I could speak to her mommy. She said "Sure, I'll go get her." Alexis sounded like she was about 10 years old. I had no idea how old William was but I had the feeling he was much younger. Suddenly a voice picked up a separate line in the house and said hello. I waited until I heard the click of little Alexis hanging up the other phone.

I said, "Hi. I think your name is Mary, right?"

"Who is this?" she asked.

"My name is Bill Johnson. Can I speak to John?" I asked. There was a silence on the phone that seemed to last forever.

"How do you know John?"

"I went to high school with him and I'm back in town. I thought it would be great to get together with him and some of our old friends from high school. I haven't seen him in years."

Mary's voice became somber. "I have some bad news for you Bill. John was killed in a car accident about four months ago."

"What?" I asked seeming shocked.

"Yes, it's true" she went on, "John lost control of his car hit a tree, and was killed instantly."

"Oh my God, Mary, I am so sorry. I feel like such an idiot. I had no idea. This is such a sudden shock to me. I don't know what to say. Are you doing okay?"

Mary said "It's been very rough. The pain is still there, and I miss him very much."

I asked, "Did you guys have children? It's been so long since I talked to John I can't remember if you guys had any kids."

Mary said, "Yes, we have two. You talked to Alexis. She's ten. William is five. They both miss their dad very much."

I then asked, "Are they starting to understand what happened?"

"Alexis knows that daddy is in heaven," Mary said, "but William is still confused. He does understand that he's not coming back. He's starting to understand what happened but it's taking him longer to grasp it. You said you knew John from high school?"

I explained that I was only in a couple of classes with him, but we really hit it off. I ended the conversation with words of encouragement. "John was a great guy. Mary, again I'm so sorry and I hope things get easier for you. I'm not a very religious man but I believe that he's looking out for you and the kids from a better place."

"Thank you," Mary said.

I wished her good luck and hung up.

After taking all this in and going through the gut-wrenching phone call, I realized how lucky I was to make it through my accident and still be around to be with my children and my beautiful wife. I knew I had to settle things with John so that he could move on. The next morning at about 10 o'clock, after the kids were at school and my wife was at work, I hobbled out to the site where John and I had talked. He was still leaning against the oak tree but now had his arms crossed as if he were waiting for me to return. I slowly walked toward John starting to feel the tingling sensation in my body and once I passed the five-foot line, I received that now familiar shock. As soon as his eyes locked on mine, he came up to me and asked how the phone call went.

"John," I began, "to be honest with you it's been very rough for them. Mary still misses you very much. Alexis has an understanding of what happened, and William is starting to grasp it. They both miss you terribly. Mary sounds like she's doing a good job dealing with her grief and the grief of your children. She seems like she really has a good head on her shoulders".

John smiled and said, "Thank you. Thank you so much for letting me know that they are getting along and starting to live life again."

"They'll never forget you, John," I told him. "I could sense it in Mary's voice. I could hear her choking back the tears as she was telling me what happened to you and how it had affected her and the children. It was hard for me to hold back the tears after talking to her as I felt so sorry for you both. But the main thing that bothers me is that you're still here. There's some sort of confusion in your mind that is allowing you to remain at the scene of the accident. I believe it was related to the fact that you had no idea what happened. Do you understand what really happened, John?" John looked confused.

"We'll let me explain something," I continued. "I have been given this gift, which I haven't decided is truly a gift or not and may be a curse for all I know. I am able to see people like yourself who have passed away but for some reason don't cross over. My grandfather appeared to me one day, maybe in a dream, and explained that I'd been given the gift to help people such as yourself. You're the second person I've seen since I talked to my grandfather."

John seemed to be starting to understand. "It's weird, but after your first visit with me, a small light by the cross started to grow. It started slowly growing and enveloped the cross overtaking the shape and brightness of the cross. It is now very bright, and I want to go into it. The light is drawing me towards it, but I'm afraid. I've been out here so long, and I don't know any other world except the one I lived in before and this one. But I want to take you with me so you can understand

and explain things to people the next time you have to do this. Because I have a feeling, you're going to have to do this many more times before you enter the light for the final time."

I answered him with a hesitant tone. "John, I don't think I can do that. Once you go into the light I don't think you're meant to come back out."

"I think they'll make an exception because you need clarification on what your gift is," John reassured me. "You helped me, and my case may not be the most complicated one. So walk with me and we'll see what's behind the light."

"Now it's my turn to be afraid," I said. "Walking into the light as I've learned on the history Channel has always meant the end. Several shows I've seen and books that I've read about the afterlife all mention the same concept. You rush through a tunnel with a small light at the end. At the end of the tunnel, family and friends are waiting. The stories these people tell who come back from the light after being revived from a near-death experience have always been wondrous to me, mainly because I'd spent so much time near death and don't remember having an experience like this. The closest thing to this is my experience with seeing my grandfather the day of the accident and then again during my recovery."

Either way, going into the light had a sense of finality to me. But I felt like I had to trust John because it seemed like the information, he was giving was from beyond his thought process. I don't think you get invited into the light without a special invitation.

At that moment I looked down at my watch and realized only five minutes had gone by. John noticed my action and said "Time stands still in the light, Scott. You won't miss anything." As hesitant as I was, all I could think about was the ability to see my grandfather again. I didn't know if they would allow me to see whatever was behind this beautiful light I was looking at, but I sure hoped they would.

John walked with me slowly towards the light I started to feel very warm and very relaxed. The pain in my leg faded away. I did not need the crutches and left them behind in the ditch. As we entered the light

John could see Mary, Alexis, and William. They all came running up to him and gave him a big hug. This confused me because I knew that Mary, William and Alexis were still alive. When I asked John how this could be he said "Scott, this is my heaven. In my heaven I can have my family with me. I think you have someone waiting to talk to you." He pointed to my left and I saw my grandfather.

Grandpa Bill was walking up to me slowly and with a look of love and a smile the size of Texas on his face. He said "Scott, do you know what kind of gift you've been given?"

I was shaking. "Grandpa Bill, I think I've got part of it figured out. It appears I can see the dead. It's a little unnerving. When it happens, I feel that my bladder might let loose and cause great embarrassment." Grandpa Bill laughed and mentioned how he had always loved my sense of humor.

"Keep that sense of humor throughout your life and bring it to others, and you'll make an impression on everyone you touch," he said. "As for the gift, my son, you've only scratched the surface. You will be given many cases like John's. Some of them old, some of them new. It will not always be easy to recognize the souls you must help, but with time you will understand. Souls get lost when tragedy happens. Not all of them can grasp what has happened and are able to proceed into the light without a problem. Some get stuck in a limbo state such as John and have trouble getting out of it. Their confusion has to be soothed. Your talents will take over and allow them to enter the light. You may share the gift of your talents with Eileen. She will worry about you and may think that this all stems from the accident, but eventually she will see the good you are doing and believe. No one else is to know about your gift. It's the only way you will be able to continue this work."

As I watched John walk away with his family while waving at me, I knew what I had done was good. He would experience the same great feelings and successes he would have experienced on Earth but in the realm of this phenomenal place, his happiness would be guaranteed. Grandpa Bill caught my attention by saying "Scott, it's time to go back. No time has passed, and no one knows where you've been. I will be here waiting for you the next time you bring a soul. John was your first test. You did well. Now go back through the light and go on with your life until you receive your next assignment."

I was nervous now. "Grandpa, how will I know when my next assignment is?"

He reassured me. "You'll know, my son."

It seemed like being with my grandfather had put me right back to the age of 10, when he was a bigger-than-life entity. Grandpa's life was not easy. He was married to a rough woman who had had eight children and should have had none. He worked hard for a living, and somehow seemed to raise all of those children in a nice brick bungalow with enough food on the plates and a roof over their heads.

I'll never forget how he passed on. He had a heart attack in the shower. He was still able to get out of the shower, call an ambulance, and make it to the hospital, where it seemed like he was on his way to recovery. Unfortunately, as in many heart attack cases, there are sometimes complications. He had a pulmonary embolism which killed him quickly. It's good to know that he didn't suffer much, but it was hard on the family, especially for the grandchildren. Grandpas play a big part in the life of most children because they've mellowed in their old age. They've become peaceful and wise and share that feeling and information with their grandchildren. Now, a lot of the parents wonder who this man is and where he came from because he doesn't act anything like he did when he was just a parent. My grandpa was strict as a father and didn't let his kids get away with anything. As a grandpa, he was much more laid back.

Grandpa interrupted my reflecting. "It's time to go back now, son. Be ready; the exit is a little rougher than the entrance." I exited the light with such a force that I couldn't help but feel like I was going to slam into something. I felt the pain starting to come back in my leg and I could see my crutches lying in the ditch. As I exited the light fully, it disappeared. I picked up my crutches, looked at the cross that said 'Dad' on it, and knew John was happy. I knew the cross would fade, and that in both worlds John's family would do well.

On my way home I realized that this gift can be a curse. How do I explain this to people? Do I explain this to people? According to Grandpa, the only person I could explain it to was Eileen. I'd have to keep this to myself and hope no one noticed the crazy guy talking to nothing at the side of the road. It seemed that when I went into the light with John, I disappeared too. But I couldn't be sure of it. My departure from reality seemed to be such a short time, but it's hard to say. I extended my drive home a little bit to go past the same area I just left to see if John was for some reason still hanging around. He was gone. I felt a sense of closure because I had helped him move on to a better place.

I kept going up the road probably slower than the people behind me wanted me to be going, but it's hard to concentrate on the speed limit after you've had an experience making a pit stop in heaven. I pulled into the driveway and realized I had the house to myself, which was both good and bad. Being alone with your thoughts after an experience like that can be a little disheartening. I was still wondering about my sanity. The headache I had was a little worse than the one I'd had before I left this morning. I figured that it might be due to the stress of the situation I'd just experienced. It was about one o'clock in the afternoon when I found myself on the couch watching the Price is Right show. The price must've been wrong, because before I knew it I was asleep.

CHAPTER 7

I woke up to my youngest child coming in the door from the bus. Dana always made a very interesting entrance into the home. She would throw her backpack about 3 or 4 feet in the air so that it landed just to the right of the shoe rack. Although most of the time I was sure she didn't want to see the backpack until the next morning, she was good about doing her homework. Casey soon followed with the same backpack toss and took a quick seat on the couch next to me. The only one left was John, who would be walking through the door at any minute. Mama would come home later, usually around 4:30. Ever since the accident, it was our tradition to sit on the couch and watch whatever the kids wanted. I would ask them about their day they would ask me how I felt. Today I told them I still had a little headache, and my leg was a little achy, but that's as far as I went. I can imagine trying to explain the experience I had to three small children. I take that back; I guess they're not really small anymore. I couldn't ask them to grasp what was going on; hell, I couldn't understand what was going on myself.

John and Dana were teasing each other, which wasn't anything new. Casey had a handful of cookies, which was also nothing new. Casey was one of those kids who could eat all day and not seem to put on any weight. Before we knew it, Mama was walking through the door, and it was time to make dinner. Our kids were pretty finicky eaters so getting one meal together for everyone to eat was almost impossible. My wife had become a short order cook. She could whip up pancakes, bacon, or whatever else the kids wanted. Eileen and I tried to settle on one thing to eat. After the dishes were done and the kids were all doing their homework in their respective rooms, my wife asked me how my day went. I said I still had a headache and it had been there all day, but it was starting to fade. Although my leg ached, I didn't mention it to her because I didn't want her to know that I was running around on it most of the day. At the end of the week on Friday, I was going to have the surgery done to remove the pins from my, so I knew I was going be pretty achy for the next couple weeks anyway.

I thought about telling Eileen that night about my experience but chickened out at the last minute. I guess I wanted to make sure that it wasn't going to be a one-time thing, and if it had happened many times, she would know that there might be some truth to it. The problem was that my curiosity had also gotten the best of me, and I wanted to see if I could help someone else. But I wasn't in any hurry to do so. The day had been very draining. My mind was racing so fast that I hoped the next time this happened, if it happened at all, I might be a little calmer afterwards.

Friday came and went, and the surgery went well. It only took them about 45 minutes to remove the three pins and two screws that were in my leg. My lower leg was pretty swollen, and I was pretty darned sore. But the doc said the bone looked like it had healed well and that it was just a matter of time before I could walk without the crutches. He put me in a walking cast but told me not to bear any weight for at least a week. Eileen was there for the weekend and my recovery. Guys are pretty big babies when it comes to being sick, even though I tried to be as tough as possible. I probably still whined a lot more than Eileen liked. So my remote and I became best friends again and I watched every stupid television show I could possibly think of while I was covered in ice packs from the knee down on my left leg. I had to skip John's practice on Saturday, as I was just too sore to make it there. Eileen went and said he did really well.

Johns got a real talent when it comes to baseball but I don't want it go to his head. I think he already knows he's one of the best ones on the team. But egos can even get in the way for men when they're 14. So, I try to keep him down to earth and make sure he knows that there's always somebody better and he has to keep working at it if he wants to become a pro baseball player. I'm not to ruin that dream if that's what he wants to do.

Sunday was pretty uneventful. It was basically a rerun of Saturday and I became even closer to my remote control. The doctor told me that for two days the only thing he wanted me to do was to get up to go to the bathroom and possibly go downstairs for dinner, but nothing else. The rest of the time I should be in bed. This is not easy for me to do. I get bored way too easy. Casey sat on the bed with me and played Scrabble; a game I despise but he loves so I play it anyway. My spelling is not exactly what you would call academic. In fact, I had trouble spelling academic. Casey usually beats me by about 100 points which doesn't really surprise me. It is a little frustrating to be beaten by a 10-year-old in the game of Scrabble. Again, Sunday night I decided I was too chicken to mention what I'd gone through to Eileen and faded off to sleep.

Monday morning came and I was ready to get up and move little bit. Putting my foot down made it throb because of the incisions and the overall swelling in the foot from the surgery. But I figured it wouldn't hurt me to get up and move around some. Again I had the house to myself, something I had grown pretty accustomed to since the accident. Little bits and pieces of the recovery time had come back to me, and I did remember some of the things that preceded one of my brain surgeries. This was something I couldn't recall until just recently.

I remembered a short conversation with one of the nurses just before I went under, telling me that I was going to be fine, but it wouldn't hurt to say a prayer two. I thought back on that day and wondered how appropriate that statement was, being that during the surgery I coded. I'd never been much for religion, but I'd always believed that there is a God. He must have listened to me that day, or at least heard my little prayer to get through the surgery so I could be with my family again. I'm still missing the first two weeks after the accident because I was pretty much unconscious about 90% of the time. With everything I went through, I'm pretty sure I don't want to remember those two weeks anyway.

So, Monday started off with me walking, or should I say hobbling, down the stairs on my crutches to have my favorite breakfast cereal, Cookie Crisp. I know it's wrong for a grown man to like cookie cereal, but it is one of my favorites. I hobbled back to the couch and turned on the History Channel to see what was going on. I'd become a big fan of the History Channel, because it sure beat the hell out of daytime TV. I was learning quite a bit about things I really did need to learn about. I had always been a history buff, so this was good entertainment for me. The History Channel had become my saving grace during my recovery. I had to watch most of the shows twice because I found myself fading in and out... so the second time I watched the show I wouldI finally comprehend the contents of the whole show. If you asked me about the Cherokee Indians, the Holocaust, or Lindbergh's first flight across the Atlantic, I'd have an answer for you. But if you tried to get me to remember what happened the first two weeks after the accident, I'd have nothing.

Looking back on it, it seems so weird to lose two weeks of your life. Having two weeks disappear without any recollection of them makes me kind of sad. I live for the smiling faces on my kids, and I think that's what kept me going during this long recovery.

I wondered often about John and his life now in heaven. It seemed that everyone had the ability to pick their own heaven and take with them the important things in their life. I was pretty sure that these things were not material in any way. I didn't see anybody driving around in a brand-new Cadillac while I was waving goodbye to John. It seemed to me that you could relive memories and spend time with the ones you loved or love, and continue on in a much less stressful world. I liked the idea of no money worries, or wondering if I still had the ability (or ever would) to change a tire again. I started to think of all the memories I would like to relive. The birth of my children, my wedding day, my honeymoon. Women might have to get the honeymoon thing cleared with the Big Guy though, because I wasn't sure if they allowed that kind of fun in heaven (although I hoped they did.) I'll probably be in trouble for that last line, but who knows.

A week after the surgery I was getting around pretty easily. The swelling had subsided, and I got the stitches out. It was time to start the long physical therapy routine to get some range of motion back in my foot and lower leg. I was told by the orthopedic surgeon that the chances of me regaining full use of the ankle were pretty slim. I was determined to prove him wrong, but I was also pretty sure I'd never run again. Not that I ran beforehand; I have a theory that I don't run unless I'm being chased.

I left therapy with the foot swollen, although not as bad as after the surgery. As instructed by the physical therapist, I iced the leg as soon as I got home. A walking cast was not a cast at all. These days things have changed. They put me in a Velcro-fastened boot that is rigid but can be taken on and off. This made physical therapy easier and also helped to support the foot when I was walking around. I still used the crutches quite often, especially if I was walking any distance, but I found my-self hobbling around the house just holding onto things. I held both handrails to get up the stairs. In the kitchen, I braced myself on the kitchen table, then on the countertops to stand by my favorite place, the refrigerator.

It's not easy to maintain a stable weight after an accident like mine; I had probably put on 10 pounds. This didn't bother me because I knew with time those pounds would fade away. Thankfully, I finally had full freedom when it came to the car. I made many a trip to the library, ran errands for my beautiful wife, and even would surprise the kids by picking them up at school on certain days. The weather was warmer now and riding around in the car with the windows down and the music playing gave me a sense of freedom I hadn't experienced in over six months. It was almost as good as being let out of prison, not that I had ever been in prison. I did get the feeling a few times that I was Andy Dufrain in The Shawshank Redemption on my way to Mexico. The Shawshank Redemption is a movie I've seen too many times. TBS runs that movie every 15 minutes or so but whenever I see it I can't seem to look away. I still find myself watching it when it's on.

Once a month I made a trip to the doctor's office so that he could tell me I was doing fine and charge me $150. He would check all my scars ask me about my head and ask me how the physical therapy was going. Standard answers would apply: I'm feeling fine, when can I go back to work? He'd laugh and say. "You're probably a ways away from going back to work, if you can go back to work at all. Until those headaches and lightheadedness go away, I can't have you up on the cherry picker in the middle of a busy highway, just to go flying out of that thing again. I'm not sure you'd get another second chance."

To which I would reply, "Thanks for the vote of confidence, Doctor." He was a great guy and had been with me since the beginning of the accident. He was a trauma surgeon and a patched me up pretty much from head to toe. The brain surgery had been done by a neurosurgeon, but I only saw him two or three times after the surgery and he handed me over to my regular doctor. I was due to see him in a month or so but was debating whether to even make the trip. His office was in Chicago and other than the headaches and the occasional lightheadedness, which were both fading, I really had no other problems. But as happens in a long-term marriage, I'll do what I'm told, which of course means I'll be going to see the neurosurgeon.

I went to physical therapy every other day. They were interested in one thing and one thing alone, and that was progress. And they would put me in any contraption necessary to gain the progress they needed and then write a little note in my chart saying how wonderful I was doing. I, on the other hand, would go home in pain looking for my favorite icepack. You don't make any progress without any pain, so I can't blame the therapists, although I would really like to. Don was now my main physical therapist. Occasionally he would pass me off to one of the newer therapists just to have them work with me so that on his days off I would be familiar with someone else. Don was about my age, so we had a lot in common. We both had three kids, and Don had been in a bad car accident when he was younger that required him to go through extensive rehab. This made it easier for me to understand why Don was making my life a living hell to try to get better. He had gone through it and knew what it took to get back to normal. I listened to Don and did what he told me. I would occasionally ask them to pass me off to one of the prettier therapists, because Don wasn't nearly as pretty as some of the other ones in the department.

After a couple weeks of therapy, I was walking pretty well. I still had a heavy limp, but I had graduated up to a cane. Not the four-pronged cane, I might add -- just a plain old-fashioned cane. My daughter Dana had decorated it for me with red tape in a kind of peppermint-stick design. Since I wasn't too afraid of someone making fun of my cane, I was more than happy to walk around with it. Dana had a knack for decorating, but unfortunately, she didn't have much of a knack for cleaning her room. I mention this in hopes that someday she'll read this book and clean her room. A guy can dream, can't he?

By the third week I was driving once a day for about an hour just to get out of the house. I must say I was looking for another roadside memorial. So far, I had seen nothing. I wasn't sure if I was relieved by that or disappointed. If I could help people, I would like to do that. Grandpa said I would know when it was time to help the next person.

Waiting patiently something I was never very good at, but that was what I'd have to do.

Before I knew it, my appointment for the neurosurgeon crept up on me. I told Eileen I would be fine going it alone. She was hesitant to let me do that but knew that I had been driving quite a bit and was able to get around much better than I had been in the past. So, like a little mommy bird she released her little chickadee into the world and off I went. This required a trip on the expressway, which is something I hadn't done in six or eight months. I forgot how crazy people are and how the expressway brings out the worst in just about every driver. I saw the usual talking on the cell phone, texting while driving, and my favorite, the guy reading the newspaper while stuck in traffic. It made me very glad I lived in a small suburb southwest of Chicago rather than in the city.

As usual, I waited in the neurosurgeon's office for what seemed to be five or six years. I was finally escorted into a room and was told the doctor would come in just a few minutes. Now, in my extensive experience with doctors, I've learned that they have their own clocks in their heads, which run at a much slower speed than the rest of the world. So basically, a couple minutes means 20 minutes. Ten minutes means 30 to 40 minutes, and God forbid they tell you a half an hour. You may as well take a nap. I was told just a few minutes, so I was prepared to wait for the generalized 10-minute interval. The neurosurgeon walked in finally at the 10-minute mark. I knew this because I was watching the clock as I had nothing else to do in the room.

He asked me the same questions he asked every one of his brain surgery patients, examined my scar, noticed that my hair had covered up the scar, and commented that the scar was actually very well healed. I asked if I could go back to my bouffant hairdo that I had before the surgery, to which he giggled. I stopped at the front desk to get my paperwork was told to see him in three months and that I couldn't go back to work. It's a good thing that the truck driver's company and their insurance policy were top-notch. They had taken care of every expense and replaced my salary after my sick time ran out. I knew their intentions were to avoid a lawsuit. They were constantly making me offers for a settlement, and I kept putting them off. I wanted to see what kind of residual problems I would be left with, and whether I would be able to ever go back to work in the same capacity. So, I kept putting them off saying I would make a decision eventually but I was pretty sure I wasn't going to sue them, I would just take their offer. It was a good way for me to put away some money just in case I couldn't work in the same capacity. I could go back to school and get a degree in something that would allow me to sit at the desk and get fatter than I already was.

On the way home from Chicago I saw quite a few roadside memorials, especially because I was on the Dan Ryan Expressway where death was pretty much an everyday thing. It had become obvious to me that not every roadside memorial produced a lost soul. I'm sure I missed a few of the crosses with flowers and pictures but I never did see a person wandering back-and-forth near one of these roadside memorials.

As I was on the last leg of my journey home, which was Interstate 80, I noticed a man standing off the right shoulder in the ditch. There were deep tire marks in the ground leading down to the spot he was standing. I was in the left lane and although I wanted to stop, traffic was just too heavy, and I figured now might not be a good time to go talk to the soul.

The next day I got on Interstate 80 and headed towards the exit just past where I had seen the man standing by the roadside memorial. I was headed east bound in the right lane when I reached the area of what had obviously been a pretty significant accident. I pulled my car off to the shoulder. It was about 11am and traffic was not that heavy. I put my flashers on, got out of the car with my trusty peppermint candy cane, and slowly walked down the side of the ditch toward the man looking down at the roadside memorial. As I got closer to him, I started to feel tingling in my body. As I got within five or six feet of him, I received that shocking feeling as I passed through what in his eyes was a dense fog. Because of the traffic and the fact that I was on a busy road, I made sure my back was facing traffic and I looked down at the roadside memorial as if I was a mourner who had just stopped to see where his friend had died. I figured I would attract less attention by doing this. I looked up and asked the soul what his name was.

He said Frank. Frank Zeski. Frank was shocked. "How can you see me when everyone else that was around the accident couldn't see me? I waved my arms at them, I jumped up and down, and did everything I could possibly think of to get their attention, but no one responded. They towed my truck away! And then this fog rolled in, and I haven't been able to see anything else other than this stupid looking cross." Frank seemed more than a little angry, mostly about where the hell is truck was. I began to gather the details.

"Frank, do you remember what happened here?" He explained that he was really sleepy when he was driving and was looking for the weigh station so he could pull over and sleep for a couple of hours. He said he lived in Tennessee and was trying to make it back in time for his 60th birthday party. He hadn't had much sleep because he had driven from Duluth, Minnesota and was trying to make it back a day.

I asked Frank if he had noticed a bright light near the cross. He said he wasn't paying much attention to it, but he did notice it. "Do you know where my truck is?" he asked. "Why would they just take away from me? I need to get home. They're waiting for me, and I don't want to be late. My buddies and I have a day filled with a ballgame and some beers."

I didn't know how to tell Frank that he wouldn't be going to a ballgame and that if beer was allowed in heaven, he might get a few in, but not with his friends. I began, "Frank, my name is Scott, and I have a gift. When I see one of these roadside memorials with a cross, I sometimes see a person pacing back and forth as you were. Do you have any idea why no one was responding to you after you fell asleep and went off the road?"

Frank said "I have no idea. People here in Chicago are usually pretty friendly. Maybe I just ran into a bunch of nasty people that night, I don't know. It just seemed that nobody was interested in talking to me."

I continued, "Frank, I want you to think back to what you saw right after you went off the road. Do you remember getting out of your truck?" He said that he did not remember getting out of the truck. "Do remember seeing flashing lights like maybe an ambulance or fire truck?"

He began remembering the pieces. "Yeah, I guess I do. There was an ambulance, but I don't remember seeing a fire truck. I must have hit somebody because they were putting some guy into the ambulance."

I tried to get him to remember more. "Frank did you get a good look at that guy?"

"No, I couldn't see much," he continued. "They were pounding on his chest and everything. I'd only seen that done the movies. Man, they really push on you when they do that."

It was time to help him see the truth. "Frank, I hate to tell you this, but that guy they were loading into the ambulance was you."

He was shocked. "What the hell are you talking about? I'm still here I just can't seem to find my way out of this fog."

"Frank, no one could respond to you that night because you had already passed away," I explained. "Now you're stuck between two worlds and it's my job to move you along to the next one."

Frank got angry. "But what about the party with my family? I don't get it. I'm fine. As soon as they bring my truck back, I'll get the hell out of here. Why don't you just leave me alone?"

I tried again to explain. "Frank, I can't leave you alone. It's time for you to move on."

Now he was really angry. "Just get the hell out of here!" Frank screamed. With that, I was lost as to what to do. I slowly backed out of the fog and hobbled back up to my car. I felt as if I had failed Frank and wondered if I really was cut out for this.

I drove home knowing that hardly any time had passed from the time I had gotten out of the car. Frank seemed like a hard kind of guy; you know, a real man's man. Truck driving fit his personality well. He seemed like a hard-driving, live fast, die young, and leave a good-looking corpse kind of a guy. Unfortunately, the latter had happened, and I couldn't seem to convince him of it. It occurred to me on the way home that maybe it was too early. The fresh tire tracks and the medical waste on the ground near the accident site made me believe that it was pretty obvious that the accident just happened one or two nights ago. Frank may not have been able to grasp the concept that he could possibly be dead. Remember, time stands pretty still after you die. To him only a short period of time at passed since he had gone off the road. To the rest of us, as I found out later in the newspaper, five days had passed. As I pulled into my driveway, I realized I would have to go back to visit Frank. I just didn't know when. Should I wait one day, two days, or maybe give him a week? I could tell no matter how long I waited; it was going to take some convincing to get Frank to cross over to the other side.

Now I was sure that this was no fluke. Grandpa Bill was not a figment of my imagination, and this gift was real. This was the second soul I had interacted with, and I was pretty sure it wasn't going to be the last. I was beginning to wonder when the right time would be to tell Eileen. How do you explain this to a person, even someone you've been with for so many years? The main thing I wanted to know was whether she would think I was completely out of my mind, or if she would listen and take my word for it. It wasn't that easy to explain, and how I would justify that me, a nobody from southwest suburbs of Chicago, could be given such a great gift.

As usual, I chickened out again, figuring I would know the right time to tell her. This didn't seem to be it. I knew I had to go back to where Frank was and see if I could convince him after a little time that he needed to cross over to the other side. So, I waited two days and decided to revisit him. Again, I took Interstate 80 eastbound, made a U-turn on Harlem Avenue and started back westbound to the accident site. I pulled off the road again. I put on my flashers, which I figured would make it look like I was just having a little car trouble, and slowly walked down to where Frank was.

Frank had sat down on the ground next to the cross looking kind of content. As the tingling started and it broke through the barrier of fog

Frank met me with a solemn look on his face. "It's true, isn't it?" he said. "I'm dead. I'm really dead. Dead as a door nail, whatever that means."

It was obvious Frank had made the connection and actually had little bit of a sense of humor about it. I asked him if he had noticed a light, maybe a bright light by the cross.

He said, "Yeah, I can't stop staring at it. I feel like its calling me, but I don't know whether to go in or stay here. I still want my truck back."

I had to reinforce the obvious. "Frank, I'm afraid your truck is probably sitting in a junkyard somewhere getting ready to be demolished."

He said, "Hell yeah, I know, the damn thing was brand-new. It had everything in it. It had a frickin' queen-size bed in it, a kick-ass stereo, and a full navigation system. Damn truck cost me $120,000. Now it sits in a junkyard waiting to be chewed up by some monster machine because I fell asleep at the wheel! Why didn't I stop earlier? If I had just stopped earlier and gotten some rest, this would've never happened."

Now I found myself being philosophical. "Frank, do you believe that everybody's given a certain time on this earth and when your time's up, your time's up?"

"Yeah, I guess I do," Frank said. "I guess my time was up huh?"

I agreed. "It would appear that way, Frank. Now I'll walk you into that light and when you see what the other side looks like, I'm sure you won't miss your truck anymore."

Frank stood up told me was scared. He said, "I can't believe I'm scared. I've had bar fights that make the movies look tame. I lost a part of a finger changing a tire just outside of Mobile, Alabama. I knew they couldn't save it because it was too crushed. I wrapped it up and went to the hospital. They sewed the end of it up and I was on the road again. But this scares me. What if I haven't been a good enough guy to get in there? What if God thinks I was an ass? I guess I wouldn't blame him, I haven't exactly been a perfect human being."

I tried to reassure him. "Frank, I don't think God judges you as much as you think he will. Heaven will be your heaven, the heaven you've always dreamed about. I'm sure you can look back on your life and apologize for what you've done wrong. I'm sure you have good qualities

Frank, and I'm sure he'll look upon those and decide that you do belong there. Now walk into the light Frank, and don't be afraid."

He looked at me with a confused look. "Are you dead?" he asked.

I explained, "I'm not, Frank, but I've had several near-death experiences and I've been given this gift. I help people move on to the next world and that's what I'm hoping to do with you. So, if you'll let me, let's go see what awaits you.

Frank said, "I'm ready, but I'm still pissed off that I missed my party."

I told Frank that I wasn't so sure he missed it, that he just may have it in another place. Frank and I walked into the light and felt the sudden speed in the tunnel's presence. Before I knew it we were standing on the other side. To the right of me was obviously the setup for a 60th birthday party. Frank's friends were all around the table, beer in hand, with a toast ready. Frank looked at me in confusion. "Are my friends dead too?"

I reassured him. "No Frank, they're not. In this world your heaven is what you want it to be. They were looking forward to your 60th birthday party just as you were. I'm not sure about this Frank, but I think the souls of your friends are allowed to leave their bodies and come up here to the other side to help welcome you into heaven."

Frank was still concerned. "But what about all those bad things I did?"

Just then I noticed that Grandpa Bill had walked up next to me. I glanced over at him wondering what the answer to this question was. Grandpa Bill was about the same age as Frank. He tried to explain.

"Frank, we learn from our mistakes and our souls become better after we accept what we've done, forgive ourselves, and apologize to the ones we've hurt. It may take several years for you to apologize to everyone that you've hurt because you can't do that until they enter heaven. But when they do, you'll have your opportunity. You'll also be given time to think back on all the people you've hurt and prepare yourself so that your apology will be accepted."

Frank looked at my grandfather and asked, "Do I know you?"

I was quick to reply. "No Frank, you don't know him. He's my grand-father and is the one teaching me how to help people like you."

Frank's voice softened. "Well, I like the old boy. He seems a lot like me and seems like a tough guy too." We all laughed. Frank was a gentle soul, and I knew it, but I'm sure he was a tough guy before now. Frank asked if he could go join his friends.

I asked, "Is that what you came up here for?"

He said, "Hell yeah! Oh wait, I guess I shouldn't swear up here, should I?" I laughed.

"I'm thinking it's probably not a good idea Frank, but I have a feeling it's something that's going be hard for you to get used to."

Frank agreed. "Yeah, it's going to take me a little while to get used to it."

As Frank joined his friends, I had a warm feeling in my heart. Frank wasn't easy to convince, but I'd gotten him over to the other side and I was kind of proud of that.

Grandpa Bill turned to me. "Frank was giving you a little bit of a hard time it seemed?"

I agreed. "Yeah, it wasn't easy, and it is amazing that we got him here."

"No, you got him here," Grandpa praised, "You're starting to get the hang of this. But it's going to get rougher from this point out. Some of the things you're going to see are going to be hard for you to handle. You've got to trust your instincts. You'll know whether it's time to bring them across or not. There's nothing wrong with letting them wait a little bit. Some people just aren't ready when they die to cross over. We try to keep them in the area of their death to contain them until they've come to the realization that they have passed away. You also may run into people who have been there for a long time. Some souls accept their death without any remorse. Others are very remorseful, but they cannot move on until they have settled their issues on earth first."

With that, I felt myself being whisked back through the tunnel and facing the cross again. I returned to my car, turned the flashers off, and again realized that I had only been there for less than 10 minutes. I started the car, and off I went. I looked back just to make sure Frank was gone, and he was.

CHAPTER 8

By the time I got back home, I decided I needed a rest. My foot was swollen, and I still had to go to physical therapy. It seems going up and down a hill is not a good idea in a soft cast. At therapy, Don looked at my leg and quickly reprimanded me for bearing too much weight on it and causing it to swell. We had to go easy that day and spend less time in the torture chamber. He iced my ankle before I even left. I told Don some made-up story about having to walk Dana to class and how I'd forgotten my cane in the car. He bought it. But he reprimanded me again about forgetting my cane. Physical therapists like to reprimand; I think it's in their DNA. I've been associated with PT for so long that I had grown to know their way. So I knew I'd have to behave myself for the next couple of days to get back on Don's good side. And that is just what I did.

The next couple of days were uneventful as I drove around town. Eileen and I began to have a weekly date night because I had been so bored over the past six months. Getting out of the house, just she and I, had become very important. We always stayed local and would usually have a few drinks and a nice dinner and be home by 9:30. I felt like I owed her a lot more than this, like maybe a trip to Hawaii. I felt like I had put her through so much over the last six or eight months. I hoped that we'd be able to do that after I was all done healing. I wondered how the change in pressure of an airplane ride would affect my headaches. A boy can dream though, can't he? God knows she deserves a trip and I hoped to be well enough soon to get her to wherever she wanted to go.

With spring in full bloom, John had baseball practice after school every day of the week. I tried to make two or three of them if I could, but it was hard with physical therapy and my daily trips looking for clients, so to speak, on the side of the road. When I did make the practices, the smile on his face was worth the price of admission. Not that there was a price of admission, but you know what I mean. He was such a good baseball player, and it was so much fun to watch him. I don't know where he got this talent, but it sure wasn't from me. I could barely catch a ball as a kid. I was a bad hitter, and I spent most of my time in right field if you know what I mean. John was a shortstop and had more balls coming at him than anyone else on the field. He would scoop up the ball, turn and fire towards first base, and get the runner out every time. God, it was fun to watch.

After practice I would take him home and pretend, I knew enough about baseball to give him some tips. He would look at me and smile and nod his head as if to say, "Thank you for your advice, but I know you know nothing about baseball." And he was right.

Casey's favorite sport hadn't started yet. He was a basketball superstar. At the ripe old age of 10 he could run circles around all the other kids, even the 12-year-olds. He was a great outside shooter and could actually make a layup at the tender age of ten. I hoped that by the time his season started, I would be able to get up and down the stands without a cane and hopefully with a little less pain.

Dana was the princess, and by that, I mean a true princess. She was all girl. Dance recitals, piano lessons, and hip-hop jazz. Sports were not her thing, nor would they ever be her thing. Dana did not catch a ball until she was five, and even then, I think it was only an accidental catch. But she always looked cute as can be in her little dance outfits trying her best to look coordinated on the dance floor. Again, I don't know where she got the dancing, but I knew it wasn't from me. I dance like a white guy. And as you know, it's against the law for white guys to dance well. We try hard but still look like fools. Especially old white guys such as myself. Dance recitals were both wonderful and painful at the same time. Usually, the girls performed two routines. If you were lucky, your daughter would perform both routines first and then you could skedaddle out of there. But it was more likely that your child would be in the first dance and the last dance, leaving you sitting through two hours of other children's dance routines and trying desperately to look in the least bit interested. It's not that I have anything against the other kids, it's just that my ass gets sore sitting in the seat for two hours.

Dana had decided to take a break from dance class for this semester because it would make things easier on her mother. She's a thoughtful child and I think she realized that Mom was doing all the running around and it would give her a break if she didn't have to take her to dance. Dana liked the dance classes but had no problem living without them for six months or so. Eventually, when I can run around freely and not get tired and sore so easily, we will sign her up for the dance classes again.

I was progressing nicely after several weeks of therapy, and on my next trip to the doctor I was told that I could start bearing full weight on the ankle. I was happy to get rid of the cane. I'd spent more time swinging it around like Charlie Chaplin than I did actually using it. Now I would only take it with me if we were going to the mall or somewhere that involved a long walk.

I had become very deconditioned from being laid up for so long, and I had never felt this out of shape. Not that I was in great shape to start with, although round is a shape as my wife says. My belly had pretty much disappeared since the accident due to the lack of nutrients I could take in during the early part of my recovery. I'd started to gain some weight back, which was a good thing. My wife and I and my trusty cane had started to take a walk every day down the street and count the houses we passed. At first, I could only make it about five or six houses and then we'd have to turn around. With time though, I could get to the front of the neighborhood. This was only a 10-minute walk, but after being laid up for six or eight months a 10-minute walk was quite an accomplishment. I don't know if I just got winded because of my poor condition or if the pain in my ankle just made it too hard to go any further. But with time I started walking past the front of the neighborhood and got to the point where I was approaching a half a mile in my daily walks. I was done going to physical therapy.

Now that I didn't need the cane, I eventually progressed to walking half a mile. There were days though, when a half a mile seemed like

10, and I felt like an Ethiopian marathon runner and 110° heat, except without being in real good physical condition.

Eileen stuck with me during these walks whenever she could. I would wait until she got home from work and give her time to change and usually from four o'clock to five o'clock, we would walk. As you can tell by the hour it would take, my pace was kind of slow. Most of the time the walk was followed by an icepack and a lovely recline on my sofa.

The weeks of summer came and went, and I had gone at least three months since my incident with Frank. I had seen many roadside memorials but none with people standing around them. I figured most of these people had moved on without a problem, so they didn't need my services. I started to wonder if I could see people in other locations than just at roadside memorials. There was a graveyard about 2 miles from my house that was quite old. Wandering graveyards had been a hobby of mine over the years since I liked history so much. I enjoyed researching some of the older graveyards in the area to find the names of the people that some of the streets in our town were named after. I remember there being a big plot of land in the graveyard dedicated to the Francis family, which is the road where I first saw John. I had hesitated to go to the graveyard since my accident because I feared what I might see. Let's face it, a graveyard is filled with memorials, and I didn't know if the only memorials that mattered in my world were roadside memorials. I couldn't decide whether or not to make a visit to our local cemetery and see what I could see. Part of me was frightened that the cemetery would be filled with people only I could see. I couldn't think of anything that would be more overwhelming than a cemetery filled with people who needed my help.

One day, my curiosity got the best of me, and I decided to take a ride towards the cemetery. I had no intention of going in; I just wanted to see if I could see anyone from the road. I slowly worked my way down Francis Road, passing the site where I'd spent so much time with John. I then moved along to the Vine Street where I made a right and headed toward the center of town. The cemetery was almost centered directly in the town square. It was old and there were some graves in there from the early 1800s. I made a left on Haven Street and headed towards the cemetery which was about a block and a half away. I checked my rear-view mirror to make sure no one was behind me so I could go at a slow pace as I passed the graveyard. The cemetery was on the hill and I could only see the outlying graves. This was the older part of the cemetery where some of the graves dated back to the 1800s. No souls.

I made a left on Oak Street which was where the entrance to the graveyard was. These graves were more on the same level as the street. From this level I would be able to see more of the graveyard. It was a bright sunny day, so I had no trouble visualizing most of the graveyard. The only thing I saw were two little girls playing. They looked about the same age as my daughter Dana, around seven. They were just to the left of the entrance to the cemetery, about 100 yards back. They were dressed as if they had just come out of the 1930s. It looked like they were playing Ring around the Rosie. I was sure they were lost souls.

I decided to keep driving slowly just to check out the rest of the cemetery. On the far-right side near the end of the cemetery there was an elderly man sitting on one of the headstones looking down at the grass and not moving. His face was wrinkled, and he walked with a cane which was by his side. He wore a fedora hat and an older suit. He would take his hat off, wipe his brow with his handkerchief, put his hat back on, and put his handkerchief back in his pocket. I saw him do this twice while I was staring at him. I figured he was another lost soul.

I was afraid of this. I was finding my own assignments now. I decided to park the car in the cemetery and research the names without entering the fog that surrounds the space that separated our two worlds. The two little girls were now sitting down in the grass picking out little flowers that had grown wild near their gravesites. The last name on the gravestones was Connor. Lisa and Emily Connor. As I got closer to the children, I realized they looked like twins. Identical twins. They were dressed alike as most children that age would be. Their gravestones were right next to each other, and the date said born August 4, 1931 and both stones said they had died December 31, 1938. This was an obvious tragedy for this family, and I wasn't sure I wanted to investigate these deaths. I wrote down the dates and the names of the two beautiful little girls and moved on to the grave of the elderly man at the end of the cemetery.

The headstone he was sitting on was somewhat obscured by weeds. It was a good thing he was sitting sideways on the headstone otherwise; I would not have been able to make out the dates of his birth and death dates, not to mention his name. His name was Elven Warden. He was born in January 2, 1901 and died in June 18, 1980. His wife's gravestone was next to his and I realized he was staring down at hers. He had tears in his eyes and was alternating wiping sweat from his brow and tears from his eyes.

From the dates on his headstone, I could see that he'd lived a long life, especially for someone who grew up in that era. I wasn't sure why he was still hanging around. Something had happened after his death that kept him here. He looked very confused and very despondent, unlike the two little girls who seemed to be playing as if they had woken up the morning after their death and continued to play like they did every day. I took my notepad, walked around the side of the cemetery to avoid entering the fog that these three souls were in, and got into my car to go home. I decided to make a stop at the library to see if I could find any information on any of the souls.

The libraries microfiche area was rarely used, but I knew I'd be spending more and more time there. I asked the librarian who was on duty to help me. I was looking for the names of two little girls that lived in the 1930s and may have died in a tragic accident. The date they died was December 31, 1938. Their names were Lisa and Emily Connor. She was able to find a newspaper from January 1, 1939, which had the information that I needed. The name of the newspaper back then was the Daily Bugle, which I thought was rather interesting.

The story about the two girls was tragic. There had been a house fire in which the mother, father, and three older brothers were able to escape. The father went in several times to try to find the girls but ended up almost dying from smoke inhalation. Firefighting was pretty crude in those days and houses were made of nothing but wood so I'm sure it was a raging inferno in no time. Getting those children out must've been an impossible task for both the father and the fire department. Obviously, they didn't succeed. The girls were buried January 3, 1938. The family was not sure if they were going to rebuild after the fire or move on to another town to forget about the horrors of the house and what they had left behind. I could not find anything else on the family in the archives, so I assumed they'd moved to a less painful place.

As for Elven Warden, I was able to find his obituary from June 19, 1980. He died of natural causes and had left behind five children, 12 grandchildren, and two great-grandchildren. He was preceded in death by his wife Maria in 1972 and an infant son in 1940. The obituary went on to describe where and when the wake and funeral would be and the usual cemetery internment dates. That was all the information I could get on Elven Warden. I decided I would start with him on the following day.

In the morning, I got all the children often off to school because Eileen had to work early. I headed out to do my work. Parking the car in the cemetery lot, I slowly walked up to Elven Warden's grave and as I got closer, I started to feel the same feelings I had felt with the two previous souls. As I crossed what I was starting to call the shock line, I entered Elven's little world. The fog surrounded both of us and he slowly looked up at me. Elven didn't look surprised or interested in my appearance.

"Looks like we got another cemetery researcher, Maria!" Elven said. He must've thought I was there only to check out the gravestones and maybe was historically interested in who Elven was.

I slowly said, "Elven Warden?"

He looked up at me with a surprised look on his face and said, "You can see me!"

I said "Yes, I can. I've been given a gift, Elven, and that gift is to figure out why you're still here."

"I know why I'm still here" Elven said angrily. "I'm waiting for Maria. I don't know where she is, and she left before me. I expected her to be waiting here when I crossed over and have been nothing but disappointed."

I said, "Elven, you know you are between worlds, don't you?" He looked confused.

"What do you mean by that?"

I tried to explain. "I mean when you died, you got stuck here for some reason. I don't know why, but you've been suspended here since the day you died. Do you see a light anywhere?"

He said, "It's over there by the caretaker shed. It widens and shrinks in size all the time, but I'm not going into it until Maria is with me."

I said, "Elven, don't you realize that Maria is already in the light? And so is your infant son, the one you never got to know because he died so young."

Elven said in a low tone, sad sounding voice, "I barely remember him. He was only a month and a half when he died. Something was wrong with his heart, and they couldn't save him. He was our first son and I thought Maria would never get over it. She was shattered. I buried myself in my work and tried to forget the tragedy we had gone through. We only had one picture of him, and it spent 40 years on our mantle in my living room. It was still there the day I died. His name was Joshua from the Bible. That's why I don't understand why I'm still here. I was a God-fearing man and did what I could to be a good person. I went to church every Sunday and even gave to the poor and yet I'm stuck here. Can you tell me how long I've been here?"

"Well, Elven, it's 2011," I explained. "You've been here for 31 years."

Elven looked surprised and also horrified. "I've been here for 31 years? I can't believe that! I feel like I just died yesterday."

"I guess time does standstill after you pass away" I said. "The other souls I've worked with have told me that."

He asked about Maria. "Can I see her now that you're here?" I

said, "I think we can. Have you been afraid to go into the light?"

He confessed, "I have been because I can't find Maria and I want her to be in heaven with me. Otherwise, I'd just as soon stay here."

"Well there's only one way to find out, Elven," I said. "Be ready to take a journey because I think it's your time to do so. Although the fog around us obscures your view of the world and how it's changed, the cemetery you were buried in 31 years ago has quite a few more souls buried in it than when you were placed here. Keep that in mind as you exit the fog. We will walk towards the light, and I will walk with you. I will even accompany you to the next world."

He said, "They let you see heaven even though you're not dead?"

"I get a slight glimpse of it and get to talk to my grandfather who passed away the same year you did. He helps me through this."

Elven asked "You weren't able to do this before your accident where you?" This caught me off guard because I hadn't mentioned that I'd been in an accident and my gift had been a byproduct of that accident. I looked shocked.

"How did you know I was in an accident?"

He said, "I just knew, I don't know why it just popped into my head. Maybe it's to help me understand."

I brushed aside his comment. "Are you ready to move along, Elven?" He wiped the sweat from his brow just one more time and the tears dried up. He put his fedora on and straightened his suit.

"I want to look good for Maria, and I don't want her to be disappointed," he said.

I tried to reassure him. "I'm sure she won't be disappointed, Elven. What I am sure of is that she is going to be very glad to see you. And something tells me she's going to be holding Joshua in her arms."

As we exited the fog, the light was about 15 yards away. This was the first time I had to walk some distance to get into the light. That's why I'd warned Elven that some things may have changed since he was placed in the cemetery. As we exited the fog, he did notice there were quite a few more graves. The day he was placed in his grave he could see the whole graveyard, but as time went by the fog rolled in and within a week or so he could only see a short distance encompassing only his and Maria's grave. He had been in that small little world for approximately 31 years. They had built a large office building next to the cemetery that was made out of glass and metal supports. It was very futuristic looking, even in 2011. Elven looked up at the building and was quite shocked.

"That used to be an empty lot," he said. "What the hell is that?"

I said, "That's an office building. Pretty futuristic looking isn't it Elven?"

He said, "It looks like a damn spaceship!"

I laughed and said, "Yeah I guess it does." Elven looked down at his feet knowing we were about to enter the light. He stopped.

"I'm still scared Scott."

I tried to reassure him. "I know that once we get through it, you'll be very happy we did. What do you say we give it a shot?"

With that we walked into the light. We were rushed through the tunnel and before we knew it we were on the other side. Again, the pain in my leg was gone and I felt a sense of peace come over both Elven and I. Grandpa Bill was there again welcoming us.

Elven said, "Thank you, have you seen my Maria?" Grandpa Bill moved slowly to his left and this beautiful young girl with black hair and a beautiful little baby in her arms was visible at a distance. She wore a 1940s style hat and a beautiful, flowered dress. She smiled at Elven, and he was gone in a flash. He kissed her and held his baby and the tears in his eyes, and mine, began to flow.

Grandpa Bill looked at me and said "I told you this was a gift! Doesn't it make you feel great to reunite people?"

I agreed. "It does, it really does. But I'm still confused. Why was Elven stuck there for 31 years?"

Grandpa explained, "I'm afraid I can't tell you that Scott. There are reasons for everything and there are also people like you with the same gift who are able to move these people along to the other side. Sometimes it's just a matter of waiting until the right person comes along. You are that right person. Elvin needed you to finally be able to see his Maria and his little baby. To Elven, he only waited a short time. You, on the other hand, see 31 years as almost forever. Don't get hung up on time. It matters little on the other side. Now go back, my son. As I recall you have two little angels to help cross over. Convincing them will take some work. Children don't understand the light as much as adults do. They know the light is there, but they usually don't know what it means. You are going to have to get down to their level and convince them that good things are waiting for them in the light. I can only help you in one way and that is to let you know that their parents and their brothers are all already in the light. They are waiting anxiously for you to do your job. I know moving someone along takes a lot of energy out of you so maybe you need to come back tomorrow and try to move the children along."

I saw Elven and Maria waving at me as they turned and walked away, heading towards what looked like a beautiful meadow and a picnic area that had been set up by Maria to welcome her Elven to the other side. Elven was still holding the baby and walking with pride. He turned one more time and tipped his hat as if to say I'm glad you showed up.

Grandpa Bill said it was time to go back, and I felt a sudden whoosh propel me back through the light. Grandpa was right; I was exhausted and knew that I needed time to think of how I was going to help Lisa and Emily cross over. I left the cemetery but went past the little girls to see that they were still picking flowers and laughing out loud. I knew they would be okay for one more day until I could get back to the cemetery.

I got home just in time to meet the kids at the door and realized I had been gone for an hour and a half. They had a half day that day and we enjoyed the afternoon outside sitting by our pool until Mama got home. She came out and sat with me and asked me how my day went. I said, "Much the same as usual, but there is something I have to tell you when we're alone."

She kind of gave me the, "What have you got in mind, big boy?" look and I gave it right back to her. You never know what a woman is thinking, so you have to be ready at all times.

I knew I had to tell Eileen about this gift. Grandpa Bill said it would be okay to talk to her about it and that she would understand. I remembered that he told me that she might be a little confused at first, but with time she would understand what I would need to do for the rest of my life. We gathered up the children and went inside to have dinner.

Grilling had become a specialty of mine and I had become quite good at it since the accident. Well, I guess I should say after the accident, when I was up and about. The kids really never wanted much more than a hamburger or hot dog on the grill, but I had become quite the steak connoisseur and believed in marinating the steaks, and grilling them to perfection. I also liked to grill the onions, some peppers, and zucchini on the grill mix them all up and use them as a topping on the steaks. I had almost gotten to the age where unbuckling my belt was necessary after eating a meal such as this. But I do emphasize the almost part.

After getting the kids off to bed that night and Eileen and I were lying in bed watching TV she reached over and grabbed the controller and turned off the TV. She asked, "What is it you have to tell me because I know you've been thinking about it for some time now. You seem preoccupied all the time like there is something eating away at you and if you don't tell somebody, it is going to keep eating away at you. So, matter what it is I'm here to listen and whatever it is we can get through it."

I explained, "There's really nothing to get through, just something for you to understand. Remember the day of the accident?" She looked at me like I had lost my mind.

"What do you think?"

I continued, "Yeah, I guess that was a stupid question. Remember the morning when I was leaving how I'd gotten out of the car and walked around the garage?"

She remembered, "Yeah that seemed so weird. You said you thought you saw something or someone."

"At the time," I explained, "I didn't think much of it because it seemed so weird. The person I saw was my Grandpa Bill."

Eileen interrupted me. "Didn't he die in like, 1980?"

"Yes, I was only 18 when he died," I recalled. "But he was the only grandpa I had. My other grandparents had died before I was born."

Eileen questioned me further. "So, you're sure the person you saw going behind the garage was your Grandpa Bill?"

I nodded, "I'm sure now, after what has happened to me over the last months. Remember our trip home from the hospital?" I asked.

Eileen said "Of course, that was the happiest day of my life! I didn't think I was ever to get you back."

"Remember me mentioning the guy on the side of the road that was standing by the cross? You know, the roadside memorial?"

She said, "Yeah, I thought you were just seeing things because you were still recovering from the head injury. I didn't think much about it. I just figured your mind was playing tricks on you."

"Well, I can tell you, it wasn't playing tricks on me. Even though you couldn't see him, I could. His name was John," I continued.

She looked shocked. "How do you know his name? He wasn't even there!"

I tried to remain calm. "He wasn't there in your eyes, but he was in mine. Eileen, this is some very weird stuff. Not too long ago, Grandpa Bill appeared to me and said I was given a great gift after the accident. As you can imagine, I thought I was going insane. But Grandpa Bill looked so real I felt like I could reach out and touch him. He told me it was going to be my job to help cross over people who were lost between the two worlds. The only thing I can think of is that my brain injury awakened a part of the brain that no one knows about or uses, because the brain is such a mystery to medicine. You know me, I've never been the most religious person in the world, but I've always believed that there was something after this. Eileen, I've gotten to look at it and it's pretty amazing. I know this all sounds like I'm flipping out, but I can guarantee you that I'm not. I've been able to research the couple of people that I've helped cross over and find out about how they were killed or died, the dates, and the circumstances in their life at the time of their death. The guy I said I saw by the side of the road was named John. He left behind three kids and a wife. He fell asleep at the wheel and smashed into the oak tree right at the corner of Francis and Gougar Roads. He was killed instantly, but somehow, in the confusion of the accident, he didn't know he was supposed to move on to the other side."

Eileen's eyes were popping out of her head by now. "Do you mean the other side as in heaven?"

"Yes, that's what I mean," I answered.

She was now right in my face. "So, what you're telling me is that you can not only see the dead but you can help get them into heaven and you've actually seen heaven?"

I tried to explain more. "I know it sounds crazy and I know you're probably questioning whether I'm having an episode of something because of the accident, but trust me, I'm not. I feel better now than I ever have, and I feel like I'm really helping. I don't know why they chose me and hope you won't leave me because you think I'm crazy. Because I'm not. I don't understand why they picked me to help move the souls along and it's not something you just turn down. So that's my story. When I go for a ride during the day I'm looking for souls. Either roadside memorials, people who are in cemeteries, or just people who look lost. I've helped three people so far. But I have a feeling eventually I'm going to run into someone that isn't associated with a memorial of any type. I don't know why I have this feeling; I just do. I haven't told anybody else about this, and they told me the only one I could tell was you. Those were Grandpa Bill's words. So I'm telling you. You have to know because it will be hard for me to explain every time, I see someone who needs my help."

I waited patiently for Eileen's response wondering if she would be calling the doctor in the morning and asking to have my head examined. But as usual she supported me and believed in me to the best of her ability. She did have questions though. Many questions. Such as, what does heaven look like, do these souls know that they're dead, and how do I get back after I've crossed through the light? Just as I'd thought, she thought once you are in the light you didn't come back.

I explained to her that there were many people who had gone through the light in near death experiences and had returned telling stories of their experiences. I told her my experiences were from the very edge of the light. I explained that I felt like I was at the entrance to heaven and wasn't allowed to go any further. I felt like an escort for the dead, the dead that were confused. My job was simply to get them through the light and to the other side. Eileen worried that I might cross over and never come back. I explained that I felt like I was just a quick visitor, and my job didn't involve staying in heaven. It was all about the souls and getting them to the right place.

Needless to say, neither one of us slept very well that night. I think Eileen was worried about my health, especially my mental health, and I was worried that Eileen was thinking about my mental health. When we awoke in the morning, I asked her if she understood what I was talking about last night and how important this job was to me. She felt like she needed to have a few days to wrap her head around it and felt that together we needed to do a little research on life after death. I reassured that I would do whatever it took to help her believe me. I'm sure she went off to work that morning worried. I reassured her that I would not tell the children anything.

CHAPTER 9

I got showered and got everybody off to school, then went directly to the cemetery. I wasn't as worried about people seeing me in the cemetery as I was about people seeing me on the side of the road. People were always in the cemetery, and they always looked reflective. I entered the graveyard and parked in the same spot I'd parked yesterday. This time I would be visiting the twins, Lisa and Emily. I slowly walked over to their spot in the graveyard. They were playing tag. As I got closer, I started to feel the tingling sensation at a greater distance than usual. It seemed like the twins had been given a little more space so they could play. As I passed through the shocking sensation I entered their realm. They looked up at me and then looked down at their feet seemingly shy and in tune with each other's feelings.

I said, "Hi girls."

They looked shocked. "How can you see us?" one of the girls asked. "No one else can see us."

I tried to explain. "I was sent from a special place where lots of people love you," I said. "Which one of you is Emily?"

A shy little voice answered, "I am." She was the twin to my left.

"Then you must be Lisa?" I asked of the other.

She said, "Yes, I am Lisa. That's my sister, Emily. We're seven. What's your name?"

I said, "My name is Scott."

They laughed. "That's a silly name. We've never heard of the name Scott."

Just then I had remembered that Scott was a popular name in the 60s and 70s. These girls were from the 1930s and probably had never heard of the name Scott. "Yeah, it is kind of a silly name," I said. "But it's my name!" They giggled. "I see that you girls like to play tag and Ring around the Rosie, don't you?" I asked.

Emily explained, "It's our favorite game, tag. We like Ring around the Rosie too, but we'd rather play tag most of the time. Most of the time we just sit and talk while we're waiting."

I was very curious. "What are you waiting for?" I asked.

Lisa replied "We don't know. Something, I guess. But we don't know what. We don't see our mommy and daddy anymore or our brothers. Do you know where they are? We saw them the day that we came here. Mommy and Daddy used to come here and cry with our brothers, but we could not talk to them. We tried to play with them and even made silly faces at them, but they never talked to us. We pretended like we were invisible to them lots of times. We must've been good at because they never could see us. Now they don't come here anymore. We just see other people come over to the other spots when they walk through our playground."

It seemed so strange to hear them refer to the cemetery as a playground. But to these two little girls, the small area they had occupied for some 70+ years was their little playground.

Emily said, "Whenever someone walks through our playground, we try to talk to them, but they still can't hear us. They just keep walking into the fog, and we never see them again."

Lisa added, "Sometimes they come back but they still don't see us, so we just keep playing."

I knew the answer but wanted to hear their reply. "Do you girls go to school?"

Emily was quick to answer. "We used to go to school every day, but we missed a day and I think we missed more than one day because sometimes it feels like we've been here for a week!"

I said, "Do you girls sleep here too?"

Lisa piped up, "No, we don't go to sleep. We just play." This was a little confusing for me because it was obvious their sense of time was a little bit elongated compared to the other souls that I had helped move along. I could only guess it was because they had been there so long. I was anxious to learn more about their lives.

"What school did you go to, Emily and Lisa?"

"We go to Schmuhl School every day. We have a nice teacher. Her name is Mrs. Roberts. She helps us a lot." I knew some history on Schmuhl School just from living in the area. Schmuhl School was still in existence and had been moved across the road from its original position so that a Walgreens could be put in. It was now a little museum highlighting small-town education in a one-room schoolhouse. And here I was talking to two little girls who had experienced that.

"I bet Mrs. Roberts is proud of you two! I bet your great students," I continued. Now came the tough part. I was going to have to get them to realize what had happened and while they were still there. I knew the history about the fire and would have to somehow make them remember what had happened and how they had passed away. I wasn't even sure if a seven-year-old could grasp the concept of passing away. I asked, "Do you girls see these big stones behind you that say your names on them?"

Emily said, "Yes!" and Lisa chimed in with the same answer. "We think it means that this is our playground. But they look kind of like those things that they put where people are dead, don't you think?"

I explained, "Lisa Ann and Emily, that's what they are. They are those things that they put where people are dead. Do you know what it means to be dead?"

"I know, I know!" Lisa was raising her hand like she was in Mrs. Roberts class and Emily told her she should be quiet, and that she was too loud. "Our grandpa is dead. He died when we were five. I still remember when they put him in this deep hole. He was in a box. They put them in the ground and covered him with dirt. I didn't think grandpa could move all that dirt off of him, so I knew he wasn't coming back he was dead. Dead means you're not breathing anymore, and you can't play. Grandpa used to play with us, and it was fun. He would chase us around the backyard, and we would laugh, and he would make silly faces at us."

I wished for a moment that I could see the headstones just to the left and right of Emily and Lisa's headstone. I'm pretty sure their grandpa's headstone would have to be in the area. I asked the obvious, "Were you girls sad when grandpa died?"

Emily answered, "Yes, we were. He was so much fun! I miss him."

At this point I figured it was time to ask them about the fire. The only approach I could take was to bring them back to that day. I didn't know how they would react, but it was the only thing I could think to do. "Girls, do you remember that you had a fire at your house?"

Both girls looked down at their feet again. Lisa looked sad as she replied, "Yes, we do; it was very sad. Something happened on the stove. And then there was a big fire in the kitchen. Emily and I ran upstairs to get away from the fire. But then it was very smoky like when we have a fire outside when we're camping. Emily said we should hide in the closet so the fire wouldn't get us. So, we hid in the closet. We heard our daddy yelling for us and we yelled back but the fire was so loud I don't think he could hear us. Then we heard the fire truck, and it was very loud. They have bells on fire trucks, and they make lots of noise. We heard other people calling our name. We figured it was a fireman, but we didn't know. Emily put her head on my shoulder, and she went to sleep and then I guess I went to sleep too, but I was coughing a lot before I fell asleep. Then the next thing I knew we were here at our little playground. It's always sunny and nice at our playground. Except when Mommy and Daddy would come; then it was sad. We don't like to see Mommy and Daddy cry. But most of the time we just have fun."

"Well girls, I have to tell you something. When you went to sleep in the closet that night, you died. Just like your grandpa did. You were supposed to go to heaven, but you got stuck here at your playground playing tag and Ring around the Rosie. That's kind of silly, don't you think? That you got stuck here? But I've got some good news for you. Do you see that light over there, the really bright light?"

Emily answered, "Yes, we see that light all the time. Sometimes we want to play over there by the light, but we get a funny feeling when we go over there. So we don't know if we should go over there or not."

"Well girls, I'm here to tell you that it's okay to go to the light. Do you know what's in the light? God is in the light. Do you know who God is?"

Lisa held her hand up just like she was in class and said, "We learned about God in Sunday school. He's the one who made us, and he made the world. He is a very nice man."

"That's right, he is a very nice man," I agreed, "and he's in the light. But I've got a surprise for you. Do you know who else is in the light?" The girls looked at me with big eyes. "Your mommy and daddy and all your brothers are in the light now. And they've been waiting for you to come over. So, they sent me to come get you. Now if I hold your hands will you walk into the light with me?"

"But what about our playground?" Emily asked. "It's our favorite playground in the whole world."

"Well Emily, I'm happy to tell you that there is a bigger and better playground for you in the light. It has slides and swings and lots of things you can climb on. And your brothers will be there to play too. So, I bet you'll like heaven, it has the best playground ever. And there will be lots of children to play with. And I bet Mrs. Roberts is even there to help teach you some more. Now let's stand up. Lisa, you hold this hand and Emily you hold this one. We are going to go into the light, and it is going to feel warm and nice. Are you ready?"

They both grabbed my hands we took one step into the light, and I held their hands through the trip down the tunnel and to the end of the light. When we got there, Grandpa Bill met me with a big smile. Emily and Lisa were laughing. "That was fun! Let's do it again!"

"Sorry, girls, we can't do it again, because you have to go play at the playground. Do you see what I see? I think there's someone waiting over there by that big, huge playground. Is that Mommy and Daddy and your brothers?"

Emily's eyes lit up. "Yes, it is! Lisa, it's them! Come on; let's run!" They let go of my hands and ran off across some beautiful green grass into the arms of their parents. The boys gathered around and hugged them like no hug I had ever seen before. So much love. The reunion seemed to take place as if time had stood still for the family even though some 70 years had passed. After all the hugs and warm welcomes from the whole family, the girls took a look at the huge playground next to the picnic area that their mom and dad had set up. Before I knew it they had been on every possible part of that playground. Dad was pushing Emily on the swing and Mom was catching Lisa coming down the slide. The boys were climbing all over the rest of the playground, and the family seemed whole again.

Grandpa Bill tapped me on the shoulder to say I had done a great job. "Now I know your heart is in this," he said. "To get those seven-year-olds to understand what had happened, and how they needed to cross over after all that time was quite an event. Several other people with the same gift had tried in the past to get the girls to cross over with no luck. I think your experience with your own family made it somewhat easy for you."

"I'm not sure it was very easy, Grandpa, but I figured if I did what you said and got down to their level, I could get them to cross over. Once they trusted me, things seem to go better. I'm just glad to see them altogether as a family again. Will the girls remember their extra time on Earth?" I asked, wondering whether or not time would matter to them.

Grandpa said, "Remember, a short time to them was 70 years. To them it was like a short camping trip for just the two of them. They will soon forget the extra time they spent on Earth."

"Grandpa, I have another question for you before I go back," I pleaded. "Are we in heaven in the biblical sense, like above the world in the clouds so to speak? Or is this just another dimension that we don't understand?"

Grandpa said, "You're right about the dimension, but that's all I can tell you. It's time for you to go back now."

Again, I was rushed backwards through the tunnel feeling the same pain in my ankle. I found myself at the gravesite, looked around to see if anybody was watching me and wondering how long I had been there. I looked down at my watch and realized what seemed like an hour was actually less than 10 minutes. So, anyone driving by would not be too alarmed with some guy kneeling down in front of a headstone. I got up and slowly walked to my car, wishing I had my cane for support. I opened the door got in and breathed a huge sigh of relief. I felt a real sense of accomplishment with my new gift.

The rest of the cemetery was empty. I looked back upon it wondering if there might be another soul hidden somewhere amongst the trees. I thought it might be worth a trip back in the next couple of weeks just to see if there was anyone else there. The cemetery wasn't huge but there were areas I could not see from my vantage point.

I drove away and headed towards home. I felt the need to start writing down my experiences in hopes that it would give Eileen a perspective into what I was going through. The souls I had helped cross over were still fresh in my mind, so I grabbed a spiral notebook and started writing down the events of the past couple of months. I was pretty sure I wouldn't forget anything because it was so fresh in my mind.

To say that this gift had made an impression on me was an understatement. I jotted down my experiences and spent the rest of the day in front of my little spiral notebook. I tucked the notebook away in my nightstand so that when I was ready, I could give it to Eileen and she could get the experiences firsthand.

CHAPTER 10

Two weeks went by without any need for my gift. I was still limping quite a bit and suspected that the limp would be with me for the rest of my life. The break in my ankle and lower leg had been pretty significant, so I knew that even with the healing process continuing it would never be normal again. Thankfully, I was able to walk without my cane. The kids came and went to school, Eileen to work, with me sitting on my ass at home being bored out of my mind.

During this two-week period, I spent quite a bit of time at the library reading about life after death experiences. It seems they are more common than people know, and there are many first-hand accounts of people exiting this world going through the tunnel towards a bright light, and even getting to see loved ones and relatives who had passed on. They always describe the same thing when they were revived. They felt almost a slamming back into their body after they were told it wasn't their time. This information usually came from a loved one who had crossed over.

There were many accounts of people telling the doctors what was going on in the room during their attempted revival from the catastrophic event. They would frequently report seeing things from above such as things on the table in the corner of the room, and the entrance and exit of staff that were not present in the room during the conscious state of the patient. Some of them could even recall what the doctors were saying and the responses of the nursing staff and technologists in the room. Some described a floating feeling that led them away from the room they were in, and down the corridors of the hospital. Some of them could even describe patients waiting on carts in the waiting area of the emergency room.

A lot of doctors dismissed these events as being the brain's reaction to low oxygen saturation and the slow death of brain tissue. But what's funny is that the descriptions from patients of near-death experiences are almost identical in any area of the world. They reported floating at a high rate of speed towards a bright light at the end of the tunnel with loved ones waiting for them who had already crossed over. Most of them were sent back because their work was not yet completed on Earth. At least this is what they reported. With so many cases being identical, it's hard to believe that this is some sort of brain reaction to lack of oxygen. You would think that people would have different experiences due to the different societies and situations that they were accustomed to. It's hard to believe that a chief from an African tribe would describe the same experience as a priest in North Dakota. They both had completely different concepts of what heaven or God would be like after they crossed over. Many other people report no remembrance after a near death experience. I wondered how this could be since a lot of people who die are brought back to life by things such as defibrillators. Defibrillators save a lot of lives, and you don't hear of many cases where people don't get the help they need immediately after having a heart attack. Obviously, the ones who are alone don't have this kind of luck. That makes me believe that when it's your time it's truly your time.

I was becoming obsessed with this topic, and I had read five books on life after death experiences within a two-week period. Two were written by emergency room physicians and two were written by people who had been through near-death experiences. The last one was by a physician who tried to explain that the effects that people experienced were due to the brain shutting down. Why I never experienced this phenomenon during the three times I coded I don't understand. But the gift I've been given has made up for that lack of experience.

I was still taking my daily rides just to get out of the house. I was never looking for roadside memorials but occasionally I couldn't help but find one. When I did see one, I looked hard at the area to make sure I didn't see a soul standing by the memorial. This had gone on for the entire two weeks I was reading up on life after death. I had also continued to take my daily walks with Eileen. The walks gave us time to talk alone, away from the children. She would ask me if I had had any experiences that day and I would gladly say no. I still wasn't sure of her belief in this gift I had been given. She seemed to go along with it, but obviously it would be hard to convince anyone of what I was going through. On our walk one day, we passed the forest preserve that had occasionally been on our route over the last month or so. There were no memorials in the area, so I paid little attention to the forest preserve. But this time I glanced at the woods a little harder than I had before.

About 50 yards back from the street, I noticed a man standing by a tree. He was dressed in 1950s style clothing and also wore a fedora hat. His suit looked freshly pressed and he did not have the same look of confusion that the others did. He looked like he was just kicking back and enjoying the view. The forest preserve was beautiful in that area with a small stream and a little tiny waterfall created by tree roots and rocks. He almost seemed to be relaxing, just watching the water go over the rocks. He seemed content in his own little world.

At first, I thought maybe this was just an elderly gentleman who had wandered back into the area just to look at the stream. He appeared to be in his 60s and we all know of people who haven't changed their wardrobe for 30 years. So, we kept walking and Eileen noticed as I eyed him up even more.

"Are you okay?" she asked.

"Yes, I'm fine," I replied.

She persisted, "Are you seeing something?"

I got defensive, "Well if I am, do you think I'm crazy?"

She got short with me, "No, of course not! I don't know what this is your experiencing, but I believe you no matter what you say. If for some reason God has given you this gift I believe you, have it. And you will do what's right with it. So, tell me, what do you see?"

I backed down, "Okay, I will. Back in the woods about 50 yards back or so there's a man standing against a tree looking down at the stream where the water falls over the rocks. Do you see where I mean?"

"Yes, I do," she nodded. "I can see a little waterfall there. I've never walked back there but I bet it would be relaxing just to sit there and watch that stream."

I agreed and said, "I think the soul back there is doing the same."

She gave me confused look. "How do you know it's a soul?"

"Well," I asked, "do you see anyone there?"

She said, "No. I don't see anything back there other than the stream." She confirmed my suspicion, and I described what I saw.

"Then it must be a soul. He's dressed in 50s clothing and has a fedora hat on. His suit is blue, and it looks like it was just pressed. He's quite a sharp dresser. He doesn't look like the other ones that I have helped though; he doesn't seem to be confused. He looks content where he's at. He hasn't looked up or away from the stream since I spotted him. He's also smoking a cigarette which I find interesting, being that I've never seen any of the souls smoking a cigarette."

Eileen chuckled, "Well I guess at this point it doesn't matter if he smokes or not."

I laughed. "Yeah, I guess you're right. Besides, in the 50s everyone smoked. So, I guess I shouldn't think too much of it."

We continued to walk until the man was out of my sight. Eileen said, "When will you go back to see if you can help him?"

I said, "Probably tomorrow." She gave me a motherly warning.

"You have to be very careful walking through those woods. Your ankle is not as great as you think it is. You're still limping quite a bit and I don't want you to re-break that ankle. I don't think I could take another six months of you around the house."

"You think you couldn't take another six months," I bantered, "I'd be out of my mind!"

We finished our walk and returned home. The children were lounging around watching TV, and of course wondering what was for dinner. Children are concerned with two and they are as follows: what time is dinner and what time do I have to go to bed. That's all. After that it's all filler time. We did like to spend time in the pool during the summer and often went for a swim after dinner. We didn't follow the rules my mom had when I was a kid. My mom believed you should not swim for half an hour after dinner, a myth that was proven wrong years ago.

I'm careful in the pool because of the slippery liner and the fact that the kids still like to jump on my back whenever they can. I don't stop them even though it hurts sometimes. It's great playtime for us. I can still pick them up and throw them into the water even though the pain in my leg is amplified by this movement. I don't mind. I just like seeing their faces when they fly up in the air. It's not easy to do with John anymore as he is really getting to be a big boy. He'll probably end up looking like his father, the poor thing.

CHAPTER 11

Early the next morning, I got in my car and headed towards the forest preserve. I parked the car in one of the available spaces and proceeded to walk towards the stream. I had brought my cane with me, just in case, but like an idiot had forgotten it in the car. So, my walk was slow, and being that the soul was about 50 to 60 yards away, it took some time to get to him.

I stood on the other side of the stream and felt the tingling that I always felt when approaching the soul. Before I knew it the shock passed through me, and I was standing in front of the man. I wondered to myself how I'd gotten across the stream without getting wet.

He looked up at me and said "Did you come to look at the stream too? It so relaxing that I come here almost every day just to check it out. It relaxes me. My job is so stressful I need something like this to keep me from going crazy."

I didn't waste any time. "What's your name?"

He wasn't so quick to give in. "Who wants to know?" he asked.

"Oh, sorry," I replied. "I should mind my manners and introduce myself first. My name is Scott."

"Scott?" he asked. "That's an unusual name."

I remembered that Scott was still a pretty unusual name in his era.

"My parents are Scotch Irish and gave me the name Scott because of it. So please, what's your name?"

"I'm William," he replied, "but everybody calls me Willy."

I tried to keep the conversation going. "What kind of work do you do, Willy?"

"I'm an accountant," he explained. "I work downtown."

"Do you take the train to work?" I asked. He said yes. "When was the last day you took the train?" He said Friday. I was trying to get a timeline out of him, so I knew where he was at in his world.

"Today's Sunday," he went on, "I just got back from church. I decided to stop at my relaxing spot and try to get ready for the rat race on Monday."

"Do you have a family, Willy?"

"No, not really. I have a wife, but I don't see her much anymore. I guess I wasn't much of a husband," he said sadly.

I tried to pry a little more. "Do you have any kids?"

His tone was very sad. "Yeah, we have one and she took him with her."

I remembered from talking to people my grandfather's age that in their era, it wasn't unusual for a woman to leave and take the children and for the father to never see them again. He explained that he last saw his child at two months of age and that he would now be 5 years old. I did the math and figured that his child might be in his 50s or 60s by this time. And Willy's ex-wife would be in her 70s or 80s.

"What's your last name Willy?" I asked. He said "Seymour. Willy Seymour. But at my work they still call me William. I guess it's more professional that way. I always hated being called William, it made me feel like I was in trouble and my mother was yelling at me again."

I laughed with him and recalled, "Yeah, my middle name is William, so anytime my mother used my middle name I knew I was in trouble." I wanted to know more about the timeline. "Willy, do you remember the day you got here?"

He looked at me like I was crazy. "I got here today."

I tried to make my question clearer. "I'm sorry, you said you went to church, and then what happened?"

"Well, for a week or two I hadn't been feeling very well," he explained. "I felt like I had flu symptoms and this pain in my left arm. I figured I pulled a muscle when I was moving my dresser at home. That's when this all started. For two weeks I felt like I couldn't eat anything, and the pain in my arm would not go away unless I rested. It got to be where walking to the train was almost impossible without stopping. The pain in my arm would get pretty intense. I didn't know if it was just because I was swinging my arm back and forth while I walked, or what. All I know is it hurt like hell. I sat in church today and wasn't feeling any pain in my arm but there was some in my chest. I figured I was catching a cold and that's why I was feeling so lousy the last couple of weeks. I walked up to the stream where I like to relax, and the pain got pretty bad. I lit a cigarette because it always calms me down. Not long after that this weird fog rolled in and now all I can see is the stream, and not much past it. When you walked up here did you see my new car? It's a 1955 Buick. It's silver and I really like it. But I can't see it anymore because of this fog. Is it still there in the parking lot?"

At this point I figured it was time to let him know what had happened. What Willy had described where the classic symptoms leading up to a heart attack. I knew that is what he died from and I was sure he had no clue he was even dead.

I continued to gather more information. "Willy, do you remember what happened after you lit the cigarette?"

He looked puzzled. "Yeah, for some reason I leaned up against this tree and then sat down. I felt sleepy. When I woke up this fog had rolled in and I've been here looking at the stream since then."

I figured it was time to tell Willy what actually happened to him and how and why the fog had rolled in. "Willy, I've got something to tell you and it's going to be a shocker." Willy looked scared as I continued. "Willy, you've passed away. That's why you fell asleep at the tree and then the fog rolled in. You didn't fall asleep, you actually passed away. But for some reason you are stuck here and haven't moved on. I've been given a gift to help people who are stuck between two worlds. I can help you move along to heaven if you'll let me."

Willy stepped back, "What the hell are you talking about? I feel fine! Other than this fog, nothing is changed."

I tried to get him to understand. "Willy, what year is it?"

"Why, it's 1955," he said in a stern voice. "I just told you I bought that new car out there."

It was hard for me to prove him wrong. "Willy, I've got something to tell you. It's actually 2011. You've been here for 56 years. For some reason you haven't been able to move along. Maybe it's because you've been so relaxed looking at the stream that you didn't even realize you had died. But I can assure you that you've passed away. Your clothes look so much different than mine because we're in another decade now. It's been five decades since you passed away. That's why my clothes look so different than yours."

Willy was still trying to put the pieces together. "But what about my car?" Willy asked.

I hated to break the sad news to him. "I'm afraid it's gone Willy. I'm sure they towed it to your house after you died."

"But I love that car. It's my only passion since my wife left me. I'm so proud of that car. I just got a huge promotion at work and was able to buy my dream car." He was very upset over the loss of the car, completely glossing over the loss of his life.

Since he was such a car lover, I decided that I would give him a glimpse of what today's cars looked like. "Willy, I will make you promise. If you come with me, I'll walk you past my car. Then you can see what cars look like 50 years after you bought your new car." I didn't have a very special car, just a Toyota Camry. It was pretty sleek looking, and we had bought it new in 2010. So, I was pretty sure he'd be impressed and maybe he would trust me more. I figured if he trusted me more, maybe I could get him into the light, and that's all that would matter.

"So, you're sure I'm dead?" he said with a confused look on his face.

"Yes, Willy, I'm sure."

He wanted to know more. "I wonder what happened to my wife, or should I say my ex-wife, and son?"

I wished I could answer that question. "All of that will be answered Willy, when you go into the light."

He was worried, "Do you think I'll be able to see them again?"

I tried to comfort him. "Yes, I believe you will, at any stage of life you want to. Now will you walk with me through the fog, and I'll show you my new car and then we'll cross over into the light?"

Willy was starting to be agreeable. "Yeah, I've looked at the stream long enough and I'm sick of standing around here." So, we crossed the stream again without getting wet, went through the fog, and came out on the other side of it. As we walked towards the parking lot I feared that there might be other cars parked in the lot. This was a remote forest reserve so I was hoping I would get lucky.

As we approached the parking lot Willy asked, "Why are you limping so bad?"

"I had a bad accident," I explained, "and broke my leg along with a lot of other stuff. I was in the hospital for two months. Not long after I left the hospital is when I realized I had the gift to talk to people who needed to cross over. I'm still pretty new at it so hopefully we'll get this right."

With that, we entered the parking lot and Willy looked up. He saw my car and said it looked like something from a comic book. His face lit up. "Does it go fast?"

"About 140 miles an hour," I told Willy.

"Will they let you go that fast now?"

"Hell no, I replied, "but it's nice to know I can if I want to."

Willy laughed. He said, "It's so low to the ground! How do you get in and out of it?"

I explained, "It isn't easy for a big guy like me, but once you're in its pretty comfortable. Do you want to see the inside?"

"Hell yeah I do, this is amazing," he said excitedly. So, I opened the door and let Willy look inside at what must have seemed like some sort of a spaceship to him. He asked me what every button did and where the radio was. He was truly amazed. When he seemed to have enough, I persisted.

"All right Willy, I kept my end of the bargain, now it's time."

He said, "Do you think they'll let me drive one of these things when I get to the other side?"

"I'm sure they will," I reassured him. "Heaven is what you make out of it, Willy, and being that you loved cars I'm sure there will be plenty of them for you to drive."

He had excitement in his voice. "I want to take my wife and kid for a ride in a car like this. They'll be amazed, especially my son. He'll think he's in a rocket ship."

We got out of the car and walked towards the light. The light appeared at the end of the parking lot near a big oak tree. As we entered the light, Willy looks scared. I assured him it would be okay. We flew through the tunnel at what seemed like 140 miles an hour which I think excited Willy due to his love of speed. We reached the end of the bright light and passed through it.

Grandpa was waiting for me and introduced himself to Willy. Willy said, "You've got a fine grandson here."

Grandpa smiled, "Thanks, I know he's a special guy."

Willy looked out to see his ex-wife and their little boy standing next to a whole line of new cars. There was one from every era. Willy's '55 Buick was there. There was a '67 Mustang convertible, a 1975 galaxy 500 with the big rims and tires on it, a 1980 Mercedes 450 SL, a 1994 Cadillac Eldorado coupe; you get my drift. He turned to me and smiled and walked slowly towards his wife and child. Even though his wife had divorced him, in his own heaven she was still his wife. It was obvious this was a one-way divorce, and it didn't go his way. He held them both and picked up his five-year-old and tossed him in the air catching him with a laugh.

Grandpa looked at me and said, "You did it again. But what was the showing him your new car routine?"

I explained, "I felt like it was the only way I could get him across, if I could promise to show him something that he had never seen before, especially a car lover like him."

"It worked, I guess," Grandpa said, "They just don't want you to take them too far away from their exit point. It can cause trouble. Sometimes if they wander too far from their exit point they get themselves into trouble. It will be hard for you to do sometimes but keep it in mind."

I understood Grandpa's warning but was a little confused by it. "All that matters is that I get them here, right?" I asked.

"I guess that is all that matters my son but remember there are rules and we don't want to cross the line too much. You can stretch the rules, just don't push your luck. You'll know what I mean when the time comes. Now head on back, we still have more work to do."

As usual I was thrown into reverse and felt myself flying backwards and landing near the site where Willy and I had met. The fog was gone, and I had to figure out how to get around the stream with my bad leg and not get soaked. I gently walked on top of some rocks and was able to cross the water. I stopped for a moment to enjoy the view of that little babbling stream. It was something I didn't even know was there and I wondered if it would be a good place to sit and relax. Willy had given me the answer to that question.

I lumbered back to my car limping pretty heavily and got in. I thought of all the gadgets I'd grown so used to that Willy thought were amazing. When I showed him the CD player the amazed look in his eyes couldn't be described. I remembered him commenting that it was like a little record player just for the car. We take a lot for granted, especially technology. It really made me think about how far we have come in 50 years by just talking to Willy inside my car. Everything was a mystery to him, even intermittent wipers. Things we take for granted.

I pulled out of the forest preserve parking lot and started to work my way home. It was around three o'clock and I met Dana at the door as she was getting ready to meet some friends down at the end of the block. I told her to be careful and to be home for dinner. John and Casey were inside watching Sports Center, something I had grown so accustomed to that it had become an everyday part of our lives. And to think they run the same program over and over every couple of hours. But you find yourself sitting there watching it over and over like something's going to change.

Three or four days went past without seeing any spirits anywhere. Being that I was usually pretty tapped out after working with one of these souls, I felt like I needed the rest. I think being overwhelmed with such a task daily would be too much. The weather was nice and we grilled outdoors, where all my cooking skills lie. My specialties are hamburgers, meatloaf on the grill (which is actually very good), and steaks. I had a chair out there next to the grill that allowed me to take a break from standing when I needed it. I was enjoying the summer months which were leading slowly to the fall. I was glad that we still had enough heat to enjoy the outdoors.

CHAPTER 12

One day as I stumbled on some old pictures, I thought of an old classmate that was killed in a car accident not too far from my high school. He wasn't a close friend, but I did have him in a couple of my classes. We would say hi back and forth in the hallways and had some mutual friends. I wondered If I drove past his accident site, would his soul still be present? Being that I had thought of him so abruptly over the last couple of days I figured maybe Grandpa was dropping a hint or two. My old high school was only 15 miles away in Tinley Park. On the night of the accident, Dave was coming home from a party. It was one of our usual late 70s kegger parties. He veered off the road near 175th St. and wrapped his car around a telephone pole going about 70 miles an hour. Back then we didn't think much about drinking and driving, it was just something we did. Obviously if we only knew the outcome of Dave's evening, we would've stopped him. Dave was kind of a loner his first couple years of high school. He started to come out of his shell about the middle of junior year. He started hanging out with some of us and would go to the parties we all went to. He even picked up a few girlfriends along the way. If you had seen him freshman year, you would think that this was impossible. He had opened up and displayed a very dry sense of humor and had the ability to drink us all under the table. Again, if we only knew.

The next day I decided to take a ride down 175th St. and see if I could remember the area Dave was killed. It was around Ridgeland Avenue, but I wasn't sure if it was north or south. As I drove south down 175th St. I looked intently on the east side of the street and tried to remember the vicinity where Dave was killed. I was pretty sure I had it narrowed down to one area but still was not positive exactly where he had met his end. As I searched, I suddenly saw him leaning up against the telephone pole smiling at me. I was still in the car and had no idea how he could see me. Every other soul I had run into was blinded by the fog. Yet Dave seemed to reach out through that fog and almost waved me down. I slammed on the brakes not paying attention to the cars behind me. I almost caused a chain reaction accident. I slowly drove past Dave and circled the block. This time I would park my car on a side street and walk up to Dave.

As I exited my car, Dave was looking down at his feet. I could tell he could not see me and probably wondered where I went. As I walked and got closer and closer, the tingling sensation enveloped my body. Before I knew it the shock was over, and I was in Dave's foggy realm. He looked excited.

"Scott, I saw you pass me by, did you see me?"

"Yeah, I did, Dave, but what I'm wondering is how you saw me?"

"Every once in a while this fog lifts," Dave said. "It's usually only for a couple of seconds, and I can only see people I know. Other than that, the fog is here all the time. So how have you been Scott?"

"Pretty good Dave," I replied.

"When did you get the gray hair? Costume party tonight?" Dave asked, thinking I had just been to a Halloween party.

"No Dave, this is the color of my hair now."

He was shocked. "Get the hell out of here! I just saw you yesterday and your hair was jet black."

This was a tough one to explain. I had jet black hair until my mid-20s when I started seeing hints of gray popping into my scalp. Now I was pretty much salt-and-pepper. I changed the subject. "Dave, do you know where you are?"

"Yeah, I'm on 175th St. near Ridgeland. Did you see my car?" Dave restored MG Midgets as a hobby. He had gotten really good at it. In fact, the way he made money in high school was to buy old rusty MG Midgets and restore them to like new condition. He'd sell them and make a pretty profit on it. He even did the paint. One time I saw him in his driveway working on a MG and I stopped by to see him. He was actually moving the steering wheel from the left side of the car to the right side of the car to make it a more authentic European sports car. That's how talented this guy was.

He had been driving a convertible MG Midget that night he was killed. He had opened it up on 175th gaining speed, and lost control around 70 miles an hour and ran into the telephone pole. He was thrown from the vehicle and killed on impact. Most of us didn't find out until the next day, but several of the partygoers passed the accident scene on the way home from the party. I lived in the opposite direction, so I was spared the vivid scene. He had been thrown some 25 yards from the car and landed headfirst on the sidewalk. His body had been covered with a yellow sheet and even though some of the friends stopped, the police would not allow them to identify the body. I'm assuming because the body was in no shape to be identified.

I continued, "Dave do you understand what happened to you the night you left the party?"

He began rubbing his head. "I remember leaving in the party in this MG I just finished. I went flying down the street and then I ended up here. I've been standing by this telephone pole for at least 20 minutes. Maybe a little longer, I suppose. So, what happened to your hair, man?"

My voice became more serious as I realized he had no idea where he was. "Don't worry about my hair right now, Dave. You see the fog around you right?"

"Yeah, what's that all about? It wasn't foggy when I left the party. Now I can't see through any of this shit."

"Dave, I've got something to tell you and it's going to come as a surprise. The night you left the party you were killed. I've been given a gift, Dave, a gift I received after a bad accident almost like yours. I was lucky enough to survive. You, Dave, didn't. You hit the telephone pole you're leaning against that about 70 miles an hour. You were killed instantly. You've been stuck here ever since. What year is it in your head?"

"What you mean by that?" he replied. "You know it's 1979. Why would you ask me something like that?"

This was hard to explain to him. "Dave, you've been here for 30-plus years. The year right now is 2011. For some reason you got stuck here and didn't move on into the light. Do you remember seeing the light, Dave?"

He nodded. "Yeah, I still see it. It's over there by the edge of the fog but I stay away from it. I'm waiting for someone to pick me up; that's why waved at you. I thought you were here to take me home."

"Well, in a way, Dave, I am. I'm here to walk you into the light so you can enjoy the other side. You remember the other side, Dave?" Dave and I had gone to Sunday school together and were taught about heaven and hell in the usual late 60's early 70's Catholic way. Maybe that's why Dave was scared to go into the light. Those nuns were pretty bitter. Maybe Dave felt like he was headed in the wrong direction. I knew Dave had a good heart and would be welcomed. "I'll walk with you and get you across to the other side."

"Scott, are you dead too?" Dave asked.

"No, I've just been given this gift to be able to see people who are stuck between worlds. I've helped several people cross over. I thought of you the other day, wondering and hoping that you had crossed over right after the accident. Now I'm glad I came out to the site where you had your accident. Now I can take you there to the other side. Walk next to me. Dave, we're headed into the light."

He stopped suddenly. "Wait a minute! What about my car?"

It was time to break the bad news. "Dave, the car you were driving was destroyed in the accident. You wrapped it around this telephone pole. But I'm sure there will be many more on the other side. A guy makes his own heaven, and for a car guy like you, it'll be filled with cars and gadgets that you'll love. Are you ready?"

"As ready as I'll ever be!" he replied. With that, Dave and I walked into the light. Dave likes speed so he enjoyed the ride. The light came upon us very quickly, and as we burst through grandpa was there.

Grandpa looked at Dave and said, "Welcome Dave!"

Dave looked at me and said, "Who's the old guy?" I explained that he was my grandpa. "Okay, I feel stupid," he said. "Hi, Scott's grandpa!"

That gave grandpa little tickle and he giggled. "Dave, you always had a dry sense of humor; I guess I shouldn't expect anything different." Dave had only met my grandpa once, but he must've made an impression on him. Grandpa shook his hand. "Welcome to the other side. We've been waiting quite some time for you."

Dave shook his head in disbelief. "Scott said it's been 30-plus years. Doesn't Scott look old, Grandpa?"

Grandpa chuckled, "Yeah, he's getting up there. Dave, look around you. This is your heaven. The one you always dreamed of."

Dave looked out to see an old junkyard with classic cars from every era. They all needed work. He wandered through the yard, and we followed him. He started naming off the makes and models of all these classic cars. Grandpa told him there was an endless supply of parts, paints, and accessories and he could restore as many cars as he wanted.

Dave said, "Well, I better get to it! Thanks for getting me out of this mess, Scott." Dave wandered off into the junkyard, or should I say, classic car yard, and disappeared around the corner.

Grandpa and I walked back towards the entrance of the light. He said "Another good one, Scott. Your tests are getting to be routine for you. Some of the future ones, especially the next one, will be very trying for you. So be ready for it. Don't get bogged down in the details, just remember what your main goal is. Just get them to me and I'll put them in their own heaven."

"Helping Dave meant a lot to me, Grandpa," I explained. "He was a friend, and that made it that much more satisfying."

Grandpa put his arm around my shoulder. "I know, my son, that's why I sent you to him. Are you're ready for your reverse trip?"

I nodded. "I guess so, although I must say I like the trip here better than the trip back."

In a blink, I was sent flying back through the tunnel into the spot near the telephone pole where Dave had met his end. As I walked to my car, I noticed a woman who looked like she had been staring at me the entire time. I glanced over and waved, and she waved back. I figured if I seemed friendly, she may not think much about me standing there for the past10 minutes. This was the first time anyone had noticed me in the process of crossing someone over. I assumed I looked as if I was in a trance-like state, though I couldn't be sure. I had no idea what had transpired in the 10 minutes it took to transfer Dave from this world to the next. As I got in my car, I could still see the lady staring at me as I drove off. It's a wonder she didn't call the police. I must've looked pretty funny standing out there for 10 minutes or so, staring at the ground. It had to be done though, and I was successful. I just figured I would drive down 175th Street for a while.

CHAPTER 13

I got home with a couple of extra hours to spare, so I decided to take a nap. I was still having headaches, although they were slowly becoming less frequent. My ankle still throbbed if I walked on it for too long, but it was also improving. I woke just in time for the kids to hit the door and the chaos to start. Today was one of those days where everyone had to be driven somewhere. Dana to pom-pom practice, John to baseball, and Casey to basketball tryouts. Eileen arrived around five thirty, and I had dinner ready even though I had to do all that running around with the kids. I guess I was trying to make up some points. The whole system runs on points, you know, the more points you accrue the more likely your life will be less complicated. That's a nice way of saying you won't get the cold shoulder from your wife.

Beef stew was on the menu tonight, easy stuff to make. I cooked it in the crock pot and with my special recipe guaranteed to cause a significant amount of heartburn later in the evening. We split the rides home for our children. I picked up John and Casey and Eileen went and got Dana. We were home altogether at six to have dinner. Eileen asked me how my day went, and I told her everything was good. John asked how my foot was and I told him it was just a little bit achy, but it was feeling better.

We went outside on the patio to enjoy the rest of the day's sunshine and talk about what went on during the day for everyone. Dana was excited about poms and told us all about the new routines they were learning. John was finishing up his season and the playoffs were coming. John was a good baseball player and looked forward to receiving a big trophy after they won the championship. I love a man who thinks big. Casey talked about the basketball coaches and how they had a psycho approach to practice. He told us it wasn't much fun, which made me sad because Casey was one hell of a basketball player and could really do the team some good. Coaching at the junior high and high school level had become a competition rather than a way to teach kids how to have fun at sports. Everything was about winning, and the coaches were only concerned with promoting their own style in hopes of landing a job at the next level.

We all decided to pile into the car and go get ice cream. We had a great ice cream place down the road with soft serve ice cream with your choice of any topping you wanted. I always went with the small cone because of my large belly. The rest of them could have what they wanted because they were all skinny.

These are the things that make having a family better than anything in the world. Realizing that I almost lost it all makes it that much more satisfying.

I was concerned about what Grandpa had said, that the next challenge would be much more significant than the previous ones. I didn't know what he meant, and he didn't let on as to the direction I would be taken. I told Eileen about Dave and how I'd moved him along and saw his little bit of heaven. She was amazed by the story and found it fascinating that I had thought of him and wondered if he had crossed over.

"What made you ride all the way up to Tinley Park?" Eileen said.

"I don't know, it was just a feeling I had. I had remembered Dave having this terrible accident and dying at the scene and wondered if he had known what had happened. It seems like the more sudden the death, the less likely the people are to understand what happened. I thought of Dave because the trauma of his accident was so significant that I had a feeling he may still be stuck between the worlds. Turns out I was right."

"It's nice to feel right every once in a while, isn't it?" Eileen said while giving me a look.

"Oh, a wise guy, hey?" I said, quoting one of my favorite Three Stooges lines. She said it had something to do with men being wrong all the time and how unusual it was for us to be right.

She said she was glad I could help Dave. Then she got a serious look on her face. "You remember me telling you about my older brother Steve, right?" she asked.

"Yes of course I remember," I replied.

"I wonder if he crossed over," Eileen said. Suddenly I understood what Grandpa meant by the next challenge being more significant. Now I was taking requests and Eileen's request was one I couldn't ignore.

Stephen was 12 when he was climbing up the side of a rocky embankment close to Starved Rock State Park. He was on a trip with his Boy Scout troop when he decided to attempt the climb. He did it without the permission of the scout leader and snuck off with a couple of his friends to climb the embankment.

His two friends got up to the top of the rock and Stephen was right behind them. But then he lost his footing and tumbled down the embankment, striking his head several times on rocks and outcroppings along the way. He died on his way to the hospital in the ambulance. Eileen was only five when this happened, so she doesn't remember much about the circumstances. But every year on the day of the anniversary of his death Eileen's parents, then after her mother died, her dad, had made the trip out to Starved Rock to place some flowers by the area where he fell. We had gone with him almost every time over the years to place the flowers.

You never get over losing a child. And even after all these years, her father still cried every time he saw the site of the embankment where

Stephen had died. I had missed last year because of my injury, but this year's anniversary was Saturday. I believe that's why Eileen brought it up. She wanted me to go with to see if I could visualize Stephen or if he had crossed over already. This made me more than a little bit nervous, and I prayed that Stephen would have crossed over many years ago.

The trip down to Starved Rock would take about an hour. That was about as much as I could take in the car with my ankle bouncing up and down over every pothole life had to offer on the way to Starved Rock State Park. I knew I had to go because it was important to Eileen, not to mention knowing that he had crossed over would make me feel better too. Grandpa made me promise to only mention my gift to Eileen so I couldn't mention anything to her father and her stepmom, who always accompanied her husband on these trips. But Eileen knowing would be enough.

A few days before the anniversary date, Eileen's stepmom asked if we were going to go along. Eileen told her that we were going to go but would be taking a separate car to get back to relieve the babysitter. Because we would be gone for a good portion of the day, we left the kids at home. John was almost old enough to be the babysitter, but we had a neighbor down the street who was 18 and was willing to sit with the kids for a price. I felt it was important for the kids to have some supervision since we would be gone so long. Though they were always good kids and I didn't worry about them getting out of line, I'd rather be safe than sorry. The family always went out to lunch after placing the flowers on the rocks where Stephen had died. Despite my trepidation, I was excited to go on the trip because I figured this would be my opportunity to see if Stephen was still in this world.

We left at 10am on Saturday to get down to the site at around 11 or 11:30. There was construction along I- 80 which we thought might slow us up a little on our way down there. I was glad we'd left a little early because I-80 was a parking lot through the construction zone.

We reached the park eventually and pulled up near the spot where Stephen fell. It was about a half-mile walk to the rock embankment.

This was difficult for Eileen's dad and step-mom in their advanced age, but they always wanted to do this and always toughed it out.

When we reached the wall, I was impressed again by the height of it and the nerve it must've taken for a 12-year-old to try to climb it. The weeds had grown quite tall, and walking through them to get to the spot was a little difficult. I led the way by knocking down some of the weeds with my trusty cane. Besides, I figured I could scare off any little varmints that were hiding in the weeds and might cause my mother-in-law to have a heart attack.

As I approached the wall, I stopped suddenly. I recognized him from his pictures and realized Stephen was sitting on a boulder at the bottom of the embankment. He was about 15 to 20 yards to the right of the place where we had always placed the flowers.

This immediately reminded me that he probably could not see the yearly ritual that his parents had kept up for so long. I knew the fog would not allow him to see his family and their grief. We all stopped and bowed our heads to say a prayer. As everyone looked down and closed their eyes I looked over at Stephen. He looked reflective and almost sad, as if he had done something wrong and knew it.

As Eileen's stepmom, Lois, finished leading the prayer, Eileen's father, Dan, placed a big bouquet of flowers on one of the rocks. He turned around and it was obvious he'd been crying. His wife gave him a big hug and they both cried for a short time. Eileen also had tears in her eyes and her brothers and sisters felt the same way. They all gathered at the site for a couple more minutes and decided it was time to make the walk back.

It was at this time that Eileen looked up at me and whispered, "Can you see him?"

I looked around to make sure that her family was out of earshot. I said, "He's here." This made Eileen cry harder. I said, "Remember, he has no sense of time or space. In his world this accident may have just happened. Most of the people that I've worked with have felt very little to no time had passed since their accident. So right now, he probably thinks it's still 1976. I need some time with him, probably five or 10 minutes. See if you can catch your dad and tell him that will meet him at the restaurant. Then come back here because I'd like to know what I do during this trance state when I'm talking to people who haven't crossed over."

Eileen hurried off and was able to see her catch her father. She told him that we would be a few minutes and would meet them at the restaurant. She came back slightly winded and said she was ready.

I slowly walked towards Stephen and felt the tingling sensation envelop my body. I stopped for a second, wondering if this was such a good idea. Having Eileen watch this whole process was a little unnerving.

I passed through the shock of the fog and entered Stephen's world. He looked up at me and said, "I'm sorry I fell. I don't know what happened. My foot slipped and the next thing I knew I was sitting on this rock."

I tried to console him. "That's okay; you don't have to feel sorry. I do need to tell you something and explain why you are here. The first thing you need to know is that I'm your brother-in-law. I married your little sister Eileen about 15 years ago."

"Eileen's only five, how could you marry her 15 years ago?" he asked, surprised.

This was not easy. "Stephen, a lot of time has passed since you fell."

He got defensive. "No, it hasn't! It isn't even dark yet!"

I tried to explain. "Remember how I told you there were things that you needed to know?"

"Yeah, what do you mean?" Stephen asked, almost angrily.

I started by explaining what had really happened to him. "Well, when you fell, you hit your head several times on the way down. Your scout leader found you and called for an ambulance. Because we're in a remote site, it took the ambulance a half hour to get here. They did everything they could, but, Stephen, you died on the way to the hospital. I'm here because your sister and dad and your whole family come here once a year on the day you died to put flowers by the area where you fell."

"If they come every year, how come I never see them?" Stephen asked.

"They are beyond the fog that's here in your little world," I explained. "Has the fog ever lifted, Stephen?"

"No, it hasn't; it's always been here."

I continued, "That's why you could never see them. They always put the flowers about 15 yards to your left. You can only see to the edge of the fog, and that's only about 10 yards. Stephen, I was in a terrible accident about a year ago. I fell while working on a light pole and was almost killed. I died three times, twice in surgery and once in the emergency room. I don't know why, but I've been given a gift that allows me to help people who are stuck between the world of the living and the world of the dead. That's where you are now, stuck between the two worlds. You've been here for 35 years. I know it seems like it just happened, but it's been a long time. Now it's time for you to move on to heaven. I've come to take you there. So if you come with, I'll get you there."

Stephen backed away. "How can I trust you? I don't even know you!"

I tried to reassure him. "Stephen, if I made this fog lift would you believe me?" I had to trust my instincts on this and hope that Grandpa would help me out.

"Yeah, I guess I would," he replied. "I haven't seen anything but this fog all day."

Suddenly the fog started to lift. Stephen got up immediately and looked up at the wall of rocks. "Wow, it looks so high from here!" he said in wonder. "And I was so close to the top! I remember my foot slipping, and I tried to grab on to that tree that's sticking out of the rocks. It wasn't anywhere near as big as it is now; it was only a stick, and my hand slipped. The next thing I knew, I was sitting on this boulder down here."

He seemed fascinated by his surroundings. Looking around, he noticed the bouquet. "Are these the flowers that you were talking about?"

"Yep," I confirmed, "those are the ones."

Stephen wondered out loud how he had never seen his family place the flowers. I told him for some reason the fog surrounds people and doesn't allow them to see outside of their own little world. "Stephen, do you remember seeing a light? You know, a bright light?"

"Yes, I do," he said. "It's been there since the beginning. But I never knew why it was there."

I said, "Stephen, we have to go into that light to get to the other side."

"I don't want to!" he protested. "I've always been afraid to see what's in there."

"You're gonna have to trust me on this one, pal," I reassured him. "I'm your brother-in-law, and I wouldn't steer you wrong."

Stephen picked up the flowers. I'd never seen any spirit pick something up from a different dimension. He walked back towards me and said, "Okay I'll go with you, but I want to take these flowers with. They'll remind me of my family."

"You might be surprised at what you see on the other side," I replied. "I have seen family members who had not crossed over waiting on the other side for their loved ones."

Stephen and I walked towards the light and entered the bright tunnel. Again, as before, the speed at which we accelerated through the tunnel was immense. The light got brighter as we got closer, and we crossed through it rather abruptly. Stephen, still holding the flowers in his hand, was amazed at how fast we were traveling.

He said, "Wow, that was cool!" I forgot how exciting a ride like that would be to a 12-year-old. As usual, Grandpa was waiting for us and met us at the exit of the light.

I thanked Grandpa for helping me lift the fog. It had made Stephen understand that the light was a good thing.

He said, "Usually I can't do that, but this time they let me. Sometimes convincing children is the hardest thing, so they give us a little leeway."

Off in the distance, I saw a picnic table with a small gathering of people. There was an older white house, and everyone was gathered in the backyard. The backyard was littered with toys, a swing set, and a fort up in a tree. The picnic table had a cover on it and it looked like dinner was about to be served. Stephen looked off in the distance at the house and said, "Looks like Mom is having another picnic in the backyard."

At that moment, I realized what he was talking about. This was his family, my wife's family, on a Sunday afternoon getting ready to have a barbecue. I looked long and hard in the backyard for Eileen. Suddenly out of the back door came a little five-year-old with my dead mother-in-law right behind her. Eileen was carrying a dish of something and placed it on the table. She looked so cute at five with her little summer dress on. I was amazed at how much she looked like Dana. Stephen looked up at Grandpa and me and said, "Can I go? Can I go see them?"

Grandpa said, "Stephen, go be with your family; they've been waiting for you." It was like Stephen had never left. It seemed as if he were coming home from his Boy Scout trip, and there would be no tragedy in this household. He ran up to the backyard and hopped the fence. He tapped Eileen on the head, and she tickled his belly. His mom gave him a big hug and he handed her the flowers. His dad tussled his hair and said, "Nice job on the flowers, son."

Stephen sat down at the table as if nothing had ever happened. He turned and waved to me, and I waved back. I could tell his mother asked him who he was waving at and he said something to her that satisfied her curiosity.

I turned to Grandpa and said, "That one was a lot harder because it was family. Is that what you meant by a challenge?"

He said, "Yeah, but they will still get harder as time goes on. You should be able to lift the fog on your own from now on if you feel like it's necessary to help you explain the situation. But try to stay in close proximity. Don't wander too far off. It's important for you and whoever you're helping to still be able to see the light. If you don't stay close, finding it again may be difficult."

I knew what to do next. "I suppose it's time for me to go back now?"

"Take a look at what you've done first," Grandpa said. "You've made that family whole up here in heaven. Up here they don't have to experience the tragedy that happened that day. As each one of the family members crosses over, they will be met by Stephen and this picnic will occur again. Stephen will climb many rock walls up here and never fall. As his family members enter heaven, they will enter at the age they feel comfortable at. The age of the children will reflect the age of the person crossing over. It represents the happiest times of their lives. So even when Eileen does cross over, which will be many years from now, she will cross with the knowledge that her brother Stephen really loved her, even as a child."

Grandpa continued, "It's time for you to go back. Eileen will explain what you experience during your visions. You may not be impressed, but there will be some things that will surprise you."

Abruptly I was thrown into reverse down the tunnel and through the entrance to the light. I looked around at the boulder and over at the place where the flowers used to be. I looked back to see Eileen standing in the field watching me intently.

I waved her over and she walked through the path I had made in the weeds with my cane. We walked to where the flowers were.

She said in wonder, "I saw them lift up and disappear. I thought I was seeing things, but it's obvious they actually disappeared!"

I tried to explain. "He wanted to take them with him. He gave them to your mother when he crossed over. It was sort of ironic. Your dad told him, 'Nice job on the flowers, son,' when your dad was actually the one who brought the flowers in the first place."

Eileen looked scared. "My dad's not dead, how could he be there?"

"Honey, everyone's heaven is different. He told me that it hadn't even been nighttime yet. So, to him no time passed all."

Eileen said, "He's been there for 35 years, how could time not pass?"

I tried my best to explain. "Things are different than you imagine for people who are stuck between the worlds. Time doesn't pass like you think it would. Sometimes just minutes and sometimes just hours pass while they are waiting. Anyway, I convinced him to cross over and we went through the light. At the end of the light was what I assume was your old house. Did it have a white fence around the backyard and a tree fort?"

She looked shocked. "Yeah, how do you know that?"

"Because I could see it," I explained. "Your mother was setting out the Sunday afternoon dinner outside on the picnic table. Stephen ran up to the fence and hopped it without hesitation."

"Did my dad yell at him for that?" Eileen smiled. "He was always yelling at him for that because he would break the fence every once in a while."

"No," I replied as I tried to describe the scene. "You were carrying out some sort of dish for the dinner and your mother was right behind you. You looked like you were five years old. Wasn't that the age you were when Stephen was killed?"

Eileen tried to remember. "I guess it was." I put my arm around her.

"So, in his mind time had not passed at all. He was back with his family as if the Boy Scout trip had ended well. There is no tragedy in heaven, so he just went right back to being a part of your family."

Eileen looked up at me. "Scott how did my mom look?" she asked softly.

I grinned down at her. "She looked great, not at all like she did when we saw her last. She was young and happy. Beautiful, really. I never realized how much you look like her."

Eileen smiled up at me with tears in her eyes. "Thanks for saying that. It means a lot," she whispered.

Curiosity was getting the best of me. "Now what did it look like from your vantage point while all of this was going on? What was I doing during the time I was over there?"

Eileen recovered quickly. "It was almost like you were in a trance. I saw you slow down just before you got to the rock, and then your body jerked as you got closer to the boulder. Your back was to me, so I couldn't see your face, but it looked like you were talking. Then you looked to your left like your eyes had been opened while you stared at the flowers. You were about two yards from the flowers when they magically rose by themselves and then disappeared. You were perfectly still for the next two or three minutes. Then you stumbled backwards and seemed to receive that body jerk like you did in the beginning. The next thing you did was wave me over. And here I am wondering how it must feel to have this kind of power."

"I don't know if I'd call it power," I said as I shook my head. "Grandpa says it's a gift, so I've got to go with that. How long did the whole process take?"

"About five minutes," Eileen said.

"It always seems much longer when I'm there," I told her. "Explaining to your brother what had happened and how he had been there for 35 years felt like it took an hour. I told him I was his brother-in-law, and he was really confused by the whole situation. He couldn't believe you had grown up and gotten married. To him you were still his little five-year-old sister. He was also amazed that the family had been coming here for so many years to memorialize his passing. He could never see you because he was sitting on the rock that was about 20 yards from where you would always place the flowers. So, he couldn't see you grow up or your dad get old. He couldn't see your brothers and sisters either. Time didn't pass for him like it passed for us. So there is no loss of time in his mind, just in ours. I moved him along, and now he's at peace."

As we walked slowly back to the car Eileen didn't say much, but her eyes were very teary. I tried to reassure her that things were okay with Stephen. He was where he should be now, and from this point forward he would be happy.

We went to lunch at the same spot we'd always gone; a little family-owned restaurant in town near Ottawa, Illinois. The restaurant had been there for many years and had changed owners many times, but always remained open. It helped that it was one of the few restaurants in town. We ate lunch and, as usual, the talk was of Stephen and how hard it was to imagine so much time had passed since they had seen him. Eileen had trouble remembering him; only bits and pieces came to mind when she thought of him. She remembered him picking her up and twirling her around, giving her rides on his shoulders, walking with her to school on her first day, and teaching her how to ride her bike very fast. The rest of it was all a blur. She wished she could remember more but was happy to hear the stories that her older siblings and father told.

It seemed that Stephen was quite the comedian and had liked to make everybody laugh. They all talked fondly of him, and it made me wish I had spent a little more time with him. It would have been great to get to know him and relay all the things he'd wanted to tell Eileen. But I guess that will happen all in good time.

The ride home from Ottawa was a long one. Eileen grilled me about the experience and explained how life-changing it was for her. She couldn't imagine how I could continue to do this without becoming emotionally drained every time.

I asked her if she noticed that she was driving. I told her that I got in the passenger seat because I was emotionally drained and figured it would be better if she drove. So yes, it was emotionally draining, but in a good way. I hadn't had any bad experiences. The emotional draining seems to be part of the process. So far, I wasn't having any trouble dealing with it. This one, dear brother Stephen, was the most draining experience I'd had. I believed it was because of the close family ties associated with this crossing.

I answered as many questions for Eileen as I could on the way home. She asked a lot of the things I would've asked if I were in her shoes. One of the questions I felt was interesting that she asked was what he was wearing. She wanted to know if he was still wearing his Boy Scout uniform. I said yes because it was what he died in. She wanted to know if he was still 12 years old when I talked to him. I explained that whatever age the person dies at is the age they stay. So Stephen was 12 just like the day he died, and it made sense that he would still be in the same outfit in which he died.

She asked me about the flowers, and I told her that he picked them up for a reason. "When he crossed over and ran to the back yard he gave the flowers to your mother. She put them in a vase with water and left them right on the picnic table. It was good to see the flowers change from a memorial to a gift of love. He patted you on the head as he walked by and sat down to have dinner like nothing had happened, because in his eyes, nothing had happened. I don't know for sure, but maybe he'll grow up and become a man in heaven. This is only a guess that I have, a feeling that the normal life he would have had will continue on the other side, but without any of the tragedy that your family was forced to go through."

Eileen was thinking deep at this point. "Do you ever see God when you get there?" she asked.

"No, I've never seen God, just Grandpa Bill," I replied. "He seems to be my liaison between this world and the next. Without him I don't know if I could do this. He's always there to meet me when I come through the light with another soul. I don't know if I'll ever get to meet God. I just seem to be helping out. I'm sure he's got better things to do than talk to me."

She shot me a serious look. "He may fool you," she said. "Who knows, maybe one of these times he'll show up to greet you. As they say, he works in mysterious ways."

"Yeah," I agreed, "I guess he does. It's a mystery that I'm still alive after all I went through. I know I've said it 100 times, but I don't think I would have made it without you. You and the kids were my only hope and my only drive to stay here on this side. Anything beyond this point, I figure, is a gift. I should've been dead and yet I'm still here."

As we finally pulled into the driveway, I was pretty exhausted. I told Eileen I was going upstairs to take a nap and she suggested I hold off because it was so late. I didn't realize it had become evening and I could go to bed a little early and sleep through the night instead of tossing and turning because I took a nap.

I still tossed and turned a lot that night with everything going through my head. I felt like I'd helped my wife's family more than anything. Eileen had thanked me before we fell asleep for doing what I had done that day for her brother Stephen. It was another gift for me, knowing that she was happy.

CHAPTER 14

On Monday I got a call from Eileen's father. He said Eileen had seemed very quiet at the dinner. "Was everything okay on Saturday?" he asked.

I said "Yeah, I think she was a little worried about me because of the walk and the long ride down there. I told her I was fine and not to worry. But after all she's been through, I guess she's going to worry."

He said, "Yeah, I guess so. There's no way around that. We're just glad that we still have you here."

I said, "Thanks, I'm sure glad to be here." I asked how he was doing after yesterday. He said it never gets any easier but he's at peace with where his son is now. I wanted so desperately to tell him about the story of Stephen, but I knew I couldn't. We small talked for a little while and he said goodbye. I had no idea it would be the last time I talked to him.

Two weeks later we got a call in the middle of the night saying Eileen's father, Dan, was having chest pain. Eileen's dad had been in good physical condition almost all of his life. He was 80 years old now and never had any problem with his heart.

We were hoping he was just having some acid reflux and things would be better in the morning. I tried to talk him into going to the hospital that night because I had heard of all the people that suffer chest pain and don't go to the hospital only to wake up dead. But he refused to go to the hospital, saying it was probably nothing.

The next morning Dan woke up, got out of bed, and collapsed on the floor. My mother-in-law was quick to call 911, and the ambulance was there within five minutes. She was far too old and frail to do CPR and didn't even know how it was performed. The paramedics never got a rhythm back on Dan. He was pronounced dead at the hospital by the emergency room doc.

We got there right after the ambulance had pulled up. I was glad that Eileen did not see them doing CPR on her father. I had seen it done on patients when I was in the ICU after my surgeries. It's not a pretty sight. I was glad most of the family was spared that experience.

Eileen was a wreck and so was I. Dan was a nice guy and a great father-in-law. He'd never interfered in our lives and was happy to see us every time we pulled up. He loved his grandchildren and spent many a day with them.

Eileen took charge of the arrangements for her dad's wake and funeral. I think it kept her busy and kept her mind off the situation. There were many tears at the wake and a lot of Dan's old friends showed up to pay their respects. Dan worked his whole life at the General Motors plant. By the time he retired he was a manager of one of the many assembly-line areas. He had worked his way up from the mailroom and over 40 years had made quite a nice living for himself. I found it amazing that there were so many people and old friends from GM that showed up. At one point, the line stretched around the building and people had to wait more than a half an hour to get in to see Dan. It was quite a tribute.

Dan's funeral was held on Thursday in a light rain at the Catholic cemetery in town. His two sons, three of the grandsons and I were the pallbearers. I felt it was a great honor to be chosen. There was a little hesitation on Eileen's part thinking that I may not be able to do it, but I knew I could put my pain to the side for this occasion. I made it through without even one stumble and we sat through a beautiful service that really summed up the life of a great father and a wonderful husband.

As we drove home from the funeral luncheon, Eileen finally broke down. She cried uncontrollably. I tried to comfort her, but knew she had to get this out rather than keep it in. She gathered herself together before we got home and spent the rest of the day up in our room. I let her be and only asked her if she wanted to come down for dinner. When she said she wasn't hungry, I brought her up a little food because I knew she just didn't want the children to see her cry. It was a long night and I held her for most of it.

Eileen was pretty grief-stricken for an entire week. She didn't say much to any of us and had quite a few tearful outbursts during this time. Her mother was having a rough time too. Even though we spent a lot of time with her, the pain was obvious.

I couldn't imagine being married for 48 years and losing your spouse so suddenly. Dan had always done all the bills and my mother-in-law, Lois, had been pretty much in the dark when it came to household finances. Eileen's dad was a lot like her and kept everything in files and well-organized.

We helped Lois go through the files and found his will along with a schedule of all the bills that needed to be paid. He also left a healthy life insurance policy which he kept up for some 30 years, leaving my mother-in-law with $300,000 and possession of the house. He left a part of his savings to each of the children. It equaled about $20,000 per child. He had managed his money well and left no stone unturned even though his death was unexpected. He even had put money aside to take care of the lawn and the landscaping for the next three years. He liked to pay bills ahead of time so he wouldn't have to worry about things. So, the only thing Lois really had to worry about was being in an empty house without the man that she had loved for 48 years.

I had purposely stayed out of the bedroom where Dan had died. I was afraid of what I'd find. I had hoped that he had just crossed over without any problem and had found his own heaven on the other side.

During the second week after Dan's passing Eileen asked me the question I had been dreading. "Do you think he's crossed over?" Eileen asked with tears in her eyes.

"I'm sure he has," I said. "He lived a long life and seemed to have everything in order when he died. The only thing that might keep him here is the confusion of the sudden death."

She looked at me with the most serious look I had ever seen on her face. "Well then, I need your help your special help. I have to know if he crossed over. I noticed you avoided the bedroom while we were at my parents' house. Why is that?"

"It's mainly because I was scared of what I'd find," I replied. "I've never had this happen to someone so close to me and I'm fearful of what

I might find. Dan was like a father to me too. I guess I'm just assuming he crossed over because he left no work here on earth that still needed to be done."

Eileen wasn't convinced. "But how do you know that? Maybe there was something. Something he wanted to say or do before he crossed over and he couldn't because of a heart attack and the quick way he went."

I was trying to talk her out of it. "I don't know for sure honey, but to be honest with you I'm pretty sure he's content."

But Eileen wasn't giving up. "I can't be sure until you go see if he has left this world."

Now I was anxious. "How am I going to do that with Lois in the house? She hasn't left there since the funeral and seems to be in a real state of depression. Don't get me wrong. If you really want me to check it out I will. But you have to figure out a way to get Lois out of the house at least for a couple of hours."

She said, "I think I can do that by taking her grocery shopping and then maybe to lunch."

Now I knew I had lost the battle. "Alright," I sighed. "When do you want to do this?"

"I don't know. I'll call her and see what I can arrange," she said.

The first conversation between Lois and Eileen did not go very well. She didn't seem ready to leave the house and was still quite depressed. Eileen tried hard to talk her into going grocery shopping and out to lunch, but to no avail. Lois said she had enough food in the house to last her a little while and that her stomach wasn't up to the lunch at a nice restaurant. Eileen tried this routine every other day for couple of weeks. During the end of the second week she finally got her to break, and Lois agreed to go out and get some groceries, but said she wasn't sure about lunch. I explained that if she could keep her in the grocery store for about an hour, it should be enough time for me to determine whether Dan was still here and if he needed help crossing over.

They decided to go do the grocery shopping on a Thursday. I went with Eileen and made up a story on how I needed to go through a few more files that the lawyer had requested. Lois opened the file cabinet, explained that she wasn't sure where anything was, and she started to cry.

"He always kept things so perfect, and I never needed to know anything about our finances. I wish I'd paid attention and let him know that I was interested in how he was keeping everything afloat."

I tried to calm her. "Lois, we can go over everything he has set up to make your life comfortable after his passing. He really had it together. I've never seen such an organized person when it came to personal finance. Everything in this file cabinet is marked and filed and a hand-written date is on every bill stating the date he paid the bill and the check number he used."

Lois smiled through her tears and said, "That was my Dan, always taking care of me. I'm so scared, Scott. I don't know how to take care of myself."

I pulled her close to me. "We'll get through this, Lois. You have to get over the shock of losing him, which is going to take some time. I want you to remember something though: he is with Stephen now."

She said, "Yes I know, I've been thinking a lot about that and how happy he must be to be with his son again."

Eileen told Lois it was time to go and with some hesitation she picked up her purse and said "I guess I'm as ready as I'll ever be. I haven't been out of this house in two weeks. Maybe it's time I got some fresh air."

Lois stepped ever so gingerly out of the house and looked back at me standing in the kitchen. "What are you going to do while we're gone?"

"I'm just going to clean up a little Lois, maybe run the vacuum or do a few dishes just help you out a little bit. And I'm going to look through the files for those papers for the lawyer. I'm still not very good at walking through a grocery store. But I can do some of the light-duty that my wife assigns me, so I figure I'll just do it for you."

Lois laughed and said, "It's good to know she has you well trained."

They both left with smiles on their faces at my little joke. They got in the car and slowly pulled out of the driveway. I hesitated in the kitchen by doing some of the dishes as I'd promised her. Lois didn't believe in the dishwasher. She thought she could do the dishes by hand just as quickly and save the money on a fancy dishwasher. I thought to myself, with the money left over from Dan's life insurance policy, maybe we could get her a dishwasher. But I was sure she wouldn't go for it.

I ran the vacuum downstairs after I finished the dishes to kind of cover for myself and the reason I was there. The whole process took me less than 20 minutes and I knew I still had some time to see if Dan remained in the house.

I walked gingerly down the hallway past the bathroom and the spare bedroom. This was not the house that Eileen had grown up in. After all the children had left, Dan and Lois had downsized to a two-bedroom ranch house that made it easier for them to get around. There was a basement, but they only used it for storage.

As I opened the door to Dan and Lois's room, my fear was at its height. I prayed that Dan would not be there. But as I walked in, I saw him sitting on the bed looking over the room. I couldn't tell if he was confused because he seemed to be preoccupied with what I assumed was the fog that surrounded him.

As soon as I had opened the door that tingling sensation entered my body. I hesitated to move through because of my fear that I would startle Dan, but I decided I couldn't wait any longer because of the time constraints. I passed through the shock and entered Dan's realm.

He looked up at me and said, "If it isn't my favorite son-in-law!"

I laughed. "You say that to all your sons-in-law!"

"I know, you're all my favorites," Dan said with a smile.

I knew had to get down to business quickly. "Dan, what are you doing here?"

Dan looked at me puzzled and said "I'm not really sure. I got up to go to the bathroom and I remember being dizzy. The next thing I know I was sitting here on the edge of the bed with this weird fog around me. I can't see anything beyond the door. I've gotten up several times, but I can't seem to open the door. What is going on, Scott?"

This was very difficult. "Well Dan, something major has gone on. Something I don't think you saw coming."

"What's that?" Dan said, seeming to be oblivious to his new state of existence.

"Dan, you remember when I had my accident, right?" Dan occasionally had memory problems, so I had to ask him this.

"Of course I do, it was the longest two weeks of my life. We almost lost you several times and I didn't know what Eileen and the kids would do without you. I prayed so hard that you would make it through, and you did, and I'm glad for that."

"Well thank you, Dan; I'm glad for that too. But something happened to me after the accident. You remember I died several times in the emergency room and in the operating room."

"Yes, I do," Dan said. "At that point I was at my lowest. You had come and gone so many times, we were almost sure we weren't going to see you alive again."

"Well, after I recovered, I started seeing things that startled me at first. I saw people standing on the side of the road by those roadside memorials that you see. No one else could see these people except me. When I finally got the nerve to approach them, I realized I was talking to the dead."

His eyes were wide open. "How can you talk to the dead?" Dan said. "The dead are dead. There is no more talking to them."

Now came the painful truth. "Well Dan, I'm talking to you right now."

Suddenly, his voice became louder. "What you mean by that?"

"Dan, do you remember when you got up to go to the bathroom and got really dizzy?"

"Yes I do, but what does that have to do with anything?" I could see he was confused by my previous statement. I was trying to break it to him easily, but it wasn't going very well, so I figured I might as well come out and say it.

"Dan, you said you found yourself sitting on the bed after you get dizzy. Do you remember ever going to the bathroom after that?"

"No I guess I don't, and I really had to go bad. When you get old you don't have much time to wait."

I laughed. "You see a fog around you, don't you?" I asked.

He thought I was crazy at this point. "Yes, I told you. Don't you see it?" he asked. "I can't see anything past that door, and I can barely make out my dresser. What do you suppose this is? Maybe there's something wrong with the air conditioning."

Oh, I was in over my head this time. "Dan, I'm afraid it's not the air-conditioning. When you got dizzy and passed out, you fell to the floor and passed away of a heart attack. You died that morning, Dan. You've been stuck here ever since."

Dan hesitated for a second. "Is that why I can't see Lois lying next to me in the bed?"

I nodded my head. "Guess that's the reason, Dan. She's been sleeping on the couch since you died. She can't seem to come in here and sleep in the bed that you two shared for so many years. She says it's too painful."

Then the truth really hit him. "Oh no, Lois must be devastated! Are you serious, Scott, am I really dead?"

"Yes, Dan, this is that talent that I've been given. I can see and talk to the dead and help them move along to the next world. I expected you to have moved along, because it seemed like everything here on earth was in order for you, and there should have been nothing holding you back. Can you think of something that might be holding you back? Maybe some unfinished business?"

Dan said, "Well, I kept everything pretty organized. It shouldn't be hard to find all my documents pertaining to my death."

I reassured him. "Yes, we found all those documents and you had one heck of a filing system. It made it easy to file all the necessary documents so that Lois would be taken care of after you went. Is there anything else though? Something else that might be keeping you here?"

Dan pondered the question and knew within almost an instant what was holding him back. "Scott, I just realized there was something that I never told Lois about that might be important for her to know. It also will make the lives of my children more stable. In the basement to the right of the furnace there is a box up in the rafters. In that box are some of my stock certificates from GM. Over the years I've stashed quite a bit of cash in that box for a rainy day. I had planned to take Lois to Italy for Christmas. I guess that dream will never come true. I don't know how many stock certificates are in the box but it's quite a few. I usually bought 50 shares at a time and did that over the years. As for the cash, I'm not sure how much is in there, but it's a pretty penny."

"Okay, Dan, I'll retrieve the box and go through it with Lois and the family. I can do this without them knowing that I talked to you. But usually, money isn't what holds a person from crossing over. Is there something else that might be keeping you here, something you need to get off your chest?"

"I was hoping you wouldn't ask that, but there is something," Dan said slowly. "When I was overseas in World War II, my first wife, Eileen's mother Catherine and I were engaged. I had been away from her for so long. I was stationed in the Pacific and met a beautiful Filipino girl named Mia. She spoke English and worked at the PX on the base. We became friendly and before I knew it, we had a relationship going. I felt guilty about Catherine being home alone waiting for me while I was having an affair with this beautiful Filipino girl. The affair lasted about three months, and as I was getting ready to be shipped back home, she told me she was pregnant. I believed her, because the sincerity in her eyes told me she wasn't lying. I didn't know what to do. I was young and I didn't want to lose Catherine. So, I just left. I left that beautiful girl to raise a child on her own, in a poor country, without any help from me. Mia had to do it all, and I felt like the lowest form of life ever put on this earth. I still have that feeling, even though my life went on and I found a lot of happiness with Catherine, and then Lois, and my family. I just wonder whatever happened to Mia and the baby. I tried to contact her at the base after I got home, but she'd left the PX and no one knew where she had gone. People in the Philippines move around quite a bit. She may have gone back to live with her parents and raised the child on her own. I often wonder what became of them and if she would ever forgive me for what I did."

I was truly in over my head now! "Well, that explains it, Dan. That guilt is keeping you here. Did you always feel guilty about not telling Catherine or Lois?"

"Yes, I did, but I figured I would do more harm than good by telling them, so I kept it to myself. Mia was halfway around the world and the chances of me seeing her again were slim to none. I didn't know what I'd do if she ever showed up in my life again. It was hard imagining how much difficulty growing up without a dad was for this baby. I felt so guilty for leaving them, but I was so young, and I didn't know what to do. Do you think she could ever forgive me?"

I said, "Dan, forgiveness is what heaven is about. Your situation was not the only one that came out of World War II. There were a lot of babies in Europe and the Pacific whose fathers were GIs. There is only one way to find out what happened to Mia and the baby, and that's to cross over. That's what I'm here for, and that's what I do. I now help people cross over, and I'd be honored to help you cross over to the other side."

Dan was scared. "I'm not sure I'm ready. I'm afraid of the consequences." Dan had been a good Catholic all his life. I'm sure he had confessed what he considered to be his sin many a time. Even in his 80s he managed to get to church every Sunday. I don't know if this makes a difference on the other side or not, but I know Dan was a good person and except for the one mistake he made as a young man, and I hoped that he would be accepted into heaven without hesitation.

"I'm glad you told me the story, Dan. It helps me to understand why you're still here. Now it's time for us to go into the light. Do you see the light?"

"Yes," he replied. "It's been over by my dresser ever since I sat down on the bed. I think knew what it was, but I was afraid to go into it. I'm afraid of what God is going to do to me for abandoning Mia and the baby."

I interrupted his thought. "Dan, I don't think you have anything to worry about. You more than made up for that mistake. You raised a beautiful family and were respectful and loving to both of your wives. The fact that you never told them was your way of protecting them. You never wanted them to be hurt, so you kept this secret. I think that's admirable. You could've destroyed a great thing. Honestly, knowing Lois, I think she would have understood and forgiven you. And from what I've heard about Catherine, I'm, sure she'd do the same."

"I'm not so sure," Dan said. "That's why I kept it from her all those years, and it's why I never told Lois, either."

We obviously didn't agree. "I think your fears are unfounded, Dan. I believe Lois will love you always, no matter what. And Catherine is the mother of your children, the children you raised together. It's time to move forward now. Walk with me, and we'll get through this."

Dan stood up and reluctantly walked with me into the light. Again, the high-speed trip was amazing. Dan seemed to enjoy the warmth and feelings of freedom that the light brings to everyone. When we got to the entrance, Grandpa Bill was off in the distance walking towards us.

Dan said, "I feel no aches or pains up here! My back feels like I'm 21 again. It's amazing! Not an ache or a pain anywhere."

"I know; that's what the light does for you. This guy walking towards us is my Grandpa Bill. He has been helping me with my new gift."

Dan was trying to understand. "So, when you get up here you see your loved ones that died when you were really young?"

"Grandpa Bill is sort of a special spirit. I guess I was about 18 when he died. I haven't seen anyone else from years back that died, but he has gotten me through this new part of my life and has helped me understand how it works. He's like my special angel."

As Grandpa Bill approached, Dan held out his hand. Grandpa Bill shook it and said, "It's always nice to welcome a veteran here on the other side. I was in Europe and was there when we drove the Germans out of France."

Dan said "I was in the Pacific fighting the Japanese. I was stationed at an airbase and was a navigator on a B-52."

This was something I'd never known about either one of them. Men from their generation rarely talked about the war. It seemed it was always something they'd left behind on the battlefield.

Grandpa Bill looked into Dan's eyes. "Dan, I understand you're worried about Mia and the baby."

Dan was visibly shaken. "Yes, I'm afraid I won't get into heaven because of what I did."

Now it was Grandpa's turn to reassure him. "Only a select few don't reach the other side, Dan. We reserve hell for special cases only, and even they usually don't stay forever. Hitler's still there and will be there forever. You were a young man far away from home and let the love of a woman enter your heart. The fact that you were engaged doesn't always stop love. The situation just didn't lend itself to a long-term relationship with Mia. But she and the baby are here. She was killed not long after you left in a bombing run by the Japanese. The baby was only six weeks old, a baby boy. But she is waiting for you over there," he said as he pointed. "Do you see her?"

Dan looked to his right to see the grass hut where Mia had lived just off the base. She was standing outside the door holding the baby and waving at him. To my surprise and to Dan's utter amazement, Catherine, his first wife, stood there as well. Dan looked back at Grandpa Bill with tears in his eyes.

"You see, Dan?" Grandpa said. "Catherine has already forgiven you, and Lois will understand too. Everyone is given total forgiveness when they enter heaven. Catherine has done her share, and Lois will give you that too when her time comes. Mia and the baby will become part of your heavenly family up here. For right now, you can spend some time with Catherine, Mia, and the baby. And as your family enters heaven, they will welcome Mia and the baby with open arms. Now go be with them. Apologize to Mia for leaving her and tell Catherine how sorry you are that you hid this from her. They'll understand. Hold your baby like you held all your other babies ... with love."

Dan started to walk away heading towards Mia. He got about 20 yards away and turned around to come back. He came up to me and said, "I almost forgot to thank you. You've been a great son-in-law. I'm proud of you. Keep taking good care of my baby, because she'll always be my little baby." That was Eileen's nickname growing up, Baby. I promised I would, and told him I was proud of him, too, for doing such a great job raising a wonderful family.

I said, "Now go and get to know your other family too."

He shook Grandpa Bill's hand again, and walked towards Mia, Catherine, and the little baby boy. They welcomed him with big hugs, and Mia handed him his little boy. At that moment I broke down and cried.

Grandpa Bill looked at me and said, "You've passed one of the hardest tests I've thrown at you, but there will be more. And your secret may have to be revealed to some other people. You will know who those people are when the time comes. They may not believe you, so get ready for some ridicule. But it's important to stick to your guns. Now go back and surprise Lois with the box from the basement. It's important to Dan; he's thinking of it right now."

I looked back at the scene enfolding around Dan. He cradled the baby, looking with joy on his son's face for the first time. Catherine stood on one side of Dan, her hand on his arm. Mia stood on the other side, beaming with happiness. All three stared down at the baby in wonder. It was the best heavenly scene I'd seen so far, and my heart warmed just looking at them.

Suddenly, I was thrown into reverse and landed back on the bed where Dan and I had talked. I had quite a headache and was physically drained. I looked down at my watch to see that only 15 minutes had passed.

I knew I didn't have much time to find the box in the basement. I had to think of a story as to why I would be in the basement when Eileen and Lois got home. I figured I could say I was just tidying up the basement and going through some of Dan's possessions to see what some of his sons might want to keep.

I found the ladder behind the hot water heater and spotted the box that Dan had been talking about in the rafters. I came down off the ladder slowly because my foot was really hurting. I put the box down on the stairs and returned the ladder to its original spot.

Bringing the box upstairs, I opened it at the kitchen table. It held a stack of GM stock certificates approximately an inch and a half thick. Each stock certificate represented 50 stocks. I counted them up and saw that Dan had over 3000 shares of GM stock. GM's stock was trading at approximately $65 a share. To the right of the box was the cash Dan had mentioned. It was also neatly bundled. "Just like Dan," I said to myself with a smile and a shake of my head. "A place for everything and everything in its place."

The cash was mostly large bills, 50s and 100s. Some of the bills were from the 1950s. Because I was a coin collector as a kid, I knew that these were silver certificates, and worth more than the denomination that was listed on the bill. I counted the money; there was $28,000. I was floored. Dan made fair money in his job, but he was obviously a better saver than he was anything else. Except for being a father, he was great at that, too.

I heard a car pull up and quickly closed the box. Eileen and Lois walked up the sidewalk and the steps to the back door. They were loaded down with groceries, so I decided to help them without explaining the box first.

We got all the groceries put away before Lois noticed the box. She said, "Where did you get that?"

I said, "After I finished the dishes and vacuumed, I decided to go down in the basement and go through some of Dan's things to see what your sons might like to keep. He had quite a tool collection, you know. I figured the boys could go through the tools and pick out the ones they wanted. I kept a small toolbox with the essentials in it, so that if I have to repair anything here, I've got some tools to work with. While I was looking up in the rafters to see if Dan had stored anything up there, I noticed this box. It looked pretty old and dry, and I was a little afraid that it was so close to the furnace. I took it down because I didn't want any kind of a fire to start."

My lie had become pretty elaborate, but I figured it was better than telling Lois I'd just talked to her dead husband. "I brought the box up here," I said, "because when I opened it downstairs, I felt you needed to go through it."

Lois said, "Please tell me it's not filled with pictures, because I don't know if I could handle that right now." Her eyes became teary, and she looked fearful of the contents of the box.

I reassured her. "There aren't any pictures in there, but it is important that you look and see what is."

Lois and Eileen slowly approached the box and opened it up. Eileen's hands went directly to her mouth, and she inhaled as if she had been surprised by a monster. Lois mimicked the same reaction.

I said, "I took the liberty of going through the box. I hope you don't mind, Lois. There are 3000 shares of GM stock in the box and $28,000 cash. The cash will be worth more because some of the bills are very old and could be sold at auction for more than their face value."

Lois sat down immediately as if she were going to faint. Between the life insurance policy and the stocks and cash, she would never have to worry about money for the rest of her life. Lois was five years younger than Dan. She was in great physical condition for a woman her age, so there was a good chance she could live well into her 90s.

I said, "Now, do you know what I think you should do? I think you should sell some of that stock, and you and Eileen should go to Italy. I know Dan always wanted to take you there. He told me a couple weeks before he passed that he planned to take you there this Christmas. I think he would still want you to go. And I think Eileen deserves a trip for having to put up with me and all my injuries for the last year. But it's entirely up to you, Lois."

Lois said, "I can't do it right now, but I think it's a fine idea. What do you say we go after the holidays, so I don't miss Christmas with the family?"

Eileen was very excited about the possibility of going to Italy. She started thinking.

"Mom, with this kind of money you could bring the whole family."

Lois was in disbelief. "I guess I could. Maybe that's what I'll do. I just wish Dan could go with us." The tears began to fall from Lois' eyes, and I knew she was still not ready to let go of Dan. It would be some time before she would start to recover.

I told Lois I would take the box to the bank and put the belongings in a safety deposit box for her. She thought this was a good idea and wondered how Dan had managed to sneak down in the basement and keep such a stash of financial stability in a box.

"I'm wondering what else is in the basement," Eileen said. "Maybe he's got a box of diamonds down there!"

This made Lois laugh, which made us all laugh. It was good to see her with a smile on her face for the first time since Dan had passed. I knew Dan was happy and was getting to know his little boy and would be proud to introduce him to the rest of the family. With time, this would all transpire. Someday, even I would get up there and get to spend time with him again. I missed the old guy and his sense of humor.

We asked Lois if she wanted us to stick around for a while, but she said no, that she would be okay. I said I would stop at the bank in town on the way home and open a safety deposit box in her name and in our name. It's always good to have more than one name on a safety deposit box.

As we left the bank and got in the car Eileen said, "He was there, wasn't he?"

I said "Yes, he hadn't left yet."

"Why didn't he cross over immediately?" she asked.

At this point I didn't want to tell Eileen the real reason that Dan had remained on earth. This was something Dan needed to tell her on his own when she crossed over. So, I told her a different part of the story.

"The box was the reason that he hadn't crossed over. He was afraid it would get thrown away when they cleaned up the basement. He just wanted Lois not to have to worry about money. He told me where the box was. I had to get a ladder out from behind the hot water heater and climb up to the rafters. The box was pretty well hidden, and I don't know if anyone would've found it. He just wanted to take care of Lois and all her needs for the rest of her life. After he told me where the box was, we went through the light, and Grandpa Bill and Dan talked about their time in World War II. Your dad said goodbye to me and told me make sure to take good care of his baby."

Eileen broke down and cried harder than I had seen her cry since the funeral. She said "You really helped him. You really do have this talent. I was having trouble believing you before, but now I know that everything you say is true. I'm sorry it took so long for me to have total faith in you, but it was a little hard to not think that this was some left-over problem from the accident."

I held her and told her I understood. "It would be hard for me to believe if it happened to you. So don't feel guilty. Just be there for me to talk to when I need to tell you about the experiences I go through. It makes me feel good to know that someone else understands why I do what I do."

We went back home and met the kids at the front door. I paid the babysitter and Eileen took her home. John told me we didn't need a babysitter anymore and that he could handle it, and from this point on, I knew he was right. The look in his eyes told me he felt he could be responsible enough to handle the task.

They asked how Grandma was and I told him that she was doing okay. Dana said, "She still misses Grandpa very much." She had a tear in her eye too.

I'd seen enough tears that day, including some of my own. I was emotionally spent. Eileen came back from dropping off the babysitter and helped me get all the kids ready for bed. Before I knew it, I was asleep.

CHAPTER 15

I woke up the next day still feeling pretty spent. I decided to take it easy and not go for my daily ride. The kids were in school, and Eileen was at work so I decided just to get some chores done around the house. This was a big event for me because chores really are chores when you've got a bad leg. But I knew Eileen would appreciate it and be happy that her house was clean. One thing my mother did teach me was how to clean a house. I knew I could always pick up a second job as a maid. Although I'd look pretty funny in the outfit, but if the light hit me just right, I'd be kind of cute ... in a nauseating sort of way.

I was amazed that Eileen had gone back to work as quickly as she did after her father's death. I think she needed to keep herself busy and hope that the pain would start to subside. It'd been three weeks now and the occasional smile was more frequently observed on her face. She seemed to cherish the little moments with the children even more. She would ask them every night how school went, what they did and how their classes were going.

We were still taking turns playing taxicab driver with all the after school activities. We were getting back into the old routine that we had before my accident.

I still limped quite a bit and suffered from the mild headaches, but I tried not to complain. I was able to get around most days without my cane but still had to use it if I was walking any distance. The physical condition of my body was still not back to normal. I was getting there but it was taking longer than I thought. I guess when they replace part of your aorta and open up your skull, your body isn't really quick to bounce back. I think my legs were my biggest problem, though. After the accident they had atrophied down to almost nothing. I really had to work on the muscles in my thighs and hips to get them back in some sort of shape. I probably shouldn't have complained, but it becomes frustrating when your body won't do what you want it to. Even though I had made quite a bit of progress, I guess I just wanted to be back to normal.

The truck driver's insurance company continued to make offers to settle out of court. I still felt bad for the driver's family, because he had no fault in this accident. He'd just had a heart attack. There was no way he could control the action of his truck. I didn't really want the case to go to court but I knew I had to protect my family in case for some reason I didn't live long. The last offer they'd made me was $6.5 million. I knew we were getting close, and like I said I wasn't sure I wanted to drag this into a court. My lawyer said he was going to try to get us $10 million if at all possible. Since the lawyer was going to take a third, I could understand his motivation. He thought it would be better if we went to court because the jury might be more likely to give us quite a bit more money. I wasn't sure I wanted to take that chance. Our lawyer had presented the case to the insurance company, stating that the trucking company had never required their truck drivers to have yearly physicals to determine if they were safe to drive. The truck driver that hit me had not been to a doctor in 10 years. This was going to be the basis of our case if it went to court. There was a law in place that stated all over the road truck drivers were to go through a physical once a year to determine whether or not they should be on the road. It's the same thing with airline pilots. I thought the law was a good law and wished the truck driver had been forced to go have his physical. He may have had a treadmill exercise test which would've picked up his heart problem and it could have been fixed. He would still be around for his family, and I wouldn't have had to go through everything I'd gone through over the last year.

But it's all water under the bridge if you ask me. The insurance company knew they were at fault for not insisting that the company follow the rules. The company was a huge trucking outfit and should have known better. All I could hope for was that the next offer would be the one that closes this case.

Fall had its full grip on us, and the temperature was dropping. This meant more achiness for me. The cold does things to an old guy's bones, especially after they've been broken to pieces. The fall colors were as beautiful as they always are. We had a lot of maple trees in our area and several around our house. Most of these turned reddish yellow and really brightened up the area. It's hard to concentrate on your driving when you've got this much beauty to look at.

John was almost finished with fall baseball and Casey was just start-ing basketball. Dana was in between gigs. She was thinking of trying out for cheerleading, something I always dreaded. I was never much for cheerleaders, although I did marry one. When I played sports in high school it always amazed me that you could be losing by 30 points and there were still 10 girls on the sidelines jumping up and down saying rhymes that made no sense. There's no use in shouting "defense" when you're down by 30 points. You can pretty much figure that the defense has already checked out. I guess I just wasn't a big fan of cheerleaders. But if Dana wanted to be a cheerleader, I would support her in any way I could. I would even buy her the little bit of glitter makeup that she needed to look like all the rest of the cheerleaders. You do what you've got to do as a parent. It's part of the deal. So, I was sure I'd be at football games just to watch my little Dana jumping up and down yelling "defense" for a team that is 30 points down. What goes around comes around. I'm sure it would just be like the old high school days when I was annoyed with the whole thing.

It had been some time since I had seen any new spirits. Because it was my own father-in-law, the last one had shaken me up so much that I was in no hurry to help anybody else. I was always looking on the sides of the road because now it had become habit. I was always glad when I would see a roadside memorial and nobody standing by it.

One sunny October day I decided to take a walk on one of the forest preserve paths just to get some exercise. I took my cane with because I didn't know how ambitious I was going to be. I drove to the forest preserve and parked my car. I got out with my cane in hand and my aviator sunglasses. Somehow, they made me feel cool. The truth is I probably looked like a dork. But who was going to see me on the path in the forest preserve?

The path was a winding one and the trees were beautiful. I saw every variety imaginable. Like I said, we had a lot of maple trees in the area, so the colors were incredible. It was a beautiful fall day, and I walked along, enjoying the weather.

About a quarter mile down the path and off to my right, I noticed what I assumed was a spirit sitting on a stump. The stump was about 50 yards away off the path. The spirit appeared to be a woman about 20 years old. She had her head in her hands and looked kind of disheveled. I kept walking, thinking I needed to get my exercise first and then I might stop and see if I could talk to her on my way back. I made it to the little bridge that crossed Hickory Creek and started on my way back.

When I approached the spot where I had seen the lady, she was still sitting on the stump with her hands covering her face. I slowly walked through the leaves that had fallen on the forest floor and approached the lady.

I knew she was a spirit when the tingling started, and I felt the shock as I crossed over into her world. I introduced myself and asked her if she needed some help. She looked a little scared. I reassured her, "I'm here to help you; how long have you been here?"

She said, "I've been here for a while."

"How long is a while?" I asked.

She said, "I think two days."

She was dressed in clothing from the 70s. She even had bell bottom jeans on. "Do you remember what year it was when you came out here?" I asked.

She gave me a confused look. "Do you mean what year is it now?" she asked.

"Sorry, yeah, I mean what year is it now?" My question must have seemed crazy to her. I kept forgetting that time stands still.

She said, "It's 1978."

I said, "Okay, why are you out here?"

She said, "My boyfriend and I were having a big fight in the car. He started to hit me. I fought him back, but he was too strong. He put his hand on my throat and the next thing I knew I was out here in the forest. This fog never goes away. I've tried to move it with my hands. It just stays where it's at. I can't seem to get past it, and I always end up back here sitting on the stump."

I knew I had come upon something I wished I hadn't. This was a murder. The girl must be buried in this spot. In 1978 there was no path going through the forest preserve; it was just a big, wooded area. So, her boyfriend must've killed her and then walked back here to the forest preserve and buried her body right by the stump.

Now I was involved in a murder case. This was definitely more than I had bargained for. I didn't know who she was because I couldn't recall a murder case from 1978. It was just too long ago.

"I'm sorry, I forgot to ask you your name," I said.

"My name is Kathy. Kathy Johnson. It was supposed to be Kathy Johnson Smith in the next couple of weeks. My boyfriend and I were getting married until our big fight happened. He wanted to break up with me with only two weeks before the wedding. He said he wasn't ready to get married, but I knew he had another girlfriend. That's why I lashed out at him in the car, because I knew he was lying to me. I just didn't think he would hit me. He never hit me before and I never saw him this angry. When he put his hands on my throat, I started to feel like I was passing out. I just wanted him to stop. I would let him have his little girlfriend and I would call off the wedding. But I never got a chance to say it because he was tightening his grip on my neck. Before I knew it, I was sitting here in this fog and wondering how I was going to tell my family that the wedding was off. It's going to crush my mother; she's been planning this for over six months. We will lose so much money when we cancel everything. My dad had to pay for everything because my jerk of a fiancé didn't have a job. He had worked at the cabinet mill on Cedar Road but lost his job because he went into work drunk one day. Now my dad is forced to pay for everything even though he wants no part of this guy marrying his daughter." This was really more than I bargained for.

"What was this guy's name?" I asked.

She said, "Mark, Mark Smith."

I said, "Where does he live?"

"He lives in Mokena. I met him in high school. In the beginning we seemed perfect for each other. We were engaged for three years while he was getting his start at the cabinet company. He started to drink heavily when he turned 21. I couldn't stop him. I told him he had a drinking problem, but he wouldn't get any help. He said he was just fine, and he was just out having fun with his friends. He was always plastered from Friday night to Sunday afternoon and several times during the week.

At first it didn't seem like such a big deal; I mean, all his friends were doing it too. But when he started drinking during the day and as soon as he came home from work, I knew there was a problem. I started to doubt my decision to marry him. He would sometimes ignore my calls for two days. When he did call me back, he would give me some lame excuse as to where he was. He'd say he passed out at Billy's house and slept for 12 hours. When I asked Billy if that was what happened he nodded his head, but wouldn't tell me anymore. I knew that jerk was screwing around on me. That's why I confronted him. I just wish I had done it many months ago."

"Kathy, do you know why you're still here in the forest?" I asked.

"No, I don't even know how I got here."

This was really hard. "Kathy, I have to tell you something and it may come as a big surprise to you," I explained. "I think Mark murdered you. You've died. I'm pretty sure he strangled you to death that night in the car. Had he been drinking that night?"

She nodded. "He was always drinking. But what do you mean I'm dead? I don't feel dead. I just feel lost."

"Well," I said, "you are somewhat lost. You're caught between two worlds. These worlds are life and death. Most people cross over to the other side immediately after they die. For some reason, and I believe it's because you were murdered, you have been here since 1978 when Mark buried your body here. Kathy, I can see spirits and I can tell you that you are a spirit. I have to tell you something else. You died in 1978, right?"

She looked confused. "Yes, if what you say is true, I did die in 1978. But how come I don't remember any part of this other than sitting here on the stump?"

"I don't know. Sometimes the trauma of a violent death is blocked out from your memory. I'm assuming that's what happened to you. The key to this is that you remember him choking you. We can pretty much assume that he murdered you. Do you remember where he lived in Mokena?"

"He lived on Third Street. I don't remember the address but it's the third house on the right."

"I have a feeling I'm here to help you get some peace and crossover to the other side. But first I have to do some research and find out about your case. I need to find out some more information about Mark, and I want to check the newspapers from 1978."

"You mean newspapers from this year, right?" she asked.

"Kathy, that's the other thing I have to tell you. We're in the year 2011 now. You've been here for 33 years. I'm assuming that no one has discovered your body, which means Mark may have gotten away with murder."

Now she looked angry. "That son of a bitch! If he killed me, how do I know if he ever was caught?"

I tried to keep a calm voice. "I don't know, and that's why I have to do the research. It may take a few days, but it would only seem like minutes to you. Just give me some time and I will see what I can find out. I'll be back shortly."

I knew that the time it took for me to research would have no effect on her. As I left the site, I walked through the fog receiving the same shock I always received. The tingling sensation faded as I walked towards the path. I was overwhelmed with the thought that this case was going to be very different than what I had experienced with the others.

I hardly slept at all that night as I was trying to put all the pieces of this mess together. I went to the library the next morning to research the newspapers from 1978. I assumed that the murder would've taken place in the summer months because they were planning a wedding that was only two weeks away, so I started with May of 1978.

The first hint of the story came on June 13, 1978. The newspaper headline read "Bride-to-be gone missing." The story went on to talk about Kathy and the fact that she was due to get married in two weeks and had simply disappeared two days prior to the article being written, on June 11th. At first the police treated the case as a runaway bride. They interviewed her parents who said there was no way she would've just taken off. She was too excited about her wedding and was looking forward to starting a new life. They also interviewed her fiancé Mark who said, "I don't know what could've happened to her. This is so unlike her to just take off." That was the only quote from Mark, who seemed convinced that she had run away from the commitment they were about to make to each other. He never mentioned anything about her safety. He seemed disconnected and unconcerned in the rest of the interview. He seemed almost disgruntled, as if he were trying to lead on that his fiancée had just gotten up and left.

But I knew otherwise, and I was quite angry at the statements he made to the newspaper. A week later, another edition of the newspaper mentioned that Kathy was still missing and that her parents had not heard from her in over 10 days. Their comments read, "She was a loving daughter who was very excited about her wedding. It was so unlike her to run away and have no contact with us. She would not want her parents to worry. Something is wrong. We think she has come upon some foul play." The newspaper had also interviewed Mark again, and he pretty much said the same thing he had said before, stating he was almost sure she got cold feet and ran away. He had mentioned a discussion they had in the car about how nervous she was. She assured him she was still going to go through with the wedding but was having a case of cold feet.

I knew this was a lie because of what Kathy had told me. Mark was the one who wanted to break off the relationship. This obviously didn't go over well with Kathy. Unfortunately, the argument led to a fight and a fight led to a physical altercation which then led to her death.

I kept looking. A month later, another story ran in the paper stating that there was no trace of Kathy and a missing person's report had gone out nationwide. A description was given, including the clothes she was wearing when she went missing. The description would have been sent to all the major police forces throughout the country. This seemed like a shot in the dark to find her if you think about all of the technology we have to help find missing persons today.

One more story ran in the fall of 1978, stating she was still missing but her parents were not giving up hope. Mark was not interviewed for this story and seemed to have dropped off the map. The parents mentioned that he had been of little help in finding their daughter, Kathy. They hadn't spoken to him since the summer. The police said they had a suspect but did not have the evidence to arrest him. I don't know nor was it mentioned what this evidence was or who their suspect was, but I'm assuming they must have found something in Mark's car that led them to believe there had been a struggle. But back then, DNA evidence was nonexistent. The police were also hampered by the fact that they didn't have a body. It is very hard to prosecute a murder without this evidence. And I knew that no one had ever found Kathy's body.

I knew that the only way to re-open the case was to discover Kathy's body in that forest preserve. I just had to figure out how to do it without making it look like I had an interaction with Kathy. The only thing I could do was to go back to Kathy and ask her if she had any jewelry on the night she was murdered. If she did, I could buy a metal detector and search the area until I found the jewelry she was wearing. Then I could dig up the jewelry and find her body and report it to the police. This could then get the investigation up and running again and maybe if Mark was still alive, we could get him put away.

I ordered a metal detector online and paid for two-day shipping. It was a high-quality model that cost me about $800. I explained to Eileen that I had always wanted to have one and that it would give me something to do while I was walking along the path. I told her that I might want to search for little trinkets. There also were several parks in our town that I could search for coins and jewelry. I hated to lie to her about why I actually bought this, but I figured I was in over my head as it was, and I didn't want her to know that I was involved in a murder case. I figured if I found Kathy's body, then I could explain the purchase of a metal detector to Eileen.

I went back to the area where I had seen Kathy and walked the 50 yards into the forest preserve and went through her perimeter. When I entered her space, she looked up at me and said, "Did you get anywhere with your research?"

I told her about the time I spent looking through the newspapers and the stories and interviews that were given by Mark and her parents. She said "Oh my God, my parents! They don't know anything about what happened, do they?" She started crying, knowing the pain her parents must've gone through during this 35-year period. She said, "They might not even be alive anymore! Oh my God, this is so terrible! How could this have happened? I have no idea why I've been here so long. This is unfair to my parents and my friends to not know where I'm at. And that that bastard Mark killed me. Did you find him?"

I shook my head. "No I didn't. There's no mention of him after the second story in the newspaper. They did say they had a suspect in your disappearance. How much did you struggle in the car?"

She said, "I fought him pretty hard. I scratched his arms and tore his shirt while he was choking me. I may even have punched him in the face once or twice. I felt I was blacking out and I don't remember anything after that."

"I wonder if the police suspected Mark," I said. "I wonder if anyone noticed the scratches and marks on him and if his torn shirt was discovered by anyone. Unfortunately, because they never found your body, they couldn't prosecute him. By the time the third story in the newspaper ran, it seemed that the police had come to the conclusion that you had met with some foul play. So at least they were on the right track. I have a question for you. Were you wearing any jewelry the night you were killed?"

"Yes, I had on my high school class ring and a necklace Mark had given me for our first month anniversary. We'd been engaged for some time, but I had never taken that little necklace off. I can still see my class ring on my hand. And I can feel the necklace around my neck."

"That's good," I said to Kathy. "I just bought a metal detector online."

She said, "What do you mean, online?"

I said, "Computers have come a long way. I don't have time to explain it all to you, but everyone has computers and people buy things online from stores, then the stuff comes from UPS. Anyway, this metal detector should pick up your class ring in this area and that will lead me to the rest of your body. With a body, the police will re-open the case and hopefully be able to charge Mark with your murder. I wanted to explain everything to you before I brought the metal detector over here. It's kind of weird looking and it makes a high-pitched noise, so I didn't want you to be scared."

She said, "I just found out I've been dead for 35 years; at this point I don't think anything could scare me."

I told her that I would go to my car to get the metal detector. I also brought a shovel just in case I came across any remains or needed to dig for the jewelry. I crossed through the fog and Kathy immediately noticed the metal detector. She said it looked like something from the future. I said "Well, technically it is from the future in your realm."

She said, "Yeah, guess you're right. We'll don't waste any time. See if you can find me."

I turned the metal detector on and proceeded to scan the area. I started at the stump where she had been sitting and worked my way outward in a circle. About five feet from the stump, I got a hit on the metal detector. It turned out to be a metal cap from an old Pepsi bottle.

She got excited. "Is that it, is that it?"

"No," I said, "just an old bottle cap but I will keep looking."

As I got to the other side of the stump I got another hit. This one was much stronger which usually means a larger piece of metal. I started to dig with my shovel and got down about a foot or so. After that I slowly went another six to eight inches so I wouldn't damage anything. The last couple inches I dug out by hand. There was a slight glimmer in the hole that appeared after I took out the last handful of dirt.

I scraped around it with my Swiss Army knife and was able to determine that it was Kathy's ring. I turned to look towards the stump and Kathy was standing over me. This kind of startled me because she had been sitting on the stump since the time I had met her.

She looked down at the hole and said, "That's my ring! I'd recognize it anywhere. It says 'Cheerleader' on the side. Class of 1976. I never took it off, I was very proud of that ring. I had spent four years as a cheerleader and earned it. I even paid for it myself by working at a pizza place during school."

I knew I had something here, because I could see the bones of her hand, and I was able to scratch off enough dirt to identify the entire hand. With this I knew I could approach the police and tell them I discovered something that they needed to see. I told Kathy that I would go to the police immediately and that there would be quite a bit of activity near her area. I asked her if she would be able to handle that.

She said, "If it helps get that bastard Mark convicted, I can handle anything." Her confidence was high, but I knew after all these years getting a conviction would be very difficult. Even with a body there was no guarantee that Mark would be convicted of her murder. I asked Kathy if they had been to this forest preserve a lot.

She sighed and said, "Yeah. this was our spot. We used to sit in the car and talk, among other things if you get my drift."

I said, "I do, I was young once too." I told her it was time for me to go to the police and I would bring them back. "Be prepared to see your skeleton as they bring it out of the ground. I don't know how much a body degrades over time but I'm assuming that there will be nothing left except the skeleton. Will you be able to handle that?"

She said, "That might be a little difficult, but I think I can handle it."

"Did anyone see you go out that night?" I asked.

"My parents did. I said goodbye to them in the living room before we left."

I said, "Your mother had given a pretty good description of what you were wearing when you left the house. So, if there is any remnant of your clothing left, that also might help identify your body. Did you have dental work done?"

"Yes, I had several fillings," she said. "I also had a tooth pulled. One of my molars needed a root canal but I just told them to pull it. It was way in the back, and I figured I didn't need it. I guess that's pretty silly now that I think about it."

"No," I shook my head. "Actually, it may help us in the long run if that tooth is missing because it will help identify you. It looks like your body is buried about two and a half, feet down. It must've been a pretty shallow grave because over the years leaves and debris have covered you even more. Mark may have come home with a lot of dirt on him from burying your body. If we can get someone to attest to that, it may also help convict him. But now I'm just playing cop. I should let the professionals handle this. I'm going to go get them, and it'll seem like only minutes by the time we get back."

I put a small stick in the ground near the hole and tied my handkerchief to it. I knew I would be able to see the area because I could see Kathy, but I had to make it look like I had discovered this on my own just by scanning the forest floor with my metal detector. I had heard that this area had once housed a French fort, so I could use that excuse as a reason that I was using my metal detector out there.

I went into the police station and was met by a very angry female police officer, for what reason I don't know, so I asked to speak to a supervisor. She said the supervisor was out on a call and I'd have to wait. I don't know what had gotten into her, but she was a whole lot of mean. I was glad at that moment I wasn't in custody for some crime. I was a big guy but I was pretty sure she could kick my ass.

I waited about 15 minutes and the supervisor arrived. I asked if I could talk to him in private and he asked, "Yes, what's this all about?"

We went back into his office in the police station. It looked like an interrogation room. I told him the story that I was in the forest preserve scanning with my metal detector and had found something.

"What forest preserve?" he asked.

I replied, "It's the one with the path going through it off of School House Road. You know, the one that used to be the Old French Fort in the 1700s. I was looking for old coins or possible buttons from the uniforms of the soldiers. But I found something much more important."

He said "Well, let's take a ride over there and you can point it out to me and I'll tell you if it's important or not." He seemed somewhat annoyed because he had to go back out after just coming in from a call.

He followed me over to the forest preserve and I parked my car. He pulled in next to me and parked. I got out of my car and waited by his. He was talking on the radio. He finished his conversation and got out of the car.

"I didn't get your name," he said.

I said, "It's Scott."

"Have you got a last name, Scott?" he said.

"Yes, of course I do," I said. It's Moss."

He continued with his questions. "Do you live in the area?"

"Yes, not too far from here," I answered.

He was all business. "Okay, so why don't we walk towards this area you're talking about."

We walked side by side until I reached the area where Kathy was. She was sitting on the stump with her hands supporting her face.

I said, "Let me see, it's right around here." I paused for effect. "There it is." I pointed to the stick with my handkerchief tied to it. It was a poor excuse for a white flag, but I pointed it out to him.

We walked up to Kathy, who was unable to see us until we got right near the white flag. She stood up rather quickly and started saying, "I'm right there! I'm right there!"

As the cop looked into the hole, I waved Kathy off as if to tell her to relax. I knew he didn't see me do this, so I wasn't worried that he would think I was crazy.

"My metal detector picked up on the ring," I said. "When I dug a little deeper, I noticed it was still attached to a hand. I just uncovered the hand so I could show you that I think we've got a body here."

He looked up at me and said, "We sure do."

"I looked at the ring," I said. "It looks like it says 'Class of '76' on it. Can you see that?"

He took out his glasses and peered down in the hole. He said, "Yes, that's what it appears to say. Dammit! I can't believe this. Of all days for our homicide detective to be off work. I'm going to have to call him in. What made you come all the way out here? You're about 50 yards off the path."

"Yeah, sometimes I get out of hand. Half the time I look up and I don't know where I'm at. I'm just concentrating on getting a signal."

"Well, you've made quite a find here."

I nodded. "Yeah, but it's not the kind of find I would want to make on an everyday basis. I almost jumped out of my skin when I saw the hand with the ring on it. I guess my heart is stronger than I think, otherwise I probably would have had a heart attack right here!" I paused, then said, "I didn't get your name."

"I'm sorry, I should have introduced myself," he said. I'm Sgt. Kowalski. No Polish jokes please."

We both laughed but with reservation. After all, there was a dead body at our feet. He continued, "I'm going to get on the radio and make a call to the station and tell them what you found."

Sgt. Kowalski was on the radio calling in some numbers, which I assumed meant a body had been found. Before I knew it, I heard squad cars pulling up into the parking lot. Three police officers entered the area where we were and looked down into the hole. They agreed it was a human body and were fascinated by the ring still being on the hand.

Sgt. Kowalski started barking orders. "We better get forensics out here. I need some help. Our forensics department isn't very big. Just a couple of people. In fact, I think I'm going to call the State Police for some help."

One of the police officers went back to his vehicle and brought back a small tent. He set up the cover, which made a little roof above the area. The forensics team arrived, and by this point I was standing back about 10 yards. The fog had lifted from around Kathy, and she was intently involved in listening to what everyone was saying. She seemed quite nervous, and I wanted to talk her down, but I couldn't get close to her because I would blow my cover. When the police officers were looking down, I would wave to her and make a calming motion with my hands trying to calm her.

The forensics team did call in the State Police force for help. They slowly dug around the area and gently lifted all the soil from around the body. Some of the clothing was still intact, although quite raggedy. I walked up to the area after they had uncovered the entire body to see the small necklace around Kathy's neck. One of the police officers mentioned the hyoid bone in the neck appeared fractured. I knew from the TV shows I had watched that this was a sign of strangulation.

The forensics team slowly removed the skeleton, keeping it as intact as they possibly could. They placed the body in a bag and zipped it up. Kathy was startled by the sound of the zipper. The police remained in the area looking for any other clues amongst the debris on the ground near the hole. They asked me if I would use my metal detector to help them. I gladly obliged them and scanned the entire area for about 10 or 15 yards beyond the hole in all directions. We came up with nothing other than a few more bottle caps. Someone must've been setting up a little camping area here and drinking Pepsi, not even knowing they were so close to a body.

The police left the hole uncovered, and after several hours they walked out of the forest preserve. I was the last one to leave and I turned around and motioned to Kathy that I'd be right back.

I followed the police officers out to the parking lot. Sgt. Kowalski shook my hand and said, "It was lucky you were scanning that area. That body would've never been found if you hadn't been out there."

I agreed. "It's not exactly what I wanted to find, but I'm glad some family will get some closure. Will you be able to identify the body?"

"There is a lot of evidence such as some remaining clothing and jewelry. Also, it appears she had some dental work done, so we might be able to match up dental records." I asked him how he knew it was a female. He said, "We can tell by the pelvis and the ring she had on said 'Cheerleader' on the side. We have several cold cases that we can look into. Hopefully we'll have some answers pretty quickly. We will need to keep in contact with you, so can we have your phone number?"

I gladly gave them my phone number in hopes that they would keep me informed. "Will you let me know if you figure out who she is? I would like to know."

"If we figure out who she is it will be all over the papers, so you'll know," he said. I followed the police cars and the van that was bringing Kathy's body to the morgue out of the parking lot. I went home knowing that this was something I had to tell Eileen about. I didn't know when I was going to do that, but it would have to be soon.

That night after the kids went to bed, I told Eileen the story. She mentioned that she thought it was very unusual that I would want to take up metal detecting out of nowhere. She said she knew that something was up when I spent $800 on a metal detector.

I told her that I ran into the spirit as I was walking on the path in the forest preserve. "When I approached her, she told me the story of how she thought she had gotten there. Honey, it appears she was murdered by her fiancé. I knew that I had to recover her body in some way. I asked her if she had any jewelry on her the night she was killed. She said she had a ring and a necklace on. That's why I needed the metal detector. I figured if I was just out searching for trinkets, I could discover her body and bring it to the police's attention."

Eileen thought that was a pretty clever way of getting the police involved. I explained the rest of the story to Eileen. "Kathy told me the story about how her fiancé wanted to break up with her two weeks before the wedding. They'd gotten into a fight in the car by the forest preserve and he strangled her. She's been out in the forest preserve for 35 years."

"Oh, the poor thing!" said Eileen. "No one knew she had been murdered?"

"No, although it seems like they suspected it. According to the paper, most people thought she went missing because she got cold feet about the wedding. But she never made contact with her parents. There was an investigation into her case, and they did come up with a suspect which I assume was her fiancé, Mark. Now I hope with her body being discovered they can put that bastard away."

"Thirty-five years is a long time," Eileen said. "He may not even be alive anymore."

"I know," I agreed. "I thought of that too. But if the police can identify her they could probably also track him down. Then Kathy can be at peace. I'm going to try to move her along tomorrow. We'll see what happens. I have a feeling she's still quite angry about what happened to her and she may not want to move on until she knows Mark has been brought to justice."

The next day I got a call from Sgt. Kowalski who said they had a pretty good idea of who this girl was. He explained, "The girl was reported missing in 1978 and her disappearance was under pretty suspicious circumstances. We are waiting for the dental records to make a positive ID. The cold case files were shipped off to a storage facility in Chicago. We're also waiting for their return. The dental records would be in that file, and we could compare them to her dental x-rays taken at the morgue."

Sgt. Kowalski called me two days later to let me know that they had identified the body as that of Kathy Johnson. I pretended that I didn't know the story.

"She was reported missing in 1978 two weeks before her wedding day<" Sgt. Kowalski told me. "At first the missing persons department thought she had just gotten cold feet and run off. But she never contacted her parents, which was very unusual for her. They started an investigation back then. Mind you, this is long before I got on the force. In fact, it was long before I thought about getting on the force. Kathy's parents are both still alive and could describe the clothes she was wearing, which matched the clothes we found on her body. Kathy's mother also remembered the ring and the necklace. They were happy to have closure but still very upset that someone had taken their little girl's life. The good news is, we think we know who that someone is."

The newspapers were all over this story the next day. The headline read "Body found after 35 years." It went on to name her and give the circumstances of the story. The police had a suspect some 35 years ago and were trying to track him down. Sgt. Kowalski was quoted as saying, "Now that we have a body, this case opens up as a new case. There is no statute of limitations on a murder case. So, if this guy is still out there where we can find him, we'll bring him to justice." I got my fifteen minutes of fame because of one sentence in the article: "Amateur collector Scott Moss was searching for war relics near the French Fort with his metal detector when he discovered some jewelry of Johnson's." The article went on to say that my find had led to the discovery of the body.

I went back to see Kathy two days later and told her about the progress they were making in the case. "They identified your body through dental records and the clothes you were wearing. Your parents are still alive, and they identified the clothing you were wearing the night you disappeared. Even though they were glad to have closure, they were still very upset that someone had taken their baby from them."

Kathy cried wondering how her parents got through the last 35 years.

"The sergeant that was here told me that they did have a suspect," I said, "and I assume it's Mark. They're trying to track him down for questioning. But that that's all the information I have. Now Kathy, I have to ask you something. Do you see a light? A bright light?"

She shook her head. "No, I don't. All I see is the fog, there is no light."

"Are you sure?" I questioned, "Because the souls I have helped always saw a light."

"Have any of the souls you've helped been murdered?" she asked.

"No," I said.

"Maybe that's why I can't see the light. I have to make sure they catch Mark and put him away before I can go into the light. Maybe I'm blocking it out because I want to see him get his due."

I realized there was still a lot of anger in Kathy's soul. She felt like her life was snatched from her way too early. And she didn't think it was fair that this bastard was still walking around living his life.

Kathy said, "I'm not going anywhere until I know they've caught him."

"Kathy," I said, "they may have to get a confession from him, and that might not be easy to do. We don't know if there's enough evidence to actually charge him with your murder. Unless he confesses, he may not get what's coming to him."

"I think he'll confess," Kathy said. "He'll breakdown. He was always kind of weak, and I think this must've been eating at him for the last 35 years. Maybe getting a confession out of him won't be as hard as you think."

"I just want to make sure Kathy," I said. "Are you sure you don't see a light?"

She looked straight into my eyes. "I'm sure."

"Well, I guess I'll come back when this case is solved. I have to let you know Kathy, it's my job to get you into the light and I won't quit until you're there."

"I appreciate that, Scott," she said. "When the time comes, I'll go into the light with you happily. But it's got to be under my terms."

"Fair enough," I said. I bid her goodbye and walked through the fog, forgetting about the shock. You think I'd be used to it by now. It still surprises the hell out of me.

CHAPTER 16

I didn't hear from Sgt. Kowalski for the next two weeks. I thought about calling him, but I figured he'd let me know if there had been a break in the case. Kathy's parents had apparently asked Sgt. Kowalski if they could talk to me. He finally called me and asked if they could speak to me.

I said I would be happy to talk to them, but I didn't know what I could do to help them. Sgt. Kowalski said, "I think they just want to thank you for finding their daughter." I asked him if they had found Mark, but he told me that all he could say was that the investigation was ongoing. I agreed to talk to Kathy's parents.

I met the Johnsons at a restaurant in town. By this time, they were well into their 70s. I greeted them sincerely. "I'm sorry for your loss," I told them.

"Thank you," Mr. Johnson said. "But what we really want to do is thank you for giving us closure in the case of our daughter. We would've gone to our graves never knowing what had happened to her. We're so thankful that you found her in the forest preserve."

I wanted to get to know their perception of the situation. "Can you tell me a little bit about her?"

Mrs. Johnson said, "Gladly. She was a cheerleader in high school and loved going to the football games. She was a beautiful girl. She wasn't perfect; she sometimes hung out with the wrong crowd. And by that, I mean her fiancé Mark. We didn't like him from the start, but we were willing to give him a chance because Kathy really seemed to love him.

"Mark had friends that were into some bad stuff. Kathy managed to stay away from it but we didn't trust Mark and were afraid he would get her involved with this bad crowd. They were two weeks away from being married when she went missing.

"We always suspected him but could never prove it. He became more distant as time went on. Eventually we never saw him again. The last thing we heard was that he moved out of state. We're pretty sure he killed our baby. But we've never been able to prove it. The cops tried so hard, but they could never get enough evidence together to charge him. I'm hoping now that we have Kathy back, they can bring him back here to stand trial for her murder. Nothing would make us happier than to see him put behind bars."

"Kathy seems like she was quite a wonderful girl," I said. "I wish I'd known her."

"You would have liked her," Mr. Johnson said, "She was so full a life. She was looking forward to starting a family and becoming a mom. It still breaks my heart that she never got a chance to do that. She would've been a great mom. She loved kids. She loved to babysit and did it quite often. Everyone loved her."

A tear gathered in his eye and his wife put her arm on his shoulder to try to comfort him. I felt a tear start to form in my eye and I knew they noticed it.

I offered to pay the bill, but they refused. "We owe you so much," they said. "At least let us buy you lunch."

I wanted to stay in touch with them. "Would you keep me informed if I give you my number? And let me know what happens in the case? It seems like this Mark guy is as guilty as hell. I'd like to know when they catch him and see if we think it's some justice for Kathy."

They agreed and I gave them my number. I watched them walk away to their car. Mr. Johnson walked with a cane and Mrs. Johnson had her arm in his. After 35 years of not knowing where their daughter had been, I felt some sort of relief knowing that they finally had an answer. I watched them drive away and hoped that they would call me with any progress in the case.

Sgt. Kowalski called me a month later to let me know that they had located the ex-fiancée Mark in Des Moines, Iowa. He had become born-again Christian and was preaching at a Baptist church just outside of town. They'd arrested him and were extraditing him back to Illinois. He didn't have much more detail, but he promised he would let me know the outcome.

Sgt. Kowalski and I had become friends because of this case. I was almost tempted to tell him of my gift in hopes that I could help solve some other cold cases. But I remembered what my Grandpa Bill had said, and I didn't know how Sgt. Kowalski would feel about my gift. Maybe he'd think I was another crazy person living in his town.

A week after I'd talked to Kowalski, the Johnsons called me to tell me that Mark had confessed to the murder of Kathy. He had always wanted to get it off his chest, especially since he had been born again. He pleaded no contest to the charge and was sentenced to life imprisonment. Now that he was 56 years old, it didn't really seem fair. He had taken so much life from Kathy and was only going to serve the remaining part of his life in prison. He had gotten all that time to be free and live his life. But at least now I could approach Kathy and possibly get her to cross over.

It was cold now, and I went into the forest preserve that was now closed. I had to park my car at the entrance and walk an extra quarter mile to get to Kathy's spot.

She was still waiting, sitting on the stump, but this time she looked up at me with a smile on her face. I knew the fog had lifted and she was feeling like something good was going to happen. As I approached her, the tingling feeling was there but the shock was much less intense as I entered her area.

She said, "Well?"

"Well, I've got some good news. They got him. Do you know what born-again means?" She shook her head. "It means a person finds Jesus and becomes very religious. Mark had been born again in Des Moines, Iowa. He was preaching at a church just outside of town."

At this point, Kathy laughed. "Mark is a preacher? I find that hard to believe. I don't think he even mentioned God the entire time we were together. He didn't even want to get married in the church. The bastard."

I explained the situation in more detail. "Kathy, they confronted him with your murder case and told him they had found your body. When they explained to him that they were sure he had murdered you and buried your body in the forest preserve, he confessed to the crime. He said since he had been born again, he felt like he could not run away from this crime anymore. He pleaded no contest, which is almost the same as pleading guilty, and was sentenced to life in prison. Your mom and dad hugged each other in court and gave him one hell of a dirty look as they took him off in tears to jail. He will spend the rest of his life behind bars with no chance of parole."

Kathy's face lit up. "Scott, I see it."

"The light?" I asked. "Do you see a light?"

"Yeah," she said. "It's been here for about two days. It seems so peaceful. I think I'm ready."

"Kathy," I said, "I'm really glad to hear that. I can help you now. We're going to meet somebody right off the bat when we enter the other world. He's my grandfather and he helps me cross people over to the other side. So don't be surprised when you see him. I don't know who else will be waiting for you. Your parents are in their 70s, so I'm sure your grandparents will be waiting for you."

She looked surprised. "My parents are in their 70s?"

"Yes Kathy, you have to remember you've been here for 35 years. People have aged and crossed over. You will have peace on the other side with some of the people that have already entered that world. Can you walk with me now into the light?"

She agreed. "Guess I can. I'm ready as I'll ever be." At that point we were almost sucked into the tunnel. I'm still amazed by the speed that we travel at when we go through this tunnel. The light at the end gets brighter and brighter and the warmth we feel accelerates as we get closer.

As we stepped through the light Grandpa Bill was waiting for us.

He welcomed me with a hug and then hugged Kathy too. Grandpa Bill said, "This was your best case yet, Scott. You've really done Kathy a great service. She was so angry that the light was not visible to her. By helping find her killer you made it visible for her. Look at what a beautiful girl she is."

Kathy smiled and blushed at Grandpa's comment. I guess I hadn't realized how beautiful she really was until we got through the light. She was in a sundress now.

"I love this sundress," she said. "It was my favorite one to wear when I was in school."

I agreed. "You do look beautiful in that dress Kathy."

Kathy looked out over the beautiful scene that she had made up in her mind of what her heaven should look like. There were mountains and a beautiful stream and lots of green grass and flowers, exactly what heaven would look like to a young girl. Off to the left was a little house with a white picket fence. In the backyard there were two little girls swinging on a swing set. A young man who looked to be in his early 20s was pushing them. He was going back and forth between the girls and pushing them higher and higher. The girls were giggling and looked to be about five years old or so.

The man turned around slowly and looked at Kathy. She took in a deep breath and said "It's Steve! I knew him in high school. He was such a nice guy, and he really liked me. But I had been going out with Mark for so long that I could not bring myself to date him. He never was mad about it; he was always so nice. He's the one I should have married."

I turned to Kathy and said, "In heaven he is the one you married. And those are your children. Heaven is what you make of it. It is what you dreamed of on earth. Steve was the man who would have taken care of you and loved you forever. You just didn't know it because you were infatuated with Mark. Now you can live, how do they say, happily ever after here in heaven."

"There are some people along the way to the house that also want to say hi," Grandpa Bill said.

"I see them!" she said. "It's my grandmas and grandpas. Both sets of my grandparents are here! And that's my friend Jill from school. Why is she here, she's still very young?"

Grandpa Bill told Kathy, "Jill passed away from breast cancer. But she is happy to have a friend up here in heaven that she can talk about the old times with."

Kathy turned and kissed me on the cheek. She shook Grandpa's hand and said, "You have a special grandson."

"I know," he said. "He's one in a million." I think what Grandpa meant by that was that about one in a million people can do what I do.

Grandpa looked at me and said, "Now you've got the girls kissing you! You're quite the charmer."

"Yes, I know, it's a gift," I said. We both laughed.

"You did a great job solving this case," he said. "And a bad man will serve out his time and answer to God when he gets up here to heaven."

"That jerk will go to heaven?" I asked.

"If he is truly sorry for what he did, he can still enter heaven, but it will take some time. He will have to convince Kathy to forgive him too. By the time he gets here maybe Kathy will have forgiven him for what he did. It's only then that he will be allowed to enter heaven. People can be forgiven even for horrible crimes. Some crimes are unforgivable. Hitler, Stalin, Pol Pot, John Wayne Gacy. None of them will ever be forgiven or ever enter heaven. Now it's time for you to go back, my son. You're doing a great job. Keep looking for the souls, and you will find them. You may never know where, but they will come to you when it's time."

As soon as he said that I was thrown into reverse again. I was getting kind of tired of reverse. This time I landed a little hard and found myself sitting on the same stump Kathy had been sitting on. I decided to sit there for a while and get my strength back to make the walk back to my car.

I drove home and got there just in time to meet Eileen as she was pulling into the driveway. As she got out of the car she said, "I bet you've got a story to tell me."

I nodded. "Oh yes, I do. And it has a happy ending I might add. I got her to crossover and she found what she had longed for here on earth. She ran into some old friends and found the man who really loved her pushing two little kids on the swing set in her heavenly backyard. Brought a tear to my eye."

Eileen said, "So she's done with this earth, right?"

"It would appear that way. Everything here has been tied up and taken care of." We walked into the house together and put away the groceries Eileen had picked up on her way home from work. The kids were home working on homework just like the little munchkins should be. Dana needed help with her math, and Casey needed help with a history project. Years ago we had decided that Eileen would take science and math as her specialties for homework helping and I would take history and geography. It's worked out pretty well -- the kids get good grades, although we don't get anything in return. Except maybe a decent grade in parenting.

CHAPTER 17

I got a call from my lawyer the next morning stating the insurance company had made another offer to settle out of court. The offer was $10.5 million, and my lawyer was convinced it was a good deal. He said, "It would be chancy to take this to a jury trial because you never know who you're going to get on a jury. You might find someone who doesn't believe you deserve this much money and will try to talk everyone down to a lower figure. You also may get lucky and end up with more money. But the process of going through a trial and then waiting for an appeal to go through, which I'm sure the insurance company would do, would make things even worse."

We had been living off of my disability, which was about 65% of my salary, and Eileen's salary. Although we had been able to make the house payment and feed everybody, there wasn't much left over for fun. Plus, I knew the way my leg was mangled, there was a good chance I would never be able to work again. Even if I could work, it may require me to go back to school so I could get a desk job. This didn't thrill me, because I was someone who always liked to be active at work.

The company had offered to train me as an indoor communications specialist, but I wasn't sure I could handle the monotony of sitting around making phone calls to people and listening to their complaints all day. Besides, I felt as if I had found a new calling and taking the settlement would allow me to do that full-time. So, after a long discussion with our attorney, we decided to take the settlement. I stipulated in the agreement that any further medical treatment would have to be paid for by the insurance company, otherwise I would let this go to a jury trial. I didn't think they would buy into this, but they did. They figured it was less risk than a jury trial. I just wanted to get back on track financially and I figured with that kind of money and the proper investments we could live pretty comfortably for the rest of our lives. I also stipulated that the insurance company would continue to pay for any physical therapy that I needed on my leg. It could take years to get to the point where I didn't need the cane anymore.

I knew I would never be able to run or dance again (not that I was ever much of a dancer) and it would be difficult and painful at times just to walk up and down the stairs. But it was time to put all this behind me. My lawyer surprised me by only taking 20% because he didn't have to take the case to court. That left more money for us, even after taxes. We started by investing in mutual funds, ones that were pretty stable. We hoped that we could continue to gather an income from these mutual funds later in life. We also decided after the two years of injury and recovery it was time to go on a vacation. We didn't know where, but I figured the warmth would do me some good.

Living in the Midwest teaches you how valuable the sun is to your overall well-being. I love the sun and the heat that goes along with it, as it takes some of the achiness out of my joints. I also notice my headaches are less frequent when we're someplace warm, even in our backyard during the summer months. I don't know why it works this way, but for some reason it does.

After getting the settlement check and practically running to the bank with it, we spread the money out between several banks in the area. If one of the banks went under, we would still have money available to us at all times. I never dreamed I'd be a multi-millionaire, but I can tell you one thing for sure, I'd give all the money back to have my health restored to the way it was before the accident. I was worried about my longevity and how it would affect the life I got to live on this earth. My body had been through hell and I'm sure there was going to be everlasting damage to it. I figured having the money put aside would help my family if I did check out early.

We decided to take the kids out of school for a week, which is a big no-no in the school district we live in, but I was willing to take that chance. I got the kids' homework assignments for the week and figured we would take it with us. We decided on a trip to the Bahamas because I always wanted to see that area. I'd heard about the white sand beaches and the clear water and the fact that it was one of the most relaxing places on earth.

We flew down the following week, and even though I was now a millionaire I was still angry that they made me pay to check my luggage. It's funny how your values don't change even if your pocketbook is stuffed. I still think they have a lot of nerve charging for my luggage when I'm paying for a plane ticket. I could see if we were taking 15 bags, but the truth is we all had one bag per person. Don't get me started.

We landed in the Bahamas on Monday morning at about 10 AM. It was a beautiful day with clear skies and the temperature was about 80°. We took the resort bus from the airport and checked in as soon as we got there. I had surprised the family by booking the best condo they had on the island, right on the beach. I figured it would be nice just to sit out every night on the beach, have a little campfire, and listen to the ocean break.

After we unpacked, we went to lunch at the hotel's five-star restaurant. The kids had chicken strips because that's what kids have. I couldn't talk them into anything else. Acting like pompous millionaires, my wife and I decided upon the lobster. We figured it was worth it just this one time. Lobster lunch and possibly a steak for dinner, what a life!

That afternoon we took a boating tour and snorkeled with some local guides. I'm a little leery about swimming in the ocean because I watch too many of those specials on the National Geographic channel about shark attacks. But I was assured that the water was too warm for the sharks. I wasn't sure I believed them, but I didn't want to miss out on this opportunity.

The water was only 12 or 15 feet deep, and the fish were so beautiful that everyone was amazed. Even my little Dana got the hang of snorkeling, and before you knew it, she was trying to pet the fish like they were dogs. Nothing better than making a nervous dad even more nervous. Eileen seemed to enjoy the snorkeling more than anyone. She was amazed by the beauty of the small reef and how clear the water was. We were out there with about 15 other snorkelers and became friends with them on the way back.

One of the kids from another family noticed my leg and how mangled it was. She said "That's a big ouch on your leg!"

Her mom shushed her and apologized for her statement. I said to the little girl, "It is a big ouch! But it's feeling much better now. Did you ever have a big ouch?"

She said, "Yeah, I fell and scraped my knee and it bled all the way down my leg. I cried a lot. Did you cry when you got your ouch?"

I started laughing. "As a matter of fact, I did cry! It hurt a lot! But it probably didn't hurt as much as your knee hurt when you scraped it."

She was about four years old and was as cute as could be. Her mother was taken by my conversation with her and said how cute it was.

I said, "You have to learn to laugh at these things, it's important in the healing process."

The little girl wandered back to her mother and sat on her lap. We talked a while with her family because the ride back was about an hour long. They also had three children, but they were younger than ours. We invited them to a campfire by our condo that night. They said they were getting a babysitter and going downtown to enjoy some dinner and dancing.

"Having kind of a date night?" I asked.

"Yes," she said. "We don't get much time to ourselves with these little kids running around."

Eileen agreed. "Been there, done that, and don't want to go back! Maybe we'll run into you later and we can get together on the beach and let the kids play." We weren't sure if we would see them again because the resort, we were staying at was pretty big, but the invitation was sincere and we hoped they'd take us up on it.

The next day we went on a tour of the island. We had to stop at some of the shops because that's pretty much required when you're with your family. Eileen bought some native jewelry and the kids all bought hats. I bought three shirts, all brighter than the next, just to look like the ultimate tourist. You have to barter with these people, otherwise they take it as an insult. I got three shirts for 60 bucks and Eileen got about $100 worth of jewelry for 70 bucks. Eileen wore the jewelry on the way back and it just made her look even more beautiful than she already did. She had a flowing white skirt on, one of those cover-up types of skirts, and her swimming suit top on. Seeing her on the beach in this outfit made me think how lucky I was to have her, not to mention the three little kids running around her.

Because he was 14, John was starting to eye up some of the amazing bikinis that were walking by. He bought a pair of sunglasses to try to cover up his roaming eyes but because I learned that trick when I was his age, I knew exactly what he was doing. I kind of got a kick out of it knowing my son was growing up. He even got a wave from one of the young teenage girls and we all gave him a hard time about it. Dana and Casey had a field day with it. John gave them hell, as a big brother usually does, and we all had a good laugh.

We decided to take a walk along the beach just to see the sights. We stopped and got a couple of tropical drinks and some water for the kids. We learned to drink bottled water pretty quickly down there.

About a half a mile down the beach, I noticed a man standing in about a foot and a half of water looking out into the ocean. He never turned around and as we passed them, he seemed unaffected by the crowds of people walking back and forth on the beach. That feeling came over me that this might be another lost soul, but I figured I'd give it some time.

We continued our walk, and I was curious to see if the man would be in the same spot upon our return trip. We spent some time playing shuffleboard, something I never thought I'd do, with the kids at the beach resort. As it turns out I appear to have a natural talent for shuffleboard and I'm sure I'll be going on tour with the shuffleboard championship very soon. I do believe there's an age limit, so I'll have to wait till I'm 65.

As we started to walk back toward the condo, all I could think about was the man in the water. He was still there. He was African American man and stood knee-deep in the water as we approached. He hadn't changed spots, nor was looking anywhere but out toward the ocean. He was not wearing traditional shorts but more of a handmade looking cloth that covered his lower area in kind of a wrap-around style. He looked out of place, so I thought he might have been a local person and may just be meditating.

We continued on past him and went to the condo. We dropped off all of our little trinkets that we had bought in town and went out to dinner. The restaurant we chose was almost like the hibachi style Japanese restaurants back home. They cooked the food in front of us. The kids really enjoyed watching the chef flip food up and down, and he made an onion ring volcano for them. I loved the look on their faces when he lit the fire underneath the onions and flame shot out of the top. The kids were amazed.

Of course, if you're wondering what they ordered for dinner, it would be chicken strips again. My wife and I had a traditional Bahamian meal of fish and some local vegetables with a sauce on it that was unbelievable. We really enjoyed the food and we laughed and had fun with the chef for about an hour and a half.

I could tell our little Dana was tired from her day and looked like she wanted her bed. We took the shuttle bus back to our condo and watched the sun set on the beach. To say it was breathtaking would be an understatement. I had not had a headache all day and the pain in my leg was minor for a change. There's something about relaxation that takes away pain.

We got the kids to bed, and my wife and I sat out on the balcony. We enjoyed the cool breeze and had a couple more tropical drinks. We drank with our pinkies out and made rich people noises. We were laughing pretty hard at ourselves and had a lot of fun just being silly. It was like we were young again and were having a great time just enjoying each other's company.

I told her about the guy I had seen standing in the water and asked her if she happened to notice him. She said, "I wasn't paying much attention, but maybe we could walk over there you can tell me if you see him."

John was still awake so we asked him if he would mind babysitting for just a little bit while we walked down the beach. He said, "No problem, I gotcha covered." John was so responsible; we really had no worries.

We locked the door behind us walked down to the beach. Less than a quarter mile down the beach, I spotted the man still standing in the water. I stopped and pointed him out to Eileen.

"I don't see anyone," she said. "It appears that you can't get away from the spirits even on vacation!"

"Yeah," I said. "I guess you're right. You know I have to help him, right?"

Nodding, she said, "Yeah I understand, it's what you do now."

"I'm going to walk out there now and just get his story really quick. Would you be okay sitting here for a little bit?"

She smiled. "There just happens to be a chair and I still have my drink, so I'll be just fine. Will you be able to hear me if I call you?"

That was a great question. "I don't know. No one's ever called me when I'm involved in one of these events."

"Go ahead, I'll be right here," she said.

"It shouldn't take long," I told her, "Because time seems to stand still when I start talking to them. I'm going to face outward, so people don't think I'm talking to nobody standing in the middle of the ocean." Eileen laughed.

I slowly walked out to him. The tingling sensation started as I approached, and the shock followed. His fog surrounded him almost like a peninsula. He could see outward towards the ocean but could see nothing behind him or to his sides. I thought this was pretty different because everyone else had been surrounded completely by the fog.

I approached him and he turned to look at me. In broken English he said, "You can see me, you can?"

"Yes, I can," I said.

"When she come back?" he asked.

I said, "Who do you mean?"

"My daughter. She come back soon, no?"

"What happened to your daughter?" I asked.

He held his hands to the sky. "Big ship take her. They chain her. They put her on a boat and take her away."

I said, "How long have you been waiting for her to come back?"

"Many, many moons," he said. This seemed unusual to me because the cycle of the moon takes about a month, and he said he had been there for many of them. That made me think he had been there for so many years that it was possible that the ship that had taken his daughter was a slave ship. Slaves were often taken from the Bahamas and brought to America, and he'd mentioned the chains.

"They no want me," he said sadly. "Too old. They take her."

"What is your name?" I asked.

"Tiki," he answered.

"Tiki," I said, "have you been waiting for her to come home?"

"Yes. I stand here until she comes home."

I wanted more information from him. "Do you remember how you got out here?" I asked.

"I fight with white man. I tried to stop taking my daughter. Men beat me with shiny sticks. I am here ever sense," he replied.

I wondered if Tiki had been killed by the slave ship crew during the abduction of his daughter. He probably had died and hadn't realized that his death had occurred. His concern was only for his daughter, the daughter he had lost probably 300 years ago. It seems kind of morbid, but I wondered what his feet must look like standing in the water for 300 years. Sometimes weird things come in to your mind and there's not a lot you can do about it.

"Tiki, you must know something. You have died. Do you know what died means?"

He looked at me sternly. "Yes, but I am not died. I am waiting. She will be here." It was going to be hard to help him understand.

"No Tiki, she is waiting for you somewhere else, somewhere very special."

"You mean God?" he asked.

"Yes, that's what I mean." Missionaries had tried and succeeded to convert most of the Bahamian people to Christianity in the 1600s. It was obnoxious to me that Christianity was okay to teach but also that slavery was okay to be ignored by these missionaries. I continued, "Tiki, God is waiting for you with your daughter. You have been here too long. You must move along to God so you can see her. She died many, many years ago." I had no way of tracking down Tiki's daughter here on the islands or anywhere else in the United States. "What was her name?" I asked.

"Mahalia. She was my last child of others taken. I must wait. She come back." It was hard to convince him.

"Tiki, Mahalia has passed over to God. You must go there now too. You can no longer wait for her."

Tiki said "No, you must go. Tiki think about what you said. I must still wait; she will come home tonight."

"I will come for you tomorrow, Tiki," I said. "If she is not here, will you let me help you to see your God?"

"She will come tonight," he said sternly. I knew I couldn't convince him at this point.

"Okay. I will come back tomorrow to see if she comes back to you." With that I slowly backed out of the fog getting the shock and feeling the tingling as I turned and headed towards the beach. Eileen was still sitting in the chair drinking her fruity tropical drink. She stood up as she saw me approach and asked how it went. I asked her how long I had been out there. She said less than three minutes.

"Wow," I said. "I felt like I talked to him for 15 minutes. You see how time stands still while I am involved in one of these cases?"

"What's his story?" she asked.

"He's been standing there for 300 years waiting for his daughter to return," I told her. "I think she was taken away on a slave ship. He has no idea that she has been dead for probably 300 years. He was killed during the abduction and appears to be the only family member who wasn't taken. I think he fought to his death to try to save his family. The last remaining one was his daughter Mahalia. She's the one he is waiting for. She must've been the last one they took. But he has been watching over the ocean for this long. He is the only one I've seen so far that can see through a portion of the fog. He sees through the front of the fog overlooking the horizon of the ocean. He's waiting for the ship to return with his Mahalia. He wouldn't go with me because he's sure that tonight is the night the ship will return with his daughter."

"That's so sad!" Eileen said. "Three-hundred years of waiting because of the love he has for his daughter! Do you think you can convince him to go into the light?"

I shook my head. "I don't know. He seems very stubborn. He's determined to wait this out. Who knows how many other people with my talent have approached him in the past and gotten nowhere with him. I will approach him tomorrow, maybe at sunset, to see if I can cross him over. He'll be okay for one more night. He's the first one who has said that he has been there for a long time. The rest of the cases all seem to think that the situation has just occurred. He referred to many moons crossing over since his daughter disappeared." Our fun night was somehow subdued after this. We slowly walked back towards the condo.

We were gone less than an hour and John had fallen asleep in the chair watching TV. I woke him up he apologized for falling asleep. I said "Don't worry, it's okay. Now go to bed, we've got a big day planned for tomorrow."

The next day was spent with jet skis, paragliding, and a fishing trip. We even ate the fish that we caught. The kids had chicken strips, which the captain of the ship knew was necessary for any child that he brought on his ship. I almost got John to try some of the fresh fish, but no dice.

We saw dolphins follow the ship and the kids were amazed. They were so close to the boat you could almost touch them. Some of them leaped out of the water completely. They are the only species that are known to play like humans do.

As the boat ride ended, I had three pretty tired children on my hands. They just wanted to go back to the condo and crash. I told Eileen I would have to go visit Tiki again. She understood and said to be careful.

I walked out the patio door right down to the beach. As I entered the water I could see Tiki standing in the same spot he had been the night before. This time he seemed more focused on something he could see in the horizon.

He said, "Bright light on the horizon."

"Tiki," I asked excitedly, "have you seen that bright light before?"

"I could hardly see before, and to me it seemed far. Now light looks closer."

It seemed to be coming towards us, which led me to believe that Tiki was almost ready to go. "Tiki, you realize you can't stay here any longer. It's time for you to move on," I said.

"Tiki want daughter. Tiki lost all family. Tiki daughter last one left -- all others went on big ship."

I realized that Tiki's entire family had been taken by slave ships and brought to the New World. The New World, that couldn't dignify his way of life and crushed his soul.

"Tiki, how many family members did you have?" I asked.

"Tiki have a wife, three sons, and one daughter."

I realized at that point that when they came for Tiki's daughter, he'd defended her abduction with his life. His soul stood on the very spot where he had lost his life. I looked up at the horizon and could see the bright light was getting closer. "Tiki, your heaven is coming. It is in the bright light you see ahead of you".

"Tiki afraid, have seen light before but have not seen family." Tiki seemed completely overwhelmed by the losses he had sustained in his life. He didn't trust the light and I'm not sure even trusted me.

"Tiki," I said gently, "if you let me take you into the light, you will be able to see your family again. They will be waiting for you in the light. All of them. Your wife, your three sons, and your daughter. All waiting for Tiki." I got closer to him in hopes of guiding him into the light. The light was rushing up upon us and would soon engulf both of us in its brilliance. "It's time for us to go. Follow me into the light and we will see your family again."

He took one step forward with me and we were rushed in through the light at high speed. Tiki seemed confused and I wondered what he was thinking. When we came to the end of the tunnel the light's brilliance was overwhelming. Tiki shaded his eyes as we passed through the light.

This time Grandpa was standing next to me. I noticed we hadn't really left the spot where I'd found Tiki the day before. Tiki pointed off in the distance and said, "I see a ship, a big ship. Tiki see many boats without sails while he wait for daughter. Many of them very fast, make a big noise. But now Tiki sees the ship, ship that take my daughter." Tiki was referring to all the leisure boats and personal watercraft that he had seen through his small opening to the ocean.

Over 300 years it must've become very confusing to him to see boats without sails. The boat coming at us looked somewhat like the ships you see in old pirate movies. The ship was moored off the reef directly in front of us. A small boat was lowered down into the water and several people climbed into it. It was too far away to recognize any of the occupants. The boat started to row towards us and the sun backlit it to make it harder to visualize the people inside.

As the boat approached it became obvious that this was a special moment for Tiki. A small girl about age 12 jumped out of the boat swam a little way and then ran up to Tiki. She jumped into his arms and hugged him tight. The rest of the occupants of the boat slowly made their way to where Tiki was standing. Three young men and a middle-aged woman got out of the boat and walked up to Tiki, and he began to cry. It was obvious that his family had been reunited for the first time in over 300 years, all because Tiki was unable to go into the light. Even though the death of his children and wife had occurred long ago, he was unable to understand. Going into the light was the only way he was able to be reunited with them.

I watched the tears roll down his face as he hugged each and every one of his family members and kissed his beautiful wife. They turned around to face the beach, a beach I had just seen, not 10 minutes ago, that was filled with high-rise hotels and personal watercraft rental areas. Now the beach was pristine. There were only small huts with various people from an age long ago. As Tiki and his family walked toward the beach, I knew they would resume their lives in eternity as they had lived them on earth. It was where they were happiest. I know the thoughts of slavery were gone, and Tiki could again enjoy his family.

He stopped and turned around to look at me. He waved and so did his 12-year-old daughter. Then they continued to walk towards the beach. I turned back towards the sunset and was facing my grandfather. "Looks like you're working even while you're on vacation," he said.

"No rest for the wicked I guess," I joked.

Grandpa started laughing. "You are anything but wicked, my son! You helped another family to be reunited, and now they live in an eternity of happiness. Tiki had been waiting a long time to be reunited. He gave his life to help save his daughter's. She was shipped off to South Carolina where she worked on an estate of the rich tobacco farmer. She was lucky enough to be what they called a house worker. But her life was miserable. She had children that were taken away from her and sold off to other slave owners. Two of the three boys died of smallpox on the way back to the mainland. One boy survived and worked in the fields of North Carolina and never saw his mother or sister again. He died at age 38 trying to escape to the north. Tiki's wife worked as a cook on a plantation in Louisiana for 40 years. She made meals for a wealthy cotton farmer for all that time. She died of pneumonia at the age of 72. So, Tiki's family has been gone for over 300 years. And it took you to reunite them! Tiki had died here in the water fighting to the death with a man wielding a knife. His last vision before his death was them carrying his daughter away. That vision prevented him from crossing over. He never gave up hope that she would return. The other family members had been taken while Tiki was out hunting. His little daughter hid up in a tree until the slave ship had left the island. When Tiki returned from his hunting trip he found only his daughter in the hut. She was crying and he knew that something terrible had happened. It was two years before another slave ship returned and confronted Tiki and his daughter. Tiki was trained as a warrior. This time he was given the chance to fight to save the last part of his family. All he had was a stick fashioned into a spear. Unfortunately, he was no match for the sailor wielding a large knife. It's a sad story but it's a story that was very common 300 years ago when man had no respect for the color of another man's skin."

"Grandpa," I asked, "why was Tiki allowed to wait so long to cross over?"

"He had been approached many times by other talented people like you. No one was able to convince him that the light was a good thing. He still believed that his daughter was coming back and that his family would be reunited again as long as he waited in the spot where he last saw her," Grandpa said. "You were able to bring him his family. After 300 years you were the only one who was able to do this. You should be proud."

"I guess I am proud," I said with a little smile on my face. It made me feel good that Tiki was together again with everyone he loved. They were right back at the same spot where they had started their lives.

Grandpa said, "You know what time it is, don't you?" And with that I was rushed backward through the tunnel and landed in 2 feet of water in the same spot where Tiki and I had once stood.

I slowly walked back to the villa where I found Eileen resting comfortably in bed with a book. "How'd it go, were you able to help Tiki?" she asked.

I thought for a while and wondered how I would explain the entire event, including the explanation Grandpa had given me about Tiki's family. I told Eileen the story of how Tiki's family had been abducted by slave traders and that he'd had died in that place trying to prevent them from taking his daughter on the slave ship. "His last vision in life was that of a slave trader taking his 12-year-old daughter away from him. He'd waited 300 years for them to come back and now they were back. When we turned around to look at the shore after the family had been reunited, none of these buildings were here. There were just some shacks made of bamboo and tree branches where all the islanders lived. When I turned back to talk to Grandpa, I was quickly thrown back into reality. I turned around to see all the large hotels, the boardwalk and all the shops along the coast. None of this was here when Tiki turned around with his family and headed towards the beach. It was like time had stood still for them and they were returning to the life they had loved."

"That story takes the cake!" Eileen said. "It all happened so long ago, and yet he stood there waiting for a family that had long since passed away. His love must've been extremely strong. I'm not sure I could wait 300 years for you." She laughed.

"I wouldn't expect you to," I answered. "But it's nice to know that we can wait that long and still be reunited with the ones we love."

The rest of the vacation was uneventful in the way of souls. We enjoyed our time together and spent a lot of time doing tourist type activities, including swimming with the dolphins and every other imaginable tourist trap you could believe. I even rode the jet skis in the ocean. I felt like I captured some of my youth jumping up and down in the waves as they broke near the shore. I was surprised that it didn't seem to hurt my let at all. My son John was with me on the back of the jet ski and had a blast.

We watched the sunset every night, and on a couple of days we even got up early enough to watch the sunrise. Watching the sunrise for me was a new experience. Like I said before, I have never been a morning person.

Eileen and I got to spend a couple of nights by us having dinner and enjoying each other's company. We even did a little dancing (I mostly stood still while she danced around me) and took nice long walks on the beach. It was almost like a second honeymoon, with three little friends accompanying us. It definitely was paradise though. And this week would be remembered by my children and me for quite some time.

During the long plane ride home, which was a nonstop flight, I was able to get some sleep. During my much-needed slumber I had a dream. I dreamed I had been rushed through the tunnel towards Grandpa. He was waiting for me with a warm and welcoming smile on his face that was so familiar to me. It seemed he was welcoming me to a permanent spot in heaven. In my dream, he said, "You've done a fine job with your assignments, and now it's time for you to rest and be at peace with the rest of us."

I woke up from the dream startled and fearful. Eileen quickly asked if I was okay and I mentioned I'd just had a dream. "I think it just startled me," I explained. I didn't go into the details, but I must say it did scare me. I couldn't tell if this was a premonition of things to come or just a dream. I was awake and somewhat anxious for the rest of the flight.

CHAPTER 18

We got off the plane in Chicago and into the limousine to take us home. The kids really got a kick out of this. A limo ride to and from the airport made them feel pretty special. I didn't let it go to their heads and quickly told them it would be some time before they rode in a limo again. I didn't want them to think that they'd be getting a limo ride to school every day just because I got the settlement for my accident.

After we were settled in for a few days, Eileen and I started talking about how to handle the large sum of money we had just acquired. Our goal was to invest the money in ways that would support us for the rest of our lives. We agreed to invest in some mutual funds and invest a small amount in some Fortune 500 companies. I figured it was a safe bet. Having a little piece of Apple, IBM, and some other big companies would be good long-term investments.

Apple was close to coming out with a new device that allowed you to listen to music digitally. Rumor had it that it would be called the iPod and would make a lot of money for Apple. That's where I put a good portion of my investment.

We paid off the house and all of our credit card bills so we were pretty much debt free. I officially had to resign my post as supervisor of my team. I knew I could never go back to work in a physical manner. My leg was just too damaged. There was also the risk of another fall. Because there were no financial worries, I wasn't upset about resigning from my position. I knew I had a new life's work in helping souls cross over, and this would keep me busy for as long as this gift would allow me to.

The settlement allowed me to rethink my future. I was now, for the first time in my life, focused on improving my health. I tried to condition my body as much as possible with some light weightlifting, along with riding a recumbent stationary bicycle to help improve my cardio health. It only took a 30-foot fall, a long hospital stay, and two years of physical therapy to get me to this point. I wish I could've been inspired by a Jenny Craig commercial instead of going through all of this just to get to the point where I knew it was important to remain in good physical condition.

It was time for another appointment with the neurosurgeon and I wasn't looking forward to it. It was a long drive to his office, and he usually asked me the same boring questions, charged me $400 and sent me on my way. But off I went, because it was important for my health. He greeted me with the same question at every visit. "How are the headaches?"

I reported that they were still there but that they were mostly just a dull ache. He maintained that I may have a problem with headaches for quite some time. He said with a skull fracture like mine, it might take a year or two for them to go away. After our visit and a prescription for

Tylenol #3, I was on my way. I had tried to stay away from the pain pills since I had gotten home from the hospital. I had been on medication for so long I wasn't sure if I'd be able to come off the pain pills.

There's nothing worse than having a terrible accident and then becoming addicted to your pain medication. I had become very good friends with Vicodin. When I came off it, they tapered me down, but I still had some withdrawal symptoms. We went with the Tylenol #3 because it was a little less addicting. I figured I would only take it when I absolutely needed it. Hopefully that wouldn't be too often.

On my way home neurologist's office, I spotted a roadside memorial about 15 miles from home. It was on the expressway, and I could barely make out a figure sitting down next to the memorial just below a hill. I was going too fast to stop and ended up getting off at the next exit. I turned around, went back to the previous exit, got off, and back on again. This time I slowed down just before I got to the memorial. I pulled over to the side and put my flashers on. I got out of the car and walked around to the side of the road. The memorial was set back about 20 feet in the grass. The grass was torn up and looked as if a car had rolled over in it. I assumed this accident had just happened because of the way the grass looked.

As I walked toward the girl sitting in the grass, I could see she wasn't much more than 20 years old. She was sitting there pulling up little pieces of grass and had a look of contentment in her eyes. This confused me, because everyone else I'd helped had always seemed a little disturbed. I slowly approached her, and she looked up, then quickly looked back down again and continued to pull up the pieces of grass.

I got within a five or six of feet of her and felt the tingling feeling, followed by the shock. She was surrounded by a fog just like the others has been. She looked up again and saw me staring at her. She said, "You can see me!"

"Yes, I can," I replied. She stood up and gave me a hug. This was the first time any of the people I helped had reached out to hug me. It felt no different than a hug from a person in the real world.

She said, "My name is Ashley."

I said, "My name is Scott, and I'm here to help you."

"Help me with what?" she asked.

"Ashley," I said, "do you notice the fog around you?"

She glanced around at the fog. "Yes, I've noticed it's been foggy for some time now. It was foggy when I crashed." This was the first time I had come across a soul who was aware that she had an accident. It seemed very strange because most of the other souls had no knowledge of this. They would remember the moments leading up to the crash but not the crash itself. But Ashley seemed to know that she had been in a bad crash.

"Ashley, do you see the cross that's in front of you?" I asked.

"Yes, I do, it even has my name on it. I know it means that I'm dead, and that this is the spot I died."

This girl was confusing me. She knew she was dead, and yet she was still here. Something was keeping her from crossing over even with the knowledge that she had passed away.

"What about a light, Ashley? Do you see a light around you, a bright light?" She looked around and her eyes fixated upon an area of the fog just in front of her.

"That light is been here since the crash. I know I'm supposed to go in it, but I've been watching my friends show up at this memorial. I'm trying to help them not feel so sad. But I don't know if it's working. They all leave here crying."

This was, to say the least, very interesting to me. Ashley was trying desperately to help her family and friends get through the rough time surrounding her own death. Just then, a car pulled up behind mine and several people got out. They walked towards the memorial with flowers in hand. There was a boy about Ashley's age, and what appeared to be Ashley's parents. The mother broke down well before she got to the memorial. The father was crying too. The boy had tears in his eyes and was fighting hard not to let them show.

Ashley didn't know they were coming because she couldn't see through the fog. I told her, "Ashley, there are some people coming. It looks like it might be your parents and a boy about your age. They're almost here; you should be able to see them in a couple of seconds."

They crossed through the fog unknowing that now Ashley could see them. "That's my mom and dad and my boyfriend, Daniel. Everyone else calls him Dan, but I've always liked to call him Daniel. They're so sad. I've got to do something to help them."

She got up and tried to talk to them. She even tried to put her arms around her mother although she seemed to only be resting them on air. "How come I can hug you, but I can hug them?" she asked.

Quietly, I murmured, "I'll explain it to you in a minute; right now try to comfort your parents and your boyfriend Daniel by thinking of them."

This was the only way I could think of to help. I didn't know if thinking about them would ease their pain, or even praying for them would help. I couldn't imagine ever losing a child, so this was very painful for me to watch. Ashley's mother placed the bouquet of flowers down by the cross and said, "I miss you, my little angel." This made me tear up.

It suddenly occurred to me that they could not see me either. I wondered how this could be, because I could still see my car parked just in front of theirs. Maybe in their grief they hadn't noticed me, but I felt as if I were invisible to them. I tried to introduce myself but there was no response. At this point I knew I was in Ashley's world and not theirs.

The mother and father were holding hands when the mother slowly reached over to Daniel's hand and grabbed it. They said a little prayer and turned to slowly walk away. Ashley began to cry. She said, "I've caused them so much pain, if I had just been more careful that night. I was looking at my cell phone because I got a text from my friend Becky. I dropped my phone and was reaching down to get it. When I sat back up, I was going off the road. My car hit the edge of the guard rail and flipped over. My mom and dad always told me to wear my seatbelt, but I forgot to put it on at night. I remember being thrown around the car and then I was here."

I said, "That must be the moment you died, Ashley."

She reached up and hugged me again crying quite heavily. I hugged her like a father would hug any daughter. I told her it would be all right.

"Your parents are going to be sad for a while and so is Daniel. I get the feeling this just happened, Ashley. Do you remember what day it was when this all happened?"

"It was two days after my birthday. My birthday is November 4, so I guess November 6, was when it happened." It was only November 16th, and I knew that wasn't nearly enough time for Ashley's parents to come to grips with the loss of their daughter. "Everybody's been here," Ashley continued. "Even my friend Becky. She feels responsible for the crash. I tried to tell her that it was my fault and that she shouldn't feel bad, but she couldn't hear me. Why can't anybody hear me?"

It was heartbreaking for me to explain. "Ashley once you pass away, you lose all contact with this side. You've entered another dimension. And now heaven is waiting for you, and it's closer than you think. Do you still see the bright light?"

"Yeah, it's still in the same spot as it was the day of the crash."

"We need to go into that light. That light will help you and your parents, and your friends get through this tough time."

Ashley knew that the light was for her but had been so hesitant to go to it because of her need to help get her friends and family through this rough time.

"Come with me, Ashley," I said, holding out my hand. "I'll lead you through the light. You don't have to be scared. There's nothing but beautiful things on the other side."

Ashley said, "I know, I've gotten that feeling since the light appeared. I just feel the need to stay here and help. My parents are so sad. I've got to find a way to help them."

"Ashley, the best way you can help them is to move on to heaven."

Ashley nodded her head and realized that she was not having much success helping her parents or Daniel get through this mess. "I guess maybe going into the light would be the best thing," Ashley said.

"Take my hand and I'll get you through the light," I said.

Ashley and I walked slowly towards the light and were sucked in and rushed through the tunnel. Ashley's hair was flying wildly in the wind as we approached the end of the tunnel. Grandpa Bill awaited us and as we slowed down and came to a stop, he reached out and hugged both me and Ashley.

"It's good to have you here, Ashley!" Grandpa Bill said.

"Are you God?" Ashley asked.

Grandpa Bill laughed and said "No, I'm Scott's grandpa. I help him cross over souls like you, Ashley. You are here in heaven now and your heaven awaits you. Whatever made you happy on earth awaits you here in heaven."

Ashley looked around and saw her family, her friends, and Daniel waiting just yards away. She ran up to her mother and father and gave them a big hug. This was a real hug, and you could tell by the look in Ashley's eyes that it was something very special to her. She kissed Daniel and hugged him tightly. I hadn't noticed the engagement ring she had on until this moment.

Daniel said, "Everything is still on up here in heaven. We're getting married in June and everyone will be here. There are two dimensions we occupy, the one in heaven and the one on earth. We continue our lives here in heaven but without the pain and suffering. As others cross over, we will be there to welcome them just like we are here to welcome you." In heaven, Daniel was wiser than his years.

They all walked away slowly, and Ashley turned back to look at me. She stopped, ran back to me and gave me a hug. She said, "Thank you. I don't know how long I would've been down there without you helping me along." She kissed me on the cheek and walked away to be with the ones she loved.

Grandpa said, "Well my son, you see how people get stuck between the dimensions of heaven and earth. There are many ways, and there are many souls you still have to help. You've done so well. God has told me to reward you with something very special. You get to ask a question; one you've always wanted an answer to. It can be anything. It can be to anybody who has passed on or about anyone, even famous people who have passed away. I know you're a history buff, so I'm guessing it will be a history question, but you can prove me wrong if you want."

This was the most amazing thing about this whole experience. I could get one question answered from anyone about anything. Unfortunately, I didn't get much time to think about a question. Should I ask about something in history? Or something more personal? I decided to go with the personal side.

"Grandpa Bill," I said. "You know Eileen's mother died before we got married. I'd like to make sure she's happy with how I've treated her daughter. I never had much time with her and only met her once. I'd really like to have a conversation with her."

Grandpa Bill said, "That can be arranged."

Suddenly I could see my mother-in-law walking toward us. She appeared to be younger and in much better physical condition than when I saw her last. She had been on oxygen then and had suffered from emphysema for quite some time. She'd been thin and quite frail while she was ill. But this woman approaching looked like she was in her 30s and was in much better physical condition than I remembered Catherine being. She approached Grandpa Bill and said, "Bill, I hear I have a visitor."

I suddenly felt nervous, as if I was being evaluated and scrutinized just like the day I met her and told her I was taking her daughter to the movies and out to dinner. Her reply at that time was, "Take good care of my daughter," and the way she said it, it was obvious to me that she meant it. I'll never forget the look on her face; it was if she knew that we would be together forever, and she wouldn't be long for this world.

I had tried very hard to adhere to her wishes. I just hoped she was satisfied with how I had done. After saying hi to Grandpa Bill, she looked me in the eyes and opened her arms and hugged me. She told me I had been a great son-in-law. She was very happy that I had treated her daughter so well and had managed to remain positive and loving even during my accident.

"There were a couple of times we were sure you were coming to stay with us permanently!" she said.

"I know," I said. "There were a couple of times I was pretty close."

"You've also given me three beautiful grandchildren," she continued, "and I love them so much. You will always have my blessing. My little girl made a great decision when she decided to marry you."

This brought a tear to my eye which she wiped with her thumb. I held her hands and said "That's really all I wanted to know. I just wanted to make sure you knew I was doing everything I could to make her happy."

"I feel honored that this was the question you asked," Catherine told me. Hugging me again, she said, "We'll see you, but not for a little while!" and slowly started to walk away.

She faded into the mist, and I looked at grandpa who said, "It's time."

"You know I don't like this reverse stuff," I told him.

Grandpa laughed and said, "I'm afraid it's a necessary evil," and soon I was flying backwards and landed near Ashley's roadside memorial. I thought of how happy she seemed and how she was with the ones she loved even in the afterlife. I thought it was great that we didn't lose our loved ones even in death. They just traveled with us to another dimension. Part of their soul remained on earth and the other part went with us.

The fog had lifted, and I walked towards my car. I got in and started it up, realizing I had only been gone for about 10 minutes. That included the time I spent talking to my mother-in-law. I quickly got back on the expressway and headed for home. I couldn't help but be proud of myself not only for helping Ashley cross over, but for being a good son-in-law in the eyes of a woman I had only met once.

CHAPTER 19

On the ride home I noticed I was getting quite a headache. This one seemed worse than the other ones I'd had recently. The pain was pretty intense and the sunlight streaming in through the car windows wasn't helping. I put my sunglasses on and hoped to deflect some of the agony. By the time I reached home I was in quite a bit of pain. I decided that

Tylenol #3 was in order. I lay down on the couch in the living room and closed my eyes. It wasn't long before the medicine kicked in and I fell asleep.

I must've been pretty exhausted because I slept for 2 ½ hours. This was unusual for me because my naps rarely lasted more than 45 minutes. That was usually all I needed to feel refreshed. I was a little worried about such a long nap and the fact that the pain really hadn't completely left my head.

I sat up on the couch and watched TV for a while and headache finally eased up. The kids came home from school and Eileen from work. Eileen asked how my appointment went and I told her it was the same as always, $400 for a trip to a doctor who told me I was making progress and that my headaches would eventually go away. I explained that I found that to be kind of funny because on the way home I got one of the worst headaches I have had since the accident.

"I had to take Tylenol #3," I told her.

"Really?" she asked. "It must've been pretty bad; you don't like taking that stuff." I agreed with her but told her that the headache had eased up and I was feeling better.

We went through the routine of the evening: helping with home-work, having dinner and cleaning up. I went downstairs to our work-out room where I tried to do some exercises. I did some upper body strengthening to help me in some sort of shape during my recovery, although I would often tell Eileen that round was a shape.

I tried to walk on the treadmill. I could last about 10 minutes at a slow pace but that was about the extent of it. I looked pretty funny walking on a treadmill with a cane, but some cardio is better than no cardio. After my workout I noticed the headache was coming back. I decided to lay down upstairs in hopes that it would go away. It did ease up after a while.

The neurologist I had seen didn't seem too worried about these headaches, but I was beginning to be a little concerned. They weren't going away, and I didn't like the idea of living with headaches for the rest of my life. I think everybody knows that you can be having a great day and a headache will change that pretty quickly. I told myself that if the bad headaches persisted, I would go back to the neurologist and see if a CAT scan was needed. Eileen always said that they would never find anything anyway; she was pretty sure things were empty up there. Always nice to have a comedian in the house. I knew I couldn't have an MRI because that would suck the screws right out of my leg and the wire out of my chest. Although this would be rather entertaining for the technologists, I was pretty sure I didn't want to go through with it.

That night I slept restlessly, waking up twice with the headache. This was very unusual because I had been sleeping like a rock. Eileen even woke up once and asked me what was wrong. I said, "This damn headache won't go away."

"How many times have you been woken up with it?" she asked.

"Twice," I answered, "and it's really getting on my nerves. Go back to sleep. I'll be fine. If it doesn't go away, I'll take another Tylenol #3." Eileen never had trouble sleeping because that's a sign of a clear conscious. She was the best thing that ever happened to me and even though I had put her through hell with this accident, she never let on that the stress might be getting to her too. I lay down again and finally fell back asleep for the night.

When I woke up the next morning, the headache was just a small, dull ache and I felt like I had gotten past the worst of it. I stopped in at the place where I had completed my physical therapy. My therapist Don told me that I could always go there to work out, even after my therapy was complete. I decided to go there to work with some of the equipment they had there that I didn't have at home. I started my routine with the help of my physical therapist.

Don was my age so we could talk on the same level. He also had three kids. They were a little younger than mine so I could give him advice on some of the challenges that parenting brings with kids that age.

I always started with a hot pack on my ankle to help loosen it up. I was using the balance board, standing on the bad foot and shifting my weight back and forth while holding onto the wall. This doesn't seem like much, but every time I stretch those ankle tendons it hurt all the way up my leg. I also worked with those large stretchy rubber bands to help me with the flexion of my foot. Things were going pretty well, and I was about halfway through my session when the headache came back.

I mentioned to Don that I was starting to get a pretty bad headache. "Trying to sneak out, aren't you!" he joked.

"I wish I was Don," I replied, "but for the last couple of days I've noticed the headaches are getting worse. I can't seem to shake them. I had to take a Tylenol #3 yesterday just to ease the pain."

Don got the hint that I was really hurting and said, "Why don't we cut things short and just have you lay down on the table with some ice?"

After a half an hour, I was ready to go. I remember sitting up but that's where it ends. From this point out the story gets very interesting.

Suddenly I found myself rushing through the tunnel but this time all alone. I wasn't scared and actually felt great. As usual, when I entered the tunnel, all of my pain disappeared. I saw the end of the tunnel and was met by Grandpa Bill.

I said, "I don't have anybody for your grandpa, why did you call me here?"

"Well son, you're going be here for a little while," Grandpa answered.

At first it didn't register with me but suddenly I got the hint. I said, "Don't tell me that after all I've been through that I'm dead!"

"I didn't say you were dead," he said. "At least not yet. But there's been an incident and you are in between worlds right now. Right now, all I can tell you is that you're going to get at least a glimpse of your heaven."

Suddenly a rush of emotions entered my body. I was scared, anxious, sorrowful and filled with regret. I felt like all I had gone through was a waste of time. If I was going to die, they should have taken me in the beginning of this mess. I was also angry; an emotion I didn't think I could experience in heaven.

Grandpa Bill said, "I know you're mad son, but there must be a reason for this. They haven't let me in on what it is, but I assure you if you are here to stay you will come to love this place."

These comforting words didn't hold much water with me. All I could think about was Eileen and the kids and how they would be able to go on without me. I asked Grandpa to send me back through the tunnel like he had done so many times before, but he said he couldn't. I even turned around to look for the entrance to the tunnel only to be disappointed when I realized that there was nothing left.

"The first part of your journey here begins with your childhood," Grandpa said. Suddenly two chase lounges appeared, and Grandpa invited me over to sit down in one of them. He sat down next to me. "Now Scott, I want you to think back as far as you can. You had many questions when you were a child that couldn't be answered. There were simple questions and complex ones. It doesn't matter what they are now, it is time to get those questions answered."

A host of memories flashed before my eyes. I could see my first day of school, playing little league baseball, running around acting goofy with my brothers and sisters, and a little sixth-grade girl that I thought I was in love with. Just then I remembered something. "Grandpa, this is going to sound kind of silly, but I lost my new baseball mitt in fourth grade. My dad paid a lot of money for it and he was very mad at me. I could never figure out what happened to it. I know it seems trivial, but to this day it still bugs me that that new mitt disappeared."

"Well that's an easy one," Grandpa said. "During little league you had a game where you hit three home runs. You probably don't remember that but were so excited about the home runs that you left your mitt under the bench in the dugout. Do you remember getting home?"

"Yes, I do," I said. "That's when I realized I didn't have my mitt. I rode my bike back to the baseball field retracing my steps. I looked everywhere but the mitt was gone. I remember crying all the way home knowing that my dad was going to be really angry. What happened to the mitt, Grandpa?"

He looked at me and said, "Two boys who were neighborhood troublemakers walked by the dugout and took your mitt. They fought over who was going to get to keep it until one of them out-wrestled the other kid for it. What's sad is the kid really didn't even play baseball.

He just saw something he could steal. He'll answer to that when he gets up here."

"Really?" I said, surprised. "Something that small can cause grief when you get up here? It doesn't seem to be the crime of the century. I hope they go easy on him."

Grandpa said, "They will, but you can believe that they will definitely remind him that he did steal something."

The entire time Grandpa and I were talking, we were overlooking mountains and streams that looked so pristine that they could only be in heaven. My mood was relaxed now, and I felt comfortable asking more questions. It seemed like whatever was going on in my existence at that time was at a standstill. I don't know what that meant for me on earth, but it seemed to be a gift to be getting questions answered up here in heaven.

"Grandpa?" I asked. "What is allowed in heaven? Can we enjoy all the things that we enjoyed on earth?"

Grandpa said, "What do you think, my son?"

"Well, I guess that if it brought you pleasure on earth then you could experience it in heaven. But I'm wondering about the things you didn't get to experience. Will I get to experience them up here?"

Grandpa said, "This is heaven. You can do pretty much anything that makes you happy, as long as it doesn't hurt anybody else. The only exception we make to this rule is for abused people. They get to abuse their abuser to inflict the same sort of pain they were subject to on earth. The reason God does this is to let the abuser experience the pain and suffering they made another go through."

I said, "I'm thinking Hitler is still pretty busy if you know what I mean."

Grandpa agreed. "He's going to be busy for quite some time. Not only did he kill a lot of people, but he also took a lot of children away from their parents. So not only do they parents get to have at him, so do the children."

I said, "Couldn't happen to a nicer guy."

Grandpa said, "What else do you remember about your childhood? I will send you some more images and you can tell me what you think."

Suddenly an entire barrage of images passed through my mind. Most of them were happy thoughts, but there were the occasional bouts of anger that my dad displayed. There were times when his patience level did not allow any communication to get through. His thought was he was the dad and what he said goes. You never got a chance to explain yourself; he just disciplined you based on what he thought, which wasn't always the truth.

I looked in Grandpa's eyes. "I guess I have another question. What made my dad so angry all the time? I never could understand why it was so important for his own children to be afraid of him. It never made any sense to me. Sometimes it was like getting run over by a freight train. He had that Marine Corps mentality, and his level of discipline didn't take into account the fact that we were just kids. Can you explain to me why he was this way and why he's such a softy now with the grandkids?"

"I'm afraid a lot of that is my fault," Grandpa said. "My father raised me in a very disciplined atmosphere, and it was the only way I knew how to raise my kids. Your father just emulated me in raising his children. It doesn't make it right, but it's the only way he knew how to do it. Do you understand what I mean? He tried hard several times to change his ways and you may remember some of those times, like when you went on vacation, and he was much more relaxed. He had no problem fishing with you, going swimming, and tossing the football around with you. He also had a lot of stress at work. Not to mention with your mother. She is an undiagnosed manic depressive. He kept things hidden from you so that you would never know the struggles she went through. Her outbursts were a product of the disease. That is why you and your siblings were subject to such hard-core discipline. Your father was interested in one thing, and that was keeping your mother happy. We know now that the illness your mother had didn't allow her to be happy all the time. So, your dad was fighting a losing battle. But he assumed if he kept you kids in line, she would be happy. We all know that this didn't work. Your mother still has these bouts, and your father still tries to keep her happy no matter what." This was a lot for me to swallow. I had no idea my mother had suffered with this disease. Back when we were kids, it was taboo to be seen by a psychiatrist. Most people bottled up their mental health problems or drowned them in alcohol. My mom was never a drinker, so I guess she just bottled up all her problems. And when they came out, there was hell to pay for everybody. There was never any doubt in my mind that my dad loved my mom with all his heart. He would do anything for her, anything to keep her happy.

"Do you understand a little bit better why your parents acted the way they did?" Grandpa asked.

I said, "I understand to a certain extent. But I don't believe in taking out your problems on your children."

"That's why they're so nice to your children," Grandpa said. "They're trying to make up for their mistakes. You feel that they are good grandparents, don't you? They have tried hard to make up for the mistakes they made with you and your brothers and sisters. They treat their grandchildren the way they should have treated their children. This is a pretty common occurrence in the world. Everybody's trying to get into heaven!"

It did make more sense to me now and Grandpa had a great way of explaining things. He said, "Now it's time for the real flashback, your teenage years!"

All I could think about was how painful this was going to be. I was a little bit awkward and a lot of overweight when I was a teenager. Before I knew it the images were flashing in front of my eyes. Eighth-grade graduation, freshman year in high school, oh God, what a mess! My sophomore year I had lost some weight and things got a little bit better. I was still pretty shy around girls, and these images were painful to watch. Images of my junior year improved, and my senior year was loaded with fun. These images seemed to pass through my mind instantaneously. But they played out in real time.

I could see myself at the senior prom dancing with a girl that was way above my level. In a burst of confidence, I had asked her to the dance and I don't know what made her say yes, but she went with it. She was my first real kiss. It was as if I could feel her lips on mine as this flashback occurred. It felt like I was at the dance, and she was as real as the night we spent together. We dated for a short time until she found someone prettier than me, which didn't take very long. Near the end of the school year I fell in love with a girl named Liz. Liz had it all. She was beautiful and had a great sense of humor. She had been my best friend's girlfriend, but he dumped her because he was a known as a player in our school. She was heartbroken and looking for a shoulder to cry on. At the time I happened to have two shoulders and was willing to let her cry on anything she wanted to.

Before I knew it, I was head over heels in love with her. We went out and had a lot of fun together. But she could never get over the breakup with my friend. She never let me fully into her life and it broke my heart. I wanted so badly to have her love me as much as I loved her. Sometimes I wonder what would have happened if I had met her at a different time and a different place.

Grandpa said, "Well those sounds like a question! Let's explore that question. I'm going to set your mind to a year later after you graduated high school, and you'll see what would have happened if that scenario had played through."

In the new scenario, Liz had gone to college in Chicago. I was taking night classes and working during the day. We met up at a party that a mutual friend was having and started talking like there had been no time in between. It took quite a bit of nerve, but I asked her out with the stipulation that it would be a real date, not just her coming over to cry on my shoulder.

She said she was way over that and that she would love to go on a date with me. Before I knew it we had been dating for several months and were so compatible that we couldn't keep her hands off of each other. We were inseparable. I looked forward to every moment I could spend with her, and it seemed like she felt the same way. This all occurred during the spring and summer months. We even talked about getting married.

That's when I found out she got accepted to a school in Nevada. It was a full ride scholarship. I knew she had to take it because financially it was better for her and her family. She said we could still maintain a long-distance relationship because she would come home once a month and I could go out there once a month for a weekend.

I had a bad feeling about this arrangement and with time I realized my worst fear. Time passed and twice a month became once a month and then once a month became once every two months. Then I got the letter saying that she had found somebody at school and had fallen for him. It wasn't my fault, she told me in the letter, it just happened. I could see myself crying and slowly throwing the letter and the trash. I never talked to her again. I still wondered about her though, we were so close. If she just didn't go away to college maybe we would've had a chance.

Grandpa said, "Does that answer your question?" "

"I guess it does," I answered. "I always wondered if things would have worked out between us. I guess I got my answer."

Grandpa said, "There's something else you should know, she's been married three times! So like God says, everything happens for a reason. There's a reason you would've gotten that heartbreaking letter. If you two had gotten married, you would have been husband number one and she would be on number four by now."

"I've got to admit that was the coolest thing I ever experienced Grandpa."

Grandpa said, "Yeah, we can do some pretty amazing things up here. You can see what any aspect of your life would have been like with just a slight change in its axis. If you had married Liz, you would've never met Eileen. Then you would've never had John, Casey, and Dana. She would've moved on and married someone else. And you'd still be single. And at your age it's not easy to be single."

My thoughts couldn't help but go to some other girls that I had dated wondering how my life would've turned out if I had married them.

"Grandpa, there was another girl. Her name was Melissa. I've been in love three times in my life. Liz was the first, Melissa was the second, and Eileen was the third. Can you show me what would have happened if I had married Melissa?

"She was a girl I'd met at work and had a great time with. She was very athletic and had a great sense of humor. We would play softball together on a mixed couples league, go bowling together, and hang out at the bar drinking beer and laughing half the night away. There was one significant problem. She was engaged. I played it off like I just wanted to be her friend, but I knew I wanted more than that. I knew I had her confused and she wasn't sure what she wanted to do.

"When she finally laid a big kiss on me, I knew she was having second thoughts about getting married. We spent quite a bit of time together including going away on vacation. She was able to hide our relationship from her fiancé.

"I begged her to break it off with him, but I think she was still trying to decide which one of us she would pick. As you know by now it wasn't me, she picked. So, what would've happened if I had married Melissa?" I asked.

Grandpa said, "Let me flash that scenario in front of your eyes." I saw myself standing by the doorway of a house I shared with Melissa. Our marriage was failing, and she had told me that she had been cheating on me with someone from work. She wanted to be with him and couldn't help it. I stood there and watched her leave, heartbroken beyond belief. We had been married five years, and I didn't see this coming at all.

I let the door close behind me and retreated to my bedroom and cried for hours. Our divorce was a bitter one. And things didn't end well. I never saw her again.

Grandpa said, "Do you understand why that wouldn't work? She cheated on her fiancé to be with you, which meant she was likely to cheat on you to be with someone else. This cycle still continues in her life. She has had many relationships that ended the same way. Even if you had stayed married to her, she would've cheated on you constantly. Eventually you would've caught her and then become enraged enough to kill her and her lover. You could have spent the rest of your life behind bars. Again, God does everything for a reason. You would've been miserable in prison, don't you think?"

"That's not really what would have happened, is it Grandpa?" I asked.

Grandpa said, "It would have been a possibility. I see it as one of the scenarios, although there are a couple of others. The one that seems to suit you best is just letting her go. She was confused and didn't know which person to pick, so she went with the comfortable choice. She had been with him for a longer period of time than you. But the other scenarios are possible, so it's hard to say which one would have played out. Knowing you, I think you would have made the correct decision. And as it turns out you did."

I continued to reflect on the early years in my life. "You know after those two trampled on my heart I really considered moving to California. I thought I could be an actor or maybe a musician, a lead singer in a band. California was so beautiful, Grandpa. I had been out there so many times and finally made the decision to move out there. A month or so before I was set to leave, I met Eileen. What would've happened if I had moved out there?"

"Well, it sounds like we have another question we have to answer," Grandpa said, "so let's go with it. You would've driven that old clunker of a car you had, remember that 1970 Monte Carlo?"

I laughed. "Yes, it was a piece of junk, wasn't it?"

"Well, it got you out there with only one stop for a repair. You moved in with your buddy Rich and started working for him. I'll let your brain take over from here, close your eyes."

As I closed my eyes, I could see myself working with Rich in the physical therapy department at a hospital in San Pedro. Rich was kind enough to let me go on auditions whenever I needed to. I would make up the time on Saturdays so we wouldn't get behind in our work. I got bit parts on TV shows and a couple of small roles in the movies. But nothing ever panned out.

I struggled to maintain a life out there because of the high cost of living. I couldn't live with Rich forever, so I got my own apartment which forced me to work even more. I spent a lot of time at the beach, which I loved.

After five years and a lot of frustration with my acting career I realized it was time to go home. I missed my family and my friends. I packed up what I could and drove home. I didn't seem to regret my time out there, but I had wished I had gotten some of the breaks other famous actors had gotten.

When I got home, not much had changed. The bad thing was I had missed my opportunity to get together with Eileen. She had married her old boyfriend and was living her new life. I was 30 years old and single, with a bleak looking future in front of me. I didn't finish my education out in California, so I was stuck in meaningless jobs for quite some time.

Grandpa said, "Well, that scenario kind of sucked."

"You're not kidding," I agreed. At this time, I realized how much fun I was having just going through the scenarios in my head. I had almost forgotten that I appeared to be dead. I was so comfortable sitting there looking at the scenery in my chaise lounge with my favorite grandfather. He had taught me so much in life and he was still teaching me even in death, or at least I thought so.

I had no idea which dimension I was destined for, and Grandpa didn't lead on or give me an answer. He was answering questions using a form of mental telepathy that allowed me to see the answers to all my questions. So far, I found the answers to be fascinating. And I was able to experience what seemed like all the things that had taken place during these episodes. Things didn't always rush by; sometimes they lingered, such as intimate moments with these two previous love interests.

Finally, I had to ask Grandpa a question that always was in the back of my mind. "Grandpa, this may seem like a weird question but I got to know. Is there sex in heaven?"

"It's not a weird question," Grandpa said. "In fact, it's one of the most common questions. Everything available to you that you enjoyed in life is also available to you in heaven. Did you enjoy sex during your lifetime?" He asked this with a grin on his face.

"Yes of course I did, probably more than others," I said, a little embarrassed to be talking to my grandpa about this.

"Why do you think I let you experience that aspect of your past with those two previous girlfriends?" Grandpa asked with a chuckle.

I guess I was amazed that Grandpa was so upfront with my question. I was afraid to ask it, yet he had no problems answering it. "There were a few others you spent sensual times with too. You can go back and relive those times if you want at any later date. But for now let's stick with the only two you experienced. Besides, you probably want to relive the most important relationship in your life and the one that all of us up here in heaven pointed you towards."

I knew he meant Eileen because I always felt she was a gift from God. The others were just warm-ups for the real thing. I didn't know what love truly was until I met Eileen. I asked Grandpa, "Can I relive my relationship with Eileen?"

Grandpa asked me to close my eyes again and I was in front of a hospital bed helping a brand-new nurse put a patient in bed. I couldn't believe how cute she was, and she even cracked a few jokes. There was something about her and I didn't know what, but I couldn't stop looking at her. It must've seemed creepy to her at first.

I wasted little time in asking her out when I noticed there was no ring on her finger. I believe it was the first date I had ever been extremely nervous about. Something told me that this was more than a special girl. I relived that first date and watched her get a salad and not eat much of anything. It was obvious to me she was nervous too. We saw a movie after dinner, and I took her home.

Before we even got to her house, I asked her out on a second date. She said yes and I told her I would pick a better movie this time. We both laughed. First Blood with Sylvester Stallone was not exactly the best movie choice for a first date. We decided just to go out to dinner and then followed it by some drinks at a local bar for our second date.

Before I knew it I had the sudden realization that there was a good chance I was going to spend the rest of my life with this woman. From that point on, we couldn't keep our hands off of each other. Before I knew it I could see us in the church getting married.

The two years before we had John were very special years. It was our time to get to know each other. I remember being in the delivery room, waiting for our surprise and being told it was a boy. It didn't matter to me if it was a boy or a girl; I just knew he wasn't going to be the last one.

I experienced holding my baby, watching him walk for the first time, and seeing him hold his little brother after he was born. I also remember being in the delivery room when Dana was born. It was so great to have a little girl, because everybody knows they're always Daddy's little girl.

I relived two trips to Disney World when they were little, and unfortunately the funeral of my grandfather. I didn't understand why this unhappy thought was placed in my vision. I guess my Grandpa had suffered so long that I was almost glad when he passed. I knew he was at peace and that made me feel good.

The vision continued on through the years of me coaching baseball, going to ballet recitals, and sneaking away on the occasional weekend with my beautiful bride. The vision ended the day of the accident. I woke up as I was backing out of the driveway and saw Grandpa ducking behind the garage wall. I was upset.

"Why did it stop there, Grandpa?"

"Well, my son," Grandpa said. "I figured you could do without the last year and a half of pain, and I didn't want to show you all the pain Eileen and the kids endured from the day you were hurt so seriously. You don't remember, but the three times that you died on the table you did enter heaven for a short time. Your memory was erased of this because it wasn't your time to be here, so we sent you back all three times.

I said, "Then I suppose this is my time to be here, is that right Grandpa?"

Grandpa said, "I did say that the decision hasn't been made yet.

You're being allowed to do this because of your special talent. It will help you to cross people over when you can tell them what awaits them. Or it may be your time and before you know it you'll be in your own heaven. So either way you'll be helped by the experience."

I couldn't help but wonder which way I was going. I was in a state of euphoria, yet still managed to feel sad for my wife and children. I knew they would have a rough time without me, and I couldn't even think of Eileen with another man. I had to find a way to get back. But I guess this decision wasn't going to be mine so I would have to wait it out.

Grandpa said, "Let's change the subject. You were always a big history buff. What kind of questions do you have from history that we can answer for you? I know you wonder about many things. What's the first thing you can think of that you want to ask?"

This took some thinking on my part. There was so much I wanted to know. So many people I would like to meet. I didn't know if it was possible but there were so many that had influenced me, I just wondered if I could meet them. I had to ask. "Grandpa, could I meet someone from history?"

Grandpa said, "I can only allow you to meet one person and it can't be Jesus. You'll get to meet him later when it's your time. So, think about who you want to meet and think hard. Right now, let's just answer some questions. What's the first question you have?"

"Well, I watched a lot of shows and read quite a few books on the Kennedy assassination. There are a lot of people who think it was a conspiracy. Can you tell me how it really went down? It's something that has puzzled me for some time."

Grandpa said, "Much to the chagrin of all the conspiracy theorists, Oswald acted alone. He was a marksman in the service and got lucky with his shots. As it turns out, the first shot would've killed the president anyway. The second shot, the one that destroyed Kennedy's head, just made sure of it. It was his time, and I don't know why God picked such a violent way for him to go out. Maybe it had something to do with showing the world how a crazy person could get to any leader if he or she wanted to. Right after that every president and world leader had a different perspective on security."

I said, "What about Jack Ruby?"

Grandpa said, "Jack was just an angry man who felt like Oswald didn't deserve to live. He had access to the police station because he was friends with so many of the cops. He seized an opportunity to kill Oswald without thinking of the ramifications it would lead to. If Jack hadn't killed Oswald there wouldn't be a conspiracy theory. Oswald would've confessed that he acted alone and just wanted to be famous. He would have been put to death anyway by the federal government in a firing squad. Does that answer your question?"

"I guess it does," I said. "It just seems so unlikely that one man could cause a whole nation to go into grief."

"It's happened many times in the past," Grandpa said. "Even the recent past. Osama bin Laden will be wasting away in hell for what he did. He caused the same amount of grief, if not more, for many families. And I also have to tell you there were no 72 virgins waiting for him. Just a spot in hell. He gets brought up every time a family member of a loved one killed on 9/11 passes on. They are allowed to give him the same pain they experienced when they found out that their loved one was killed that day. He's also had to endure the pain that each one of those 3000 people felt at the time of their death. Just like Hitler and Stalin, they have to relive the death of everyone they killed directly or indirectly. It's part of the punishment of hell for people like this. Pol Pot is also suffering in hell. He killed so many people that he may not ever get out of the hell fires. These people are known as hell's demons, and I'm not talking about the motorcycle gang. They are demons from hell who envelop a body and turn it evil. The only good thing is that there is a limited supply of these demons. And they only come along at rare times. It's the constant battle between good and evil. Occasionally evil wins, but not without retribution."

"What about you Grandpa Bill? Is this place everything you thought it would be? Or are you making it up as you go along, having your heaven evolve as time goes on to suit you?"

"It's not quite that simple, my son," grandpa said. "Things evolve after a certain amount of time, and you feel the urge to help people more than help yourself. I've already experienced the wants and needs from my previous life. Now I spend my time helping others cross over and welcoming them to heaven. I need you to continue to help me if that's in God's plan. We just don't know yet. I'm waiting for an answer as to whether you're going back or not."

I was overwhelmed with how much had happened since I got here. It felt like I had been sitting on the chaise lounge with grandpa for hours and hours reliving my past. I'd gotten the chance to rekindle old flames, experience the meeting of the love of my life, and experience my favorite thing of all, fatherhood. I got to ask questions and get answers that no one else had.

Just as my heart was feeling full, grandpa announced that he had a surprise for me. "Scott, I want to let you experience something very special. I want you to meet someone who has had a very special spot in your heart throughout your whole life. In the open field in front of us, a heavyset man approached. He was short in stature and wore a fedora hat and was dressed in a nice suit. A chaise lounge appeared next to me and as the figure approached, I was amazed to see the man I had always wanted to meet. Jerome Horwitz, also known as Curly Howard.

He sat down next to us and said hi to Grandpa Bill as if he had known him all his life. I sat there with my mouth wide open, in a blank stare at Curly and in awe of his presence.

Curly said, "I hear you've always wanted to meet me. Well, here I am in the flesh, or should I say in the spirit. Did you want to say something to me, or did you have a question you wanted me to answer? You can throw anything at me; I've answered just about every question possible."

I looked at him and said "Do you realize that for 75 years you've made people laugh out loud? Generation after generation, your humor has made people happy. You've been a hero of mine because I can sit and watch the same episode over and over and still laugh at how funny you were. Even my boys get such a kick out of your humor. It's fun to watch them laugh so hard."

Curly interjected. "Well, I did have some help. Without my brother Moe and Larry Fine, none of it would've happened. We were a good team, and we tried really hard to make people laugh. I'm proud of the work we did, even though not everyone thinks it's real comedy. Either you like us, or you don't! That seems to be the running theme. I appreciate guys like you who respect our work. It wasn't always easy, but we made it work. What was your favorite scene?"

I was thrilled that he asked. "Well, I guess it's when you were in the hospital working as doctors, and you ran down the hallway away from the camera and Moe and Larry turned right and you turned left. Then Mo whistled for you, and you slowly walked towards him in such a funny way that every time I see it I still end up on the floor laughing."

"You know that was an improv scene," Curly said. "I was supposed to turn right with them but at the last second I decided to turn left. Moe had the presence of mind to whistle for me and I just walked like I was out for a stroll. It worked so well that we left it in. So it wasn't by any means genius, it was just luck and a little bit of goofiness."

Curly's demeanor was pretty serious, and I could tell he was very proud of his work. My real desire was just to thank him for all the years of laughter and make sure he knew how much influence he had on the world. Curly started to get up from the chair and I asked him to stay because I had one more question. "

"Curly, why did you die so young? I know you had a stroke or a couple of them, but what caused the strokes?"

Curly said, "I had what's called malignant hypertension. The arteries leading to my kidneys were narrowed and it caused my blood pressure to skyrocket. We didn't have medicine to keep it under control, so I pretty much had to suffer with it. I got bad headaches all the time near the end of my life. And when I had my first stroke, I was on the set filming one of our shorts. I couldn't speak or move the right side of my body. I eventually got some of that back and you know when I came back, I talked a little slower and moved a little slower too. The second stroke pretty much ended my career. I spent the last number of months in a nursing home in a semi-vegetative state. And then one day I found myself up here." Curly seemed to put this all together and deliver the information so nonchalantly. It was obvious he had told this story before. He said, "As they say, when it's your time, it's your time."

Curly rose from the lounge chair and started to walk away. He turned and looked at me and said, "Thank you for being such a fan. If you ever want to talk, just ask and I'll be here. That's if they decide to keep you. Any word on that yet, Bill?"

Grandpa Bill said, "I'm still waiting for an answer. It should be coming soon."

I was still confused as to the hesitation in my case. Was I dead or not? I finally had to ask Grandpa for an answer.

"Grandpa if I'm dead, I want to know what happened. I worked so hard to get better and I feel like I've been ripped off. I'm sorry to sound so harsh but after going through all that I went through and eventually getting better, I didn't expect to find myself here so quickly after my recovery."

Grandpa said, "I can tell you what happened, but I can't tell you the outcome. The outcome still has to be determined. You remember lying on the table in physical therapy, right?"

It seemed like hours had passed but I did remember lying on the table and sitting up to go home. But that was all I remembered. The rest of it is a blur.

"Scott, you know your headaches were increasing in both frequency and intensity, right? During your injury and the subsequent brain surgery, one of the arteries in your head was weakened by the fall. It wasn't noticeable during your brain surgeries. But as the healing process began, the artery started to bulge outward. The more it bulged outward the worse your headaches became. The artery finally burst when you sat up from the physical therapy table. You were in a good place to have this happen. There were plenty of medical people around you who quickly called 911 and got you to the hospital before your heart stopped. They revived you twice in the emergency room and now you're in surgery with everybody feverishly working to repair the artery and save your life. You're stuck here because your life is in the balance. The surgeon working on you is the best one in the area, so you've got a good chance of making it out of this alive. But there's always a chance you won't come back from it. Eileen is waiting in the surgical waiting room at the hospital saying more prayers than a single human being should be able to say in one incident. The kids are very worried about you. They know you're sick, but they don't know how sick you are. God is trying to make a decision as to whether to keep you here or send you back to continue using your gift. He likes what you've done so far, and I think is leaning toward sending you back. You know when you go back, they'll be more recovery time for you right?"

I said, "Well if anyone is used to recovery time it sure would be me. I think I can make it through another brain surgery. But my hair is simply going to be a mess!"

Grandpa laughed out loud. The truth is, I was afraid of what I would come back as. Would the aneurysm do some serious damage to my brain? Would I be stuck in a wheelchair for the rest of my life? Would Eileen have to take care of me for the rest of my life? If any of this was going to be true, I didn't want to go back. I would rather stay here and have my family move on without me. I didn't want to be a burden. I would just as soon stay here and start living in the next dimension.

Grandpa looked at me and said, "I just got the answer; are you ready for it?" All of a sudden, I found myself flying backwards in the tunnel at an incredible speed. The pain in my head was getting progressively worse to the point of being almost unbearable. I slammed into a bed in the ICU at the same hospital where I had started my long recovery nearly two years ago.

I slowly started to open my eyes, but the light was very painful. Eileen must've seen me open my eyes and crept up towards my ear.

She said, "You dodged another bullet my friend. You had an aneurysm in your head that burst. Your heart stopped twice in the emergency room, but they got you back both times. Everything fell into place rather quickly and thank God the neurosurgeon was already in the hospital. He was able to clip the aneurysm and save your life. He doesn't think you lost any brain tissue or had a stroke."

Even though the pain was extreme, nothing Eileen had told me was a surprise to me. It had been exactly like Grandpa said.

My head throbbed and I slipped in and out of consciousness. From the snippets of conversation I could gather, I guess I was nearly dead in the physical therapy office. By the time the paramedics had gotten there, I had pretty much flat-lined. They brought me back after the second shock and loaded me up as quickly as they could into the ambulance. Don even went with me to the hospital and called Eileen from the ambulance to let her know what happened. How Don got home from the hospital I don't know, but I guess he just didn't want to leave me alone. Eileen arrived and relieved Don in the surgical waiting room. John wanted to go with and wait with Eileen. She couldn't talk him out of it no matter how she tried. I guess he was protecting his mom and wanted to be there in case something bad happened. I also think he just wanted to make sure I was going to be okay.

Eileen's sister stayed with Casey and Dana. After I was out of surgery and out of the woods, Eileen went home and got some rest. John wanted to stay at the hospital and wait for me to wake up. Little did he know it would take 24 hours for me to wake up.

John ended up going home after Eileen got some sleep and came back later on that day. I woke up with both of them at my side and felt quite groggy. But they were a sight for sore eyes.

It took a while before I could focus and feel well enough to sit up. I had quite a bit of nausea after the surgery, and after someone tiptoes through your brain cavity a headache is definitely in order.

They started me walking on the second day. For the first couple of days I walked with old Silver, my trusty companion from the old days. I had hoped I would never see this walker again, but it sure made walking a lot easier. I was uneasy on my feet and a little lightheaded. Eileen would mention to the nurses that I was always a little lightheaded, that's why she married me. She felt the need to help the handicapped. It hurt to laugh, but I still did.

As usual I don't know what I would've done without her. I probably would've just gone ahead and died. Heaven is rather inviting and if you don't have something waiting for you on earth; I could see why you would want to check out. I was lucky enough to have such a beautiful family waiting for me here on earth. Even though all my troubles would've been gone if I'd stayed in heaven, there was too much for me to live for here on earth to commit to staying with Grandpa.

I spent four days in the ICU and another three days in a hospital room. After a week passed, I could walk on my own and I didn't have any trouble talking. There was some tingling in my left foot, but the doc said that would go away. I was still walking with my cane and even though my balance was a little off, I was able to support myself.

After the seventh day I was finally in my own bed recovering once again from a near-death experience. I must say, I was getting tired of these experiences. I went back to the neurosurgeon at the two-week mark and he removed the staples and said it looked like everything was healing up as planned. He definitely recommended I stay away from any kind of MRI machine now that I had all these metal clips in my head. Between the metal I had in my leg in the metal I had in my head I was beginning to feel like a Transformer. At any moment I could turn into some sort of race car.

He said I could now start doing things around the house but not to drive for another month. I had to wear sunglasses when I went outside even if it was cloudy. The sun caused an instant headache. The sunglasses really helped avoid this. I wandered around the house while my wife and kids were at work looking for things to do that weren't too stressful. I looked back on my experience with Grandpa and my short time in heaven. I smiled when I thought about meeting Curly and thought of my old relationships with girlfriends and how things always work out for the best. I was tempted to look up my old girlfriends just to see the results of Grandpa's statements. Not to rub it in their faces for leaving me but... Oh who am I kidding? I did want to rub it in their faces! Other than having to go through two years of rehab with me, I thought 'd missed out on a good thing. But I took the high road and let it go.

The answers I got to my questions still amazed me. But in my time of recovery I had thought of so many more. Did Abraham Lincoln die because of a conspiracy? How many stories in the Bible are fables? What was Jesus really like? The list goes on and on.

Of course, you think of these things after the fact, and under pressure I came up with the questions that I had always wondered about. I spent many hours sitting in my recliner thinking of the extra time I got to spend with Grandpa Bill. It'd been very special, and I realized it was a gift given to me by Grandpa Bill and God for the work I was doing. Although heaven was a wonderful experience, I wasn't sure I wanted to be a permanent resident yet. Getting sent back meant that I wasn't done with my work. I didn't know what assignments I would be given or even if I still had my gift, because so much had happened in the last couple of weeks. I figured when it was time, and I was healed sufficiently I would find out quick enough whether or not my abilities were still intact.

CHAPTER 20

I started to get my strength back and went back to physical therapy where they were all glad to see me alive for a change. On the third trip back from therapy, I saw a roadside memorial off the expressway about 10 yards from the drainage ditch. There was no one around it so I assumed that this person that crossed over. I was glad for this because I wasn't sure I was ready to make the trip back. I was still pretty worn out and needed to sleep quite a bit during the day. They say sleep is the body's way of healing, and I must say I was getting plenty of healing.

I always took a nap after lunch and sometimes would doze off after dinner. I usually went to bed at 9:30 and was asleep by 10:30. I had to watch my favorite show before I could go to sleep. I really liked the Daily Show with Jon Stewart. Not only did he make me laugh, but he put a real interesting perspective on the world. When you can't trust any of the cable news networks, it's nice to have somebody make fun of them. So after Jon Stewart was over, I would usually shut down. Most of the time I remembered to turn the TV off but there were quite a few times where Eileen would get up in the middle of the night come around to my side of the bed and turn it off. I'm sure she wasn't happy about getting up in the middle of the night.

Eileen was one of those people who could put her head on the pillow and be asleep 3 seconds later. It doesn't surprise me after all the work she did every day that she was able to fall asleep so quickly. I only wished I could do the same. There was always something running through my head that kept me awake.

Lately I had been wondering whether or not my gift was still available to me. Sometimes my thoughts kept me awake past 10:30, and on a bad night I could be up till midnight or 1:00. I tried to limit my naps so I could sleep at night. I still found myself dozing off after dinner, sitting up in my recliner, but I asked Eileen to wake me up whenever she saw me sleeping. I must admit, that would sometimes get pretty annoying. But if it helped me sleep better at night, I was all for it.

I was approaching the six-week mark after my surgery. We had one more visit to the neurosurgeon before he could clear me to drive again. I looked forward to this day even though I didn't really look forward to seeing the neurosurgeon and his $400, ten-minute interview. I had all the money I needed, but for some reason it still bugged me. You think I could get at least 20 minutes out of them for $400! Hell, for $400 he should wash my car. But then again he did save my life, so I should stop bitching. And he did do what I wanted him to do, which was clear me to drive again. Eileen let me drive home and I must say it was one of the more pleasant rides I've taken in a car. You don't realize how independent the car makes you feel until it's taken away.

I felt much steadier on my feet and the only thing that bothered me was bending over. Eileen would give me small errands to run during the day and that kept me pretty busy. I was in charge of picking up the kids from school, getting them to their various practices, and doing some of the grocery shopping. Grocery shopping gave me a headache before the aneurysm so I wasn't surprised to get a little headache during my shopping trips. Ever try to find Q-tips in the middle of the 50,000 square-foot Wal-Mart? Now you know why I had the headache.

I was getting antsy about not seeing any spirits for the last six weeks. I guess Grandpa was also giving me a break and letting me heal. Finally, I couldn't take it anymore and I took a ride past an old cemetery in the town next to ours. The cemetery was overgrown and had not been cared for very well. The fence and gate had been broken in several places. It was called Founders Cemetery; I assume after the founders of the town. I slowed down and looked carefully into the cemetery to see if I could find any spirits.

Just as I was about to give up, I saw a little boy peeking his head out from behind an oak tree appearing to look at my car. He couldn't have been much more than seven or eight and was wearing an outfit that looked like it was from the 1950s. I stopped the car and got out. I had to squeeze through the broken gate of the cemetery and walk through the tall weeds. Most of the gravestones were from the late 1800s to the mid-1900s. I assume this little boy was one of the last ones buried in the cemetery. He had tucked his head back around the tree as if he were hiding from me.

As I got closer to him, I realized I had not received the shocking feeling. I found this somewhat startling because of the recent surgery I had, and I had wondered if I was just seeing this boy. But then the fog appeared and at the same time I got the shocking feeling. The shocking feeling was much milder than usual and only seemed to affect my legs. I also noticed when I entered the fog that it was only about 4 foot high, and I could see above it and all around it. The sky was very visible and the oak tree that this little boy was standing behind was easily recognizable by the upper branches and the acorns growing on it.

The little boy was inching around the tree still trying to hide when I said "Hi, my name is Scott, what's yours?" He didn't answer and just stared at me. I tried to get him to warm up. "I came here to help you and I saw you peeking around the tree. Did you see me?"

"I did see you in your fancy car. It doesn't look like the cars we have."

Now mind you I wasn't driving a Corvette; it was a Toyota Camry that was about five years old. But to him it must have looked like a futuristic car.

"Can you tell me your name?" I asked.

"My name is Tommy, Tommy Johnson. I'm nine years old and I go to Mokena Elementary School. I like to play basketball and a lot of other sports. But I can't find my basketball and there's nothing but grass here anyways. Do you see my basketball anywhere?"

"No I don't Tommy," I said. "Did you have it when you got here?"

"Yes, it was in that long thing I was laying in when my mommy and daddy said goodbye to me."

I realized Tommy was referring to his own coffin. They must've buried him with a basketball. The basketball must not have made the journey to the world Tommy was living in now. "Tommy, do you remember what day it was when you said goodbye to your mommy and daddy?"

"I don't know what day it was, but I remember it was April and our basketball season was just starting," Tommy said. "We had two practices when I got sick. I was coughing a lot. I couldn't run and my chest hurt. I had to stay home from school and Mommy took me to the doctor. The doctor said there was something wrong with my heart. They took me to the big hospital in Chicago. There were a lot of machines that went beep. And I was getting more and more tired every day. Then one day I fell asleep. And when I woke up I was here dribbling my basketball. It bounced off my foot and went into the fog over there. I can't seem to go into the fog because it stops me every time. Can you go over there and get my basketball, Mr. Scott?"

"You can just call me Scott, Tommy."

"My dad always said to call adults Mr. and Mrs. and I don't want to make him mad," Tommy said solemnly.

"Okay Tommy, you can call me Mr. Scott if you want. I came here to help you. Do you see this big stone over here with your name on it?"

"Yeah," Tommy answered." I don't know why it's there but there are a couple of other stones here that have other people's names on them. That one says Barbara Winters and that other one says John Hendrickson. I don't know why they have their names on these rocks. But my rock has a basketball on it. I think it means that this is where I'm supposed to play basketball."

The little boy seemed very confused about his origin "Tommy, do know what that stone means?" He shook his head no. "It means that you're supposed to be in heaven." I figured this might be the best way to break the news to him.

"Is that why Mommy and Daddy would come see me and cry by my stone?" Tommy asked, becoming a little upset.

"Yes Tommy, that's why. They miss you very much."

His face looked sad. "They haven't been here in a long time. They used to come a lot but my mom was always crying so hard that I think my dad and her decided not to come anymore because it made them too sad. Maybe they thought I was in heaven I and couldn't see me. It made me sad to see them crying. I didn't want them to cry, I wanted to help them feel better. So I've been waiting for them to come back and maybe I can cheer them up. Maybe me and Daddy can play basketball again. Mom used to like to watch us play basketball so it would make her happy too. When do you think they'll come back Mr. Scott?"

I tried to break it to him gently. "Tommy, I don't know if they're coming back. You've been here for a long time. Do you see the date on your stone? It says you died in 1952. Did you know you died, Tommy?"

"I kind of thought I died but I was hoping that I could come back alive again and play some more basketball with my daddy. I miss my mommy and daddy a lot."

"Tommy, I need to tell you something that may surprise you. Do you know what year it is now?" I asked him, hoping to shake him out of his sadness.

"Isn't it 1952?"

"Not any more Tommy. You've been here a long, long time. This is the year 2011. You've been playing here for almost 50 years. I know you could see the cars changing and looking almost like they were space-ships. Is that right Tommy?"

Tommy looked at me and then I think he realized that a lot of time had passed. "I bet that means my mommy and daddy are in heaven now. They had me when my mommy was 34. My daddy was 38. I guess they could still be alive, but they would be really old, wouldn't they Mr. Scott?"

"Yes, they would be very, very old, I told Tommy. "In fact, I'm pretty sure they might already be in heaven. I could check for you if you want me to, Tommy."

"Can you come back after you check and tell me?" he asked, the frist glimmer of hope I'd seen lighting up his eyes.

"Of course I will Tommy; it will only take me a couple of minutes," I smiled. His child-like hope softened my voice.

"Okay, he said, "I'll be here."

"I'll be back in just a couple minutes okay Tommy? Don't go anywhere."

"Don't worry Mr. Scott I can't go past the fog," Tommy grinned.

I went through the fog and got the tingling feeling in my lower legs. I got in my car and turned back to see Tommy peeking around the tree looking at me. I waved to him and he waved back at me. I wondered how many people he'd waved at over the years that couldn't see him. It made me incredibly sad that this boy had died so many years ago and was buried with his basketball. It must've been devastating for his parents.

I went home and tried to access the Mokena township archives through the Internet, since that was the town in which the cemetery was located. There were records back to 1975 but the rest were in storage. I decided that I had to check for obituaries of Tommy's parents. I found it interesting that Tommy's parents were not buried near him and wondered if they would still be alive.

After digging through the archives of the Mokena records, I found Tommy's parents were named Margaret and Herman Johnson and had moved to Tampa, Florida in 1980. I called the Tampa archives looking for obituaries on either one of them. They were able to find both of them. Herman had died in 1988 followed by Margaret in 1996. That was why they weren't buried near Tommy. I'd bet they were laid to rest down in Tampa.

It appeared that Tommy had no siblings. Margaret's obituary read she had been preceded in death by her son Tommy and her husband Herman.

Now that I knew the facts of Tommy's parents and how they had already crossed over, I could go back to talk to Tommy. I drove slowly through the cemetery area and reached the broken gate. I parked my car on the side of the road, got out and squeezed through the gate.

Tommy peeked around the oak tree like he had done before and greeted me with a big smile. "Hi, Mr. Scott! I knew you'd come back. You know what else came back? That light I saw a long time ago."

I went through the fog and saw the light Tommy was talking about. "Do you see it over there? It keeps getting bigger. I'm not afraid of it now like I was before. Can you help me go into the light or can you even go with me into the light?"

"Tommy, that's what I'm here for. I checked on your mommy and daddy and they're already in heaven waiting for you. I think they are the ones who put the light there so you could go through it. And of course I'll help you go through the light. Besides, I want you to meet my grandpa."

Tommy looked at me and slowly reached his hand up towards mine. We took about six steps and entered the light, rushing through at a speed I can't describe. We exited the tunnel to find Grandpa, Herman, and Margaret in front of us. Margaret and Herman appeared to Tommy at the same age they were when Tommy left them.

Tommy ran into them and jumped in his dad's arms and his mother hugged him at the same time. They kissed him on his cheek and Herman reached down behind him and picked up a brand-new basketball. He gave it to his son and he and Tommy immediately started to dribble the ball. A basketball hoop appeared just off to our left and Tommy and Herman started shooting around just like a day had never passed.

Margaret smiled as she watched her two men played basketball to-gether. She walked over to me and gave me a great big hug. She thanked me for helping Tommy cross over and making their family whole again. They had waited so long. Margaret said, "You're a gift from God and so is our little Tommy."

"Tommy was ready," I told her. "He missed you two. He was peeking around the oak tree in the cemetery and was at looking right at me. I'm sure he was ready to come up and see you. And now that I see you all together, I can't help but think that Tommy realized he needed to go somewhere else."

It's hard to understand or even conceive what heaven is when you're nine. Tommy asked me if I wanted to shoot some baskets with them and I asked Grandpa if that would be okay. Grandpa looked at Tommy. "He can only shoot for a couple of minutes and then he has to go back and help other people." I played basketball with Tommy and Herman for what seemed like 10 minutes or so. Tommy was a great little basketball player. He hit outside shots like a high schooler. Who knows, he may have been on the way to the NBA if his heart hadn't given out. In the 50s it was all about the outside shooter. There was no such thing as a slam dunk. I think Tommy would've stood a chance to make it. And if that were the case he could experience that up here in heaven.

Finally, grandpa said, "It's time now, Scott."

I waved goodbye to Tommy and Herman and gave Margaret a hug. She whispered in my ear "Thank you one more time."

, grandpa said "You were beginning to wonder if you were going to get your gift back, weren't you?"

"Yeah, I guess I was, Grandpa. After my visit up here and then the recovery time from my aneurysm I wasn't sure if I'd lose it all. But I'm glad to help Tommy, and I'll be glad to help anybody else you want me to help. Just say the word. Or better yet just show me the spirit."

"You're beginning to sound a little bit like Superman," Grandpa said.

"I guess it just makes me feel so good to reunite these families that I feel a little like Superman." Before I knew it, I was in reverse, heading back to my earthly dimension. I landed in the cemetery next to Tommy's grave. I rested my hand on it and cleared some of the weeds from around the headstone. Although it was almost impossible to see

Tommy's grave from the road, I didn't want it to be covered in weeds. The least I could do was open up a space so that maybe someone would notice that a little boy with a potentially great future was buried here.

I glanced around the rest of the graveyard just to make sure there weren't any other souls to help. The cemetery was empty from what I could see. But I had this eerie feeling. Something was telling me that there might be another soul here. I wandered through the thick grass pushing away some of the weeds that had grown to almost 4 feet high. I stumbled upon gravestones of soldiers from World War II and World War I. The earliest gravestone I could find was from 1851.

I assumed that my eerie feeling was just a remnant of my experience with Tommy until I turned around and headed in the direction of my car. Suddenly I got the tingling feeling and was quickly greeted by a shock. A spirit in a full World War II sailor's outfit appeared to me.

He seemed startled when he saw me. "You can see me, can't you?" he said in excitement.

"Yes, I can. What is your name?"

"Harry S. Kaplan," he replied. "I was stationed in Hawaii. I was studying to be a naval officer and was getting mighty close."

"When were you stationed in Hawaii?" I said, obviously wondering if this man was involved in the attack on Pearl Harbor.

"Most of 1941," Harry said. "The last thing I remember is being attacked by Japanese bombers on December 7. Those bastards came out of nowhere. They flew low and dropped torpedoes and bombs into our ships. They got almost every one of our ships. I remember running towards the USS Oklahoma. It was starting to capsize, and I could see the sailors jumping into the water. I tried to get to them. They were so badly burned. I remember a loud sound and being thrown further underwater. The next thing I know I'm here."

I looked around for Harry's grave and found it hidden in the weeds. It was so hidden I almost tripped over it. It was a small stone with his name date of birth and death and a small plaque that said he was killed trying to save others in the Pearl Harbor attack. The grave was limestone, and it was getting harder to read the name and the dates engraved on it. The plaque was more visible. It had weathered to that green color. The letters were still easy to make out and there was an anchor symbol on the bottom of the plate signifying that he was in the Navy.

Harry was a true American hero who was lost in a cemetery that was completely forgotten. It really bugs me that so many of these heroes have been forgotten over the years. Talk about the greatest generation, these men lived through hell. Fighting on two fronts, watching their friends die right in front of them, and being forced to be away from their families for years at a time. So many of them came home maimed but they never complained. They went on with their lives as if nothing had happened.

My grandfather was in World War II and never said anything about it during my childhood like I've said before. I guess it was a part of his past that he wanted to forget about. So many of these men were true heroes and yet their stories were never told, mostly because they refused to tell them. So many of them received Medals of Honor, Silver Stars, and Bronze Stars, many of them put them away in the top drawer of their dressers and never shown to anyone. I didn't know my grandfather had received the Silver Star until after his death. He saved several men in a tank by grabbing a grenade that had been thrown under the tank and tossing it as far as he could. The grenade exploded in midair, and he was hit with some shrapnel. His wounds were not severe, but the tank surely would have exploded if the grenade had been left underneath it. He never made mention of this and the only way my grandma ever knew was because of the letter the Army had sent. She read it and put it back in the envelope for him to read. She said he looked it over quickly and stuck it in the top drawer next to the medal. She never saw him take it out again.

"Harry, do you have any idea how long you've been here?" I asked.

Harry looked at me in kind of a funny way, his head cocked to one side and said, "It feels like only about a week, but it could be wrong, it could be longer. I remember my family standing over there crying and seeing the stone with my name on it. I couldn't believe I was dead.

I figured there must have been some sort of a mistake, and I would wait here until was straightened out. I saw a bright light right after the explosion at Pearl Harbor but didn't go into it. Not long after arriving here I saw the light again over there by the two oak trees that are close to each other. I didn't want to go into the light. I'm only 21 years old, how can I be dead?"

I don't think he saw me shake my head, but I was both disappointed and upset that this man didn't get a chance to live his life, all because the people in the world can't get along well together. "What's your name?" Harry asked.

"My name is Scott."

"Scott?" he said. "What kind of a name is Scott? Sounds more like a last name than a first name."

With a grin, I explained to Harry that my parents gave me the name and I had nothing to do with it.

"I don't recall ever meeting a Scott before," Harry said with a smile on his face.

"Yeah, I get that a lot," I said, chuckling. "It wasn't a very popular name in 1941. But in the 1960s it became pretty popular." Then I became serious. "Harry, you're right about being dead. You've been dead for quite some time now, about 70 years. A lot has changed since you passed away. Unfortunately, most of your family has probably passed on, too. While you've been waiting to go into the light, I'm sure most of them have crossed over into it. I know you feel like you were shortchanged. But what's on the other side is better than a life here."

I noticed the fog around Harry's grave and his area was not as dense as some of the other areas I had seen. "Harry, can you make out anything beyond the fog? A lot has changed around you."

Harry reached up under his white sailor's cap and scratched his head, knocking the cap askew. "I know nobody takes care of this place anymore. You can barely find my marker. And some of the other people that are buried here, their headstones are gone. They were knocked over and taken by some teenage kids. I tried to stop them, but it was like I was invisible to them. I even tried to make some scary sounds to get them to leave but they didn't seem to hear anything, even though a couple of them were pretty spooked about being in a graveyard at night. I also notice the sound of the cars going down the road in front of the graveyard sound a lot different than they did when I was a kid. They sound a lot faster. How fast can a car go now, Scott?"

"Well, I've got my family car out there that'll do 150 miles an hour. But they won't let you go that fast on the road. Most big highways will only let you go 65 miles an hour."

"Wow," Harry exclaimed. "The fastest my car would do is about 50 mph. A friend of mine named Jimmy used to work on cars. We got his up to 75 one time. I guess everything changes doesn't it, Scott?"

"You wouldn't believe it if I told you, Harry. Japan is now a friend of the United States and so is Germany. But I got to tell you, we kicked their asses in World War II, which is the war in which your life was lost. December 7, 1941, was the first day of that war for the United States. A lot of good men died that day. You were one of them. But we got them back and we got them back good. Japan surrendered about four or five years after the war started. Hitler blew his own brains out just as the Russians and the Americans were about to capture him. We later found out he was responsible for killing about 6 million Jewish people. It was an awful war and one that will never be forgotten. There are only a handful of veterans of that war left. I always say thank you to them for their service when I meet them, just like I'm going to say thank you for your service, Harry."

"I didn't get much of a chance to serve," protested Harry. "I was killed the first day the war started! I wish I could've hung around long enough to do my duty and take out some of the enemy. I would have loved getting back at those dirty Japanese for what they did to us at Pearl Harbor. I hope we made them pay."

"Oh, don't worry about that, Harry," I said. "They paid dearly with a new weapon we dropped on their country, a very scary weapon that wiped out tens of thousands of their people. It was called the atomic bomb and it wiped out two cities. They finally surrendered after the second city was bombed. It was both a high point and the low point for the United States. We had to kill a lot of people, most of them innocent civilians, just to get the Japanese to surrender. But we saved a lot of American GIs by not having to invade Japan. So, in the long run I guess it was the thing to do."

Harry seemed both happy and confused at the same time. I don't think he understood the power of the atomic bomb. He was just glad we'd won the war. I guess I would be happy too if the people who killed me got the living crap kicked out of them.

Harry was a pacer. He kept walking back and forth between his grave and the oak trees where the light had been. I don't know if he was looking for the light to come back or if he was just pacing because he was nervous. "Well, Harry, now that I've explained what happened to you and what happened to the earth around you, are you ready to go into the light?"

"One more question, Scott. What are these silver things with the long white tail that fly overhead and make so much noise?" I realized Harry could see above him and was talking about jet planes. Jets really hadn't been used much in World War II. Only near the end of the war did they start using them, and then only as experimental aircraft. So Harry really didn't have much of an idea as to what they were. He said, "I'm pretty sure they're planes right? If they are, they fly very high and are very big. I've never seen one up close, they're always way up in the sky."

"Those are jet airliners," I explained. "A lot of people nowadays fly on those big jets from one place to another. You can take a jet airliner from New York to Los Angeles in about six hours. They travel at about 500 miles an hour. Some of the plane's seat 300 people. There are thousands of them in the sky at any given time during the day or night. A lot of people use them to get around for vacations and business. Pretty cool stuff, don't you think?"

Harry agreed. "I wondered what they were, but I didn't know they held that many people. That's amazing! I wish I could fly on one of them." I blew me away that something I took for granted was so incredibly mystifying to Harry. I didn't even pay attention to planes overhead anymore. Yet every time he saw one, he wondered what they were.

This was one of the great parts of my gift, being able to explain to these people what has changed and how important it is for them to go into the light so they can realize all the great stuff that the world has accomplished. Harry told me, "The light is back. It's right where it was before between the trees and it's getting bigger. I'm still afraid to go into it, Scott."

"I know you are Harry, that's why I'm here. I'm here to get you through the light to the other side. That's what I do. Are you ready to go? Because I have a feeling a lot of wonderful people are waiting for you on the other side. So, what do you say we make the trip?"

"Well, I've been here long enough," Harry said after a pause. "What the hell; let's take a chance! I'm not as scared as I was before, and I'm not as angry about dying so young. So maybe it's time for me to go."

I walked next to him, and we were quickly in the tunnel with the light in all its brilliance facing us. We came through on the other side and of course Grandpa was waiting for me. Grandpa said, "You brought me a hero this time, didn't you Scott?"

"Harry," I said. "This is my grandfather. He was also in the war. He was lucky enough to make it out alive. He greets me every time I bring someone up here. It's always good to see him."

Harry introduced himself to Grandpa and they shook hands. "I know your story Harry," Grandpa said, "and I'm sorry you felt short-changed. A lot of guys were shortchanged. But up here you'll get to live the life that you didn't on earth. Look to your right, Harry."

Harry turned his head to the right to see a beautiful woman walking towards him dressed in 1940s style clothing. She walked slowly towards him with the brim of her hat just slightly obscuring her face. As she approached, Harry's eyes widened. She looked up slowly to reveal a beautiful young face with ice blue eyes and a beautiful complexion. "Margaret is that you?" Harry asked in disbelief.

She looked directly into his eyes and touched his face ever so gently. "Yes, Harry it's me. I've waited so long for you to come. And now you're finally here and we can start our life together like we had planned before the war. Do you remember the plans we made? We can live those plans up here. The war won't get in the way."

"I missed you so much, Margaret while I was away at Pearl Harbor. Did you get my letters? I wrote you almost every day. Even as busy as we were, I would sometimes sneak to an open window and write in the moonlight just so I knew you would get another letter from me. I didn't want you to forget about me."

Shyness in her voice, Margaret said, "I still have all your letters. I would rush to the mailbox every day just to see if another letter was waiting for me. I read your letters over and over again, each one of them touched my heart just like you did, Harry."

As Harry and Margaret talked some more, I asked Grandpa what Margaret had done after Harry's death and how her life had progressed.

"Harry was her true love," Grandpa said, "and she never found another. She tried but could never seem to get him out of her head. Everyone was second-best compared to Harry. She worked for Inland Steel in Chicago for 40 years and remained single the entire time. Once a year on December 7 she would take out Harry's letters and read them. For years she cried when she read them. But as time went by, she learned to appreciate every word on the page as her only remaining memories of him. She passed away at the age of 85 of cancer. She's been waiting for Harry ever since. Because Harry was trapped in the other world, she came to me and asked if I would point you in the direction of Harry's grave in hopes of freeing him from his tether."

I looked to my right to see Harry and Margaret dancing slowly, Margaret with her head on Harry's shoulder. It was like time had stood still and their life was just beginning. Harry turned to me, took off his sailor hat, and reached out his hand. I shook it vigorously as was the custom in the 1940s.

"I don't know what I would've done if I hadn't run into you, Scott," Harry said." I may have been stuck there forever. You made it safe for me to go into the light. Now I'm with my best girl Margaret and we're going to get married."

Margaret was not surprised by this statement. She knew Harry was her only love and marriage was what she'd always had wanted for the two of them.

A small clear glass box appeared in my left hand almost magically. I looked at it, knowing what it was. I handed it to Harry and said, "I do believe this is for your bride-to-be."

Harry took the box from me, looked at Margaret and bent down to one knee. He opened the box in front of her without even looking at the ring, knowing for sure that it would be perfect. He said, "Margaret Marie Smith ... will you marry me?"

With both hands covering her mouth and tears streaming down her cheeks she said the one thing that she had waited to say for 70 years, "Yes!"

Harry picked her up and spun her around with such excitement that her hat blew off revealing her beautiful blonde hair. They slowly walked away holding hands and fading into the mist.

I turned to Grandpa, looked him in the eye and said, "Alright that one was the best one yet."

"Yeah, that was a special love story, one that you won't soon forget. I thought you would enjoy it and Margaret was the one who approached me to get the ball rolling. How could I turn down a beautiful woman like that?"

"Did she really keep his letters all those years?" I asked.

"Yes, she did, in a special box in the top drawer of her dresser. Every morning, she looked at the box and remembered Harry but she only took the letters out once a year. Too much sadness in the beginning, and regret later on for a life she felt was never fulfilled. That life will be fulfilled now up here in heaven."

We walked together back to the tunnel so I could return. "Well Scott, are you ready to go back?"

I asked Grandpa if I could stay just a little while longer because I saw that Harry and Margaret had come back out of the mist and Harry was being thrown a welcome home party by some of his sailor buddies. A lot of them looked young like Harry and I assumed they were his buddies from Pearl Harbor and passed the same day Harry did. There were banners and what looked like Harry's parents and family members all around. Margaret was showing off her ring and Harry was toasting his arrival. He held Margaret tightly around the waist and introduced her to all his friends.

Watching this from a distance warmed my heart. Again, I realized what I was doing was truly a gift from God, or at least a good gift from my Grandpa. Grandpa asked again if I was ready to go back. I nodded my head and was quickly thrown into reverse flying down the tunnel backwards and landing rather abruptly near Harry's grave. I spent several minutes clearing the grave site so that people would see Harry's grave if they chose to wander through the cemetery.

I got back in my car and slowly drove away from the long-forgotten cemetery. I wondered how many other cemeteries I was to visit in the near future. These were different than the roadside memorials, but when you think about it most cemeteries are roadside memorials, just not as crude. From this point forward, I felt I would have to look hard at every cemetery I went past.

CHAPTER 21

I reached home at the same time John was walking in from school. I asked him how his day went, and he seemed a little disappointed about something.

"I didn't do so well on my math test, Dad," he said.

I knew John was always hard on himself. What kind of grade did you get?" I asked.

"I got a B-."

I smiled and said, "As I recall all the rest of your math tests resulted in an A. So I don't think a B- will be a real big deal for you. Maybe you'll just have to work a little harder for the next one."

When I was in high school, I would've been jumping up and down for a B- on a math test. Here this kid was beating himself up because he got a B-. I would've proudly displayed that test on my refrigerator at home if it were me taking the test. Being that I was lucky to get out of high school, I appreciated John's hard work to maintain good grades. I wasn't that ambitious. I was more interested in sports and girls than I needed to be. And all it got me was 30 feet up in the air in a bucket that got hit by a semi-truck.

I wondered if things would be different if I had gone to college and was pushing papers at a desk somewhere. Most people don't get hit by semi-trucks when they're sitting at their desk. Maybe I'd have lived all my life without my amazing gift.

While lying in bed that night I explained to Eileen how touched I was by Harry's story and how the ending was so beautiful. After telling her the story she even had a tear in her eye.

"How can you keep doing this without getting emotionally attached to all these souls you've helped bring home?" she asked.

"Too late for that, Eileen," I said. "I've become pretty emotionally attached to every soul I worked with. It doesn't really bother me. I consider it a privilege to be working with them. I'm sure this is now my life's work. It's kind of nice to go to work and actually enjoy it." Though the rushing in and out of heaven was a little hair-raising, I'd seemed to adjust to it and knew the pitfalls of coming back every time.

And don't get me wrong, I always wanted to come back, but it was nice to be pain-free in heaven. I still had aches and pains and suffered with the ankle on a daily basis. My head had healed up nicely and most of my hair was back now. I had to grow it a little longer than before to cover the scar that had been left by the surgeon's knife, not to mention his saw. Because it was the second time, I'd had my head opened, the scar was worse. I think anytime it's a rush job their main concern is to get in there and fix the problem. Aesthetics are left in the dust. It really didn't bother me though. I wasn't up for any beauty queen contests and knew that I was lucky to be alive. Who cares about the scar when you get a second chance? I guess I'm like a cat. I seem to have more than my fair share of second chances. Nine lives I suppose.

Since the settlement, we'd paid off all our bills and now had very little money worries. The kids' college educations were already paid for and even though I could afford a new car I decided to stick with my old one. I bought Eileen a two-seater Lexus just to drive around because I felt like after all I had put her through, she deserved to have something fancy to drive. She wanted me to take it back, like most of the gifts I've given her, but this time I refused. She had not quit her job completely but had gone to more of a part-time schedule. She liked nursing and didn't want to leave it for good.

On the other hand, I was happy to leave my job because it had left me with scars and pain and probably a shortened lifespan. I couldn't imagine living well into my 80s with all the injuries I'd suffered. I'm sure at one point in time the warranty on one of these fixes was going to wear out. Whether it would be my brain aneurysm or my aorta or one of the many orthopedic problems, something was bound to take me early. Maybe I'd make it to my mid-sixties or even push to my 70s, but I had an eerie feeling that I wasn't being given the lifespan that most people are given.

Eileen always looked so cute pulling up in her little sports car and parking it in her own special space in the garage. Even though she'd wanted to take it back, she seemed to love the car. It made me happy to see her enjoying her little toy.

I continued to drive my Toyota Camry mainly because I figured I'd be stopping on the side of the road quite a bit in the future and didn't need to worry about the condition of my car while it was sitting on the side of the road. Besides, Eileen would let me drive her car whenever I needed a little spin in a sports car.

John was also eyeing up the car, but he had a couple years to wait before he could get his hands on it. And I was pretty sure Eileen wasn't going to let him touch it unless she was in the car with him.

Casey came home from school one afternoon and mentioned to me that the school's janitor had been killed in a car accident on the expressway near our house. Casey was young and didn't know it was I-80. He didn't have many details on the accident. They'd had an assembly at school to break the news to the students about the janitor, whose name was Darnell.

I'd met him several times while coaching basketball at school. He always had the basketballs out of the storage room lined up for me and would sometimes stay and watch practice. Darnell was tall probably about 6' 5" and I figured had played basketball in high school. Sometimes before the kids got there, he and I would shoot around, and he obviously had some skills. Occasionally he would stay and help me with some of the basic drills that we would assign the children. Nothing fancy; these were 10-year-olds. But he loved kids and I think really enjoyed working with them.

I called the school the next morning to ask when the funeral and visitation would be held. After talking to the secretary Gina and getting the information, we started to small talk about what a great guy Darnell was.

He was a favorite of all the employees, not to mention the children. He was kind and always there to help. His demeanor was that of a big teddy bear and he never let the rowdy kids get to him.

I asked Gina if she knew the details of the accident. She said some idiot was coming home from the bar after an eight-hour binge and had cut him off, slamming into the front of his car and rolling both cars over. Unfortunately, Darnell did not have a seatbelt on. He was ejected from the car and died on his way to the hospital. The other driver was also killed. So often the drunk walks away and ruins the life of another person, and I guiltily felt that maybe there had been some poetic justice. I guess I shouldn't be so hardnosed about it, since somewhere his family was suffering too.

"Gina, do you know exactly where the accident happened?" I asked her for an obvious alternative motive.

"On I-80 just south of Cedar Road," she said. "Both cars flipped and went down the embankment. They landed up against the fence. A friend of mine drove past the accident. She didn't know it was a friend of mine, and she gave me a really detailed description of the scene. A little too descriptive, honestly."

"I'm sorry to hear that," I said. "It's a shame to lose him. He was a great guy and fantastic with the kids."

"We're really going to miss him around here," Gina said. We said our goodbyes and I knew I had a trip to make. Not everyone stays between worlds, but I had to make sure Darnell wasn't trapped between the two dimensions.

I decided to get in my car and get on I-80 going eastbound and make a U-turn, somewhere east of Cedar. Traffic was too heavy so I ended up going all the way to LaGrange Road and turning around there, in a legal fashion I might add, since it's illegal to make a U-turn on that part of the highway. I got back on going westbound and slowly approached the Cedar Road bridge. I stayed in the right lane going slower than I should have been and pulled over on the shoulder.

I could see the torn-up grass and the destroyed fence at the bottom of the embankment. I put my flashers on as I always do and started to walk down the embankment. To my surprise the only person visible was the other driver in the accident. Darnell had obviously passed on without a problem. I guess it didn't surprise me as much as I thought. Darnell was a good man and had led a pretty clean life. He probably knew to go into the light.

This other man obviously did not. Part of me wanted to walk away and head back to my car. Why should I help this guy cross over after taking away one of the nicest guys I've ever met? But something was pulling me towards him. I assumed it was my grandfather and I proceeded to the area near the fence where he was sitting. As I approached, I felt the tingling in my legs and the shock as I entered the fog that surrounded him.

He looked up at me and quickly said, "Who the hell are you?"

"My name is Scott. Who the hell are you?" I replied sternly. I figured I'd match my demeanor to his, because at this point, he wasn't one of my favorite people in the world.

"My name is Tom," he replied.

"Well now that we've got the niceties out of the way, why don't you tell me why you're still here?" I said still with a little attitude in my voice.

"I'm sorry I'm being such a jerk, I don't remember what happened or why I'm here. I can't seem to get out of this fog. I've been sitting up against this fence wondering what the hell happened. I remember leaving the bar at about 5am. I worked 3 to 11 and got off at about midnight. I hate working overtime; it just ruins the night. I stopped at the bar to have a few before I went home."

"According to the reports you had more than a few," I said in an accusing tone.

"What do you mean, 'the reports?" he asked.

"Well let me tell you what happened, Tom," I said in a sarcastic manner. "You had way too many drinks at the bar to even consider driving. You got in your car and decided to drive home instead of being a bigger man and calling for a cab or having a friend come pick you up. On the way home you must've been weaving and hit the front end of a car driven by a friend of mine. His name was Darnell. Both of your cars flipped over, and both you and Darnell were killed in the accident."

Tom seemed to realize the finality of my statement, and looking up at me said what so many have said before, "You mean I'm dead?"

"Yes Tom you're dead," I reported. "The fog you see around you is the only world you can see right now. For some reason I've been given a gift. I can see you even though you've passed away. You're stuck here for some reason, most likely because you haven't realized that you're dead."

Tom began to cry. "What about my wife and my little daughter? She's only two."

This statement made me feel a little more compassionate towards Tom. He had obviously made a huge mistake and was realizing how much it would affect his loved ones. I realized there was nothing I could do about Darnell being gone, but maybe I could help cross Tom over.

"Tom, you obviously had a pretty significant drinking problem."

"Yeah, my wife was always on me about it, especially when I would drive home from the bar. I figured I was a good driver even when I was drunk, and nothing like this could ever happen to me. I don't even remember hitting your friend's car. I never should've never gotten behind the wheel that night. I should have never gotten behind the wheel any of those nights. I already have had two DUIs and was driving on a suspended license. But I had to go to work. So I took my chances and drove. I'd been trying to stay away from the bar. The day just got to me and I figured it wouldn't hurt to stop for just one or two. I ran into some friends and before I knew it, it was five o'clock in the morning and I was drunk out of my mind. I snuck out of the bar as it was just about to close so none of my friends would bug me about drinking and driving. If I'd stayed a little longer maybe one of them would've given me a ride home. Now I've lost it all."

Tom seemed remorseful but also surprised that he wasn't able to navigate his way home in the state he was. It's what most drunk drivers think. "I'm not that drunk, I can make it home." I have grabbed many a set of keys out of people's hands at parties. In my job I had seen too many drunk drivers and the results of their actions on the road. We'd find a roadside memorial next to a light pole that had been knocked down. It was always our job to put the pole back up or replace it. It was sad to see the memorial and then find out later in the paper the accident had been caused by a drunk driver.

"Tom, did you see a bright light after the accident?" I asked him.

"I saw it, but it wasn't here long," Tom replied. "After that I saw a circle of fire in the place the bright light was. Then that went away. Now that I know I'm dead, I must be destined for hell. That must be what the ring of fire meant. If hell is my only choice I might as well stay here."

I had never heard of or seen this ring of fire he mentioned. Grandpa had never mentioned it either. But I've never come across a man with so many demons in his past. Tom obviously was going to have to pay for his sins, or whatever you call them, when he crossed over. I think maybe the ring of fire was a signal for that. Suddenly I started to see the bright light. "Tom," I said, calling his attention to the glow. "I see the bright light. Look to your right, do you see it?"

"I do," said Tom with some excitement in his voice. It looked like Tom was going to be given a chance to enter heaven, but I assume with some stipulations.

"Walk with me towards the light and we'll see what it has in store for you. You might as well face the music now and get it over with. You're obviously being given a chance to enter heaven, but I have a feeling you're going to have to answer some serious questions."

We walked towards the light, Tom with a hesitant gait, and we were sucked into the tunnel and rushed through at high speed. As we began getting closer and closer to the light, it began to dim, and flames started to appear at the sides of the light. We went through and landed on the other side.

Grandpa was there and looked at me and said in a quiet voice that wasn't audible to Tom. "You're about to see something that may scare you a little. Try not to let it bother you. Tom has some demons following him. He will have to fight them off to enter heaven. They're not demons as you imagine. They are people in his life that he's hurt greatly by his drinking."

Tom was picked up by a mist and slammed into a chair sitting upright. A white screen appeared before him, and images started to flash across the screen. It started with his parents greeting him at the door after a drunken teenage party where he had driven home in his dad's car and wrecked the front end of it. His mother was crying, and his father was screaming at him. Not about the car, but about how he could've killed himself or someone else.

It flashed to the parents lying in bed and Tom's father trying to console his mother. She stated how she worried so much that Tom was going to kill himself with his drinking. That obviously not been the first time Tom had come home this way.

As he watched the flickering, heart-wrenching scene, Tom began crying inconsolably and I could tell he was actually feeling the pain his mother and father had felt all the nights he had come home drunk.

The screen then flashed to what appeared to be Tom's prom night. It showed him drinking in the backseat of the limousine. All his friends looked disgusted as Tom continued to drink himself into oblivion. His date was embarrassed and when she walked into the prom she immediately sat Tom down and lectured him about how he was ruining the evening. He told her to go to hell and continued to drink. His date stormed off to a corner and cried with her friends. She said, "I really liked Tom, but I can't handle his drinking anymore."

Tom passed out at the table they were sitting at about midway through the prom. He had to be carried by some of his friends to the limo. The limo driver was kind enough to drop him off at his house. Tom's friends carried him up to the front door and rang the bell. Tom's parents answered the door and were shocked by the condition of their son. The boys carried Tom up to his bedroom and laid him in his bed, still dressed in his tuxedo. Tom's mother stayed awake all night watching Tom to make sure he didn't choke on his own vomit when he threw up.

After he was out of danger, she cried herself to sleep again. Tom's date for the prom never spoke to him again.

By this time Tom's tears were streaming down his face at a steady pace. The screen flickered and we were taken to a scene in the Dean's office at a college. Tom was being expelled for excessive drinking on campus. It was obvious Tom had a good brain and had been given a great opportunity to get an education at a fine college. He drank that opportunity away. The scene changed to Tom at home drinking daily after being kicked out of college. He got a job as a night watchman where he could continue to drink on the job. After all the executives left around 6:30 or 7:00 at night, he could start drinking. By the end of his shift at 11 o'clock he was already half in the bag.

It was embarrassing for Tom to see what he had become. He squirmed uncomfortably in his seat as he continued to sniffle and sob. It was obvious to me that this was part of the ongoing punishment he was receiving for wasting his life at the bottom of the bottle.

Finally, Tom found someone who thought she could change him, his wife. He seemed to try to give up the bottle at the beginning of their relationship, but it soon fell by the wayside. Their marriage was rocky to say the least. There were many fights and drunken evenings with Tom passing out on the couch. When his wife got pregnant Tom made another attempt at giving up alcohol. This attempt lasted about three months, though it was halfhearted, and Tom had snuck many a drink during this time.

The night of the baby's birth, Tom was in the bar and noticed his wife was calling him on his cell phone. The screen flickered as Tom checked his cell phone, noted that it was his wife, and ignored the call. She was in labor, and Tom was as drunk as ever sitting in a bar missing the birth of his child. His beautiful little girl was born without his presence.

The marriage went downhill from there and they were not speaking to each other. When he was sober, Tom would take the time to play with his little daughter and genuinely enjoyed it. But these moments were few and far between. He spent most of his nights sleeping in his recliner after a night of binge drinking. He had missed two birthday parties and forgotten at least one anniversary. During these three times a flash of his wife's face and her general disgust with him crossed the screen. She had many sleepless nights wondering if he was going to come home alive.

The screen flickered again, and it was the night of the first DUI. Tom's wife had been awakened by a phone call from the police saying her husband had been picked up for DUI. She was forced to pick him up the next day from the police station, where two police officers helped load him into the car because he was so sick with alcohol poisoning. His license was suspended for six months, and the court costs drained their savings. His wife's worries turned to anger and as he realized that he continued to squirm in his chair.

The second DUI occurred only two months later, and Tom's license was suspended indefinitely. His wife begged him to take the bus to work but he said he was going to drive no matter what the court said. His ignorance and arrogance towards his wife and the system could not be surpassed.

Now with a flash we were at the accident scene where two paramedics were pounding on Tom's chest trying to revive him. Tom saw himself getting out of his own body and sitting up against the fence.

He also saw Darnell exiting his body, looking at him with total disgust, and then entering the light.

By this time Tom was crying inconsolably and asking for Grandpa to make it stop. Finally, the screen went blank and disappeared.

From a distance a figure walked towards us. As he approached, I could see the big frame of Darnell. A chair appeared directly across from Tom. As Darnell reached us, his face was filled with anger. He grabbed Tom by the lapels and pulled him out of his seat, lifting him at least a foot off the ground. He slammed Tom to the ground and Tom cowered in fear.

Darnell picked him up again and got directly in his face. "Do you realize what you've taken from me? I had a life, a family, children that love me and you took it all away with one night of drinking. All because you didn't have the guts to stop yourself!" Darnell slammed Tom back into his seat and slapped him hard in the face. Tom hit the floor again this time shaking with fear.

Darnell walked towards me and Grandpa. "I'm sorry you had to see that Scott, but God gave me the right to confront Tom and express my anger towards him. It was not my time to leave the earth. Tom cut my time short, and I wanted to make sure he paid for his mistake."

"Darnell," I said, "I can't say I blame you; I would've done the same thing."

Grandpa chimed in. "Darnell, you're going to have to find it in your heart to forgive Tom for what he's done to you. That's what heaven is about. It may take you years and Tom will suffer the consequences until you do. Tom's demon was alcohol. We don't expect you to forgive him immediately but maybe someday you'll find it in your heart to forgive him for what he's done to you."

"Don't count on it," Darnell sneered. "The son of a bitch took every-thing away from me. I want him to suffer like my family's suffering right now. Then maybe someday I'll forgive him."

With that Tom was picked up by what seemed to be an evil mist and swept away beyond my view. I asked Grandpa where he was going.

"He will feel the pain he caused by his actions," Grandpa answered.

"The pain he caused to everyone, from his little baby growing up without a father all the way to Darnell's children knowing that they would never see their dad again. He will feel that pain deeply and realize the mistakes he made in his life. He will ask Darnell for forgiveness many times before he accepts. Then he will be let into heaven. But the suffering he will have to go through will never be forgotten even as he enters paradise. It will always be a scar on his soul. Most people who enter heaven have no remorse. Tom will feel remorse until everyone he affected in life has crossed over to heaven. He will have to ask for their forgiveness too and hopefully by then they will forgive him.

"He will be back at the beginning of the light someday and will move on into the heaven that most people call paradise. Right now, he'll be in a transition state."

"Is that like purgatory?" I asked, remembering my Catholic upbringing.

Grandpa said, "Purgatory was just a name one of the Popes made up. It's not really filled with fire and brimstone, whatever brimstone is. This is just an area that houses people who have failed at being good. It's a learning experience and is taught by people who have led exemplary lives. It's like school in heaven. Tom won't be there as long as some others. Not that his crimes were minor, but there are a lot worse people than Tom. And remember time almost stands still up here. So it may not seem as long for Tom as you think."

"What about Darnell?" I asked. "He was a great guy. He was so good with the kids and really loved working with them. He made an impression on a lot of people, and it was always good. Will he be able to get over his anger?"

"He already has," Grandpa said. "Once Darnell left our area his anger was gone. He could move on to enjoy his heaven; one surrounded by his family and friends and also children. Darnell is a lot like you. He has a special talent with children. We put children who have no families with people like Darnell and yourself to give them the families they never had. That reminds me, Eileen is going to suggest something to you soon about adopting a baby. I want you to consider this with all your heart.

It is something you can afford to do now, and it would be nice to give a little child a home who has never had one."

This completely took me by surprise. I would've never thought to adopt another child. Not that I have anything against adoption, but after all we've been through, I think it would be a lot of stress on the family to add another soul to the mix. But Grandpa suggested it for a reason. I wasn't sure what the reason was, but I figured it must be a good one.

"Just consider it," grandpa said. "You don't have to do it, but I want you to think about it."

"Well now that you've told me, how can I do anything but think about it?" I admitted.

"You don't have to do it Scott, but there are a lot of lost little children on earth who've been either given up on by their parents or abandoned by the system. Many of them are practically in your own backyard. You won't have to go far to adopt a baby, you just have to be open-minded about what kind of baby you want."

Grandpa's words rang loud and clear with me. You see so many people running off to China and spending tens of thousands of dollars to adopt the little Chinese girl when there are thousands of African American children here in the United States who need to be adopted.

I looked at Grandpa as he looked outward towards the open field and the mountains we always had as a backdrop. There were thousands of little children playing. The entire field was converted instantly to a huge playground. These children played together and had access to every piece of sports or playground equipment they wanted. They all had smiles on their faces and the sound of laughter was almost deafening. There was a section for little babies and toddlers that were being supervised by what appeared to be angels. Most of the younger kids were running and playing, but they were under control.

"You see out there, don't you?" Grandpa asked. "More than a thousand children are available for adoption in your state alone. As you can see most of them are African American or Hispanic. A lot of them were born to unwed mothers in their teens and were given up for adoption immediately after birth. Unfortunately, a lot of these children go un-adopted. So out of all those children in that field, I'm sure you and Eileen could find one to give a home to. Just think about it. You and I love children and you would have a blast with a new baby. It would be a lot of work, but you would be rewarded greatly."

"You make a good point grandpa; I just wonder if I'm too old to put myself through this again. Eileen may have the energy, but I'm not sure I do. I guess there's only one way to find out, but once you commit, you commit for life." I spoke.

Grandpa looked at me and smiled in almost a childlike manner and said, "I'm going to play with the kids, but it is time for you to go back. I love to play with the kids, it makes me feel young again."

At that point I began my trip back to reality with Grandpa's words ringing in my ears. Young again, huh?

Before I knew it, I was back at the site where Darnell and Tom had left this world. My car was still parked on the side of the road with the flashers on and no one seemed to have noticed that I had been standing near the fence for five or 10 minutes. I had been lucky so far not to have had a police car pull up behind me and interrupt my work. Maybe it was meant to be that way. They say timing is everything, so maybe God was controlling the time I saw the souls so I could avoid contact with the world around me while I was helping these lost souls. Who knows? This thing has been a mystery to me since day one. But I was enjoying the entire experience. I got back into my little Toyota Camry, signaled to get back on the expressway, and took off toward home.

CHAPTER 22

Darnell's wake and funeral were attended by many people. I stopped in at the wake to pay my respects. I saw his family and his kids, all teen-agers. I wanted so badly to tell them that their father was okay but that wasn't possible. I couldn't share my experiences with others because it would be too hard to explain and certainly wouldn't be understood.

As I walked into the funeral home, I noticed Darnell standing to the left of the casket by his own head. Not only did this shock me and make me speechless in the receiving line, but I couldn't take my eyes off of him. I gathered my wits by the time I reached his immediate family in the receiving line. I told them that I worked with Darnell while I was coaching basketball at school, and he would help me work with the kids. I told them that he did it without my asking; that he just seemed to enjoy helping the kids learn how to play basketball.

Darnell's oldest son spoke up and said, "That sounds like my dad, did he tell you that he played professional basketball?"

"He never mentioned it," I said. "But I often wondered if he had some experience at a higher level. Where did he play?"

"He spent most of his time in Italy playing for one of the teams over there. He came back to the states and played for a couple years with the Boston Celtics. He saved his money from his professional career and put it away for his kids. He didn't have to work, he just loved being around the kids."

To say I was shocked would be the understatement of the year: first seeing Darnell by his own casket, and then finding out he was so much more than just a janitor. Everyone has a life before you meet them. What goes on in their life will be a mystery to you unless that person decides to share it. For some reason Darnell never felt it necessary to brag about his time as a professional basketball player. The only thing that was important to him was his family and the kids at school.

I approached his wife, gave her a big hug and told her how sorry I was. She had heard the conversation I'd had with her oldest son and knew who I was.

"Darnell mentioned you very fondly. He loved the way you coached. He said you were all about the kids, not about winning. That's the way it should be for every coach." I didn't know what to say except thank you. I nodded my head and approached the casket. As I knelt, I looked to my left to see Darnell's spirit start to bend over towards me.

He said, "Good turnout, don't you think?" Darnell always had such a great sense of humor it was hard not to giggle. I nodded my head but didn't say anything.

Darnell continued, "You don't have to say anything; you've done enough for me already. I've forgiven Tom for what he did to me, and I know my family will be okay. I'll miss seeing you around the gym." I nodded again and tried to look like I was deep in prayer. "You think about what your grandpa said. You'd make a great dad even the second time around." I nodded my head a third time and got up from the casket. He waved to me, and I went on my way.

This left me wondering if every time I went to a funeral or a wake, I would see the dead next to the casket. I wasn't sure how I could handle that and hoped that it would be quite some time before I would have to find out.

CHAPTER 23

Eileen met me at the door when I returned home. The kids had been fighting and she was a little frazzled. I put on my big daddy hat and went to have a talk with them.

"Listen," I scolded. "I don't know what you've got your mother all frazzled about, but it's going to stop right now."

They stood with their heads down and looked ashamed by being yelled at by their dad. Most of the time I could just shoot them a look and that was enough to stop the fighting. Most of the time the fighting was about nothing. All siblings fight as part of growing up. I think this one involved John teasing Dana and then Casey getting in on the action. It's tough to be the little girl in the house. But we straightened everything out and went on with dinner.

Eileen was quite a cook, which would explain my growing girth around the spare tire region of my body. I'd lost so much weight during the accident that I was making up for lost time. Things kind of got out of hand. I'd put on an extra 20 pounds and Eileen was trying to make our dinners healthier. Healthy eating was not as much fun as putting on the extra 20 pounds, but any extra weight I could take off would probably be good for my bad ankle.

The kids asked if I went to Darnell's wake. I said, "Yes I stopped by and there was quite a crowd of people there. People really loved Darnell. Your principal was there Dana, and so was yours, John and Casey. I saw a lot of teachers too. Darnell's family was genuinely touched by the turnout. He was a great man and we're all going to miss him."

"Dad," Dana asked. "What do you think happens to you when you die?" Needless to say, this took me by surprise. I guess it shouldn't have with all that had gone on in the last couple days. The children hadn't really experienced losing anyone that was young before Darnell died, so this was all new for them.

Eileen and I had never been much for organized religion. We wanted our children to make their religious decisions on their own when they were adults. They had been baptized in the Catholic Church near our house, but we rarely attended any services. Religion has caused more wars and deaths than all the world wars put together. I wasn't a big fan of religion, to say the least.

But Dana seemed to be looking for more of an answer than I had given her in the past. I tried to explain. "You know what heaven is, don't you? If you're a good person and treat people well, including your mom and dad (I had to throw that in there), when you die you go to heaven. Heaven is a beautiful place where you get to do so many wonderful things. They call it paradise for a reason. Remember how beautiful the beach was when we went on vacation?"

She nodded. "Yes, I do Dad. It was the prettiest thing I ever saw."

"Well, I imagine heaven is a lot like that, 24 hours a day."

She smiled and seemed satisfied with my answer. If she only knew that I had contact with heaven and knew so much more about it than I could tell her. Eileen looked at me with a nod and seemed satisfied with the answer I'd given Dana. We finished up dinner and got to the homework. The homework was slowly growing beyond my knowledge base, and it was getting tougher and tougher to help the kids. Thank God for the internet, that's all I have to say.

I had taken on my new role as a house husband with some reservations. Most of my time was spent cleaning up after the kids and doing all the reading I missed out on while I was recovering from my accident.

Since my aneurysm repair the headaches had pretty much disappeared, so I could read again without any pain. I joined a health club to try to continue my goal to improve my health and get rid of my spare tire. I went there at least three times a week and worked mostly on upper body type exercises. I could ride a recumbent bike which gave me some cardiovascular workout, but that was about the extent of it.

I also began to enjoy planning vacations. Now that we had no money problems, I wanted to see the country. I was constantly bugging Eileen with brochures and ideas about where we could take our next vacation. She always seemed interested but I'm sure sometimes I got on her nerves.

I had never seen the Grand Canyon and really wanted to go see it. She was worried that this would be pretty boring for the kids. I said as long as the kids had a pool and a nice hotel they would be just fine. We could even take a mule trip down to the bottom of the canyon. I just wanted to see Eileen and the kids on mules. The thought of it made me laugh. I also wanted to check into camping down at the bottom of the canyon for the night. It sounded like fun to me and I think I would be able to convince them of that. We had already been to Disney World a couple of times and I figured it was time to see some of the natural beauty in the United States. You know; Mount Rushmore, Yellowstone National Park, and maybe San Diego.

CHAPTER 24

Although I knew this was coming, it was still a surprise to me. Eileen came home from work at the hospital and mentioned how a little baby girl had been abandoned by her teenage mother at the hospital. She was African American and seemed to be in good health. The mother was not a drug addict, she was just very young.

"Scott," Eileen said, "this baby is so cute I could just bundle her up and take her home."

"I'm sure the hospital would frown upon that," I said with a smile. I reflected back on what Grandpa had said to me about taking in a new family member.

Eileen said, "I really think I want to adopt this baby." The look on her face was that of a loving mother who had already accepted the challenge of raising another child. Although I couldn't protest the idea, I did have to point out that it would change our lives pretty significantly.

"Are you sure you want to start this all over again?" I asked.

She snuggled up to me, which was her way of getting anything she ever wanted, and said, "We can afford to give this baby a life. A real-life. Not one in a foster home or an orphanage. One with our family. She'll have brothers and a sister and two loving parents."

"Well, how would we go about doing this?" I asked.

She looked at me in surprise as if she were expecting an argument. The excitement welled up in her face when she realized I wasn't against the idea. "I already talked to social services," she said. "They would have to interview both of us and the family to make sure the baby would be a good fit for us. We'd have to go through small court proceedings and then the baby would be ours." She made it sound really easy, but I knew it would involve more than that. I was willing to go through it because Grandpa said it would be a good idea and I loved the way Eileen looked at me when she talked about adopting this baby.

"I hope you don't mind" she said, "but I already have a name picked out for her. How does Catie sound to you?" We would be naming her after Eileen's mother, Catherine, known as Catie. Since I'd had that encounter with Catherine in heaven, I thought it would be a great idea.

"Catie it is," I said.

The next month was filled with social worker visits and court proceedings. But within two days of the month end, we brought Catie home from the hospital. With John, Casey, and Dana, it was like having three little extra mamas running around the house. They'd get diapers and bottles and help in any way they could. They all tried to make Catie smile whenever they could. They were something to watch, let me tell you. Eileen carried Catie around just like she had done with all three children before. She looked so comfortable with a child at her side.

Of course, I was no different. I played with her and tried to make her laugh and hoped that she wasn't just smiling because of gas. I must say I was pretty excited about having this new little life in our home.

We never knew the mother or father of Catie and didn't want to know them. We figured they could go on with their young lives and maybe someday start families of their own. We were just glad that their little mistake became our little gift.

We were told Catie had been abandoned by her mother at the hospital. We had no reason to doubt this, but the hospital was pretty vague on the reasons she had abandoned the child. The father was not in the picture from the time of conception. We had her all to ourselves and that's all that mattered to us. She was spoiled by her brothers and sister and of course by mom and dad. My parents were amazed that the whole process went so quickly. Eileen's family was excited to have the baby around again. She had greenish hazel eyes and was light skinned. She had a thick head of hair and was a little on the chunky side. She was already smiling and had a little laughter by her three-month birthday. John carried her around like he had a new best friend. Casey and Dana never stopped trying to make her laugh. We were fixated on her from the day we brought her home.

We brought Catie back to the doctor for her three-month checkup. The pediatrician's office was in the same hospital where she was born. After Catie's checkup we decided to bring her up to the nursery to see all the nurses that it helped us get through the adoption. They took care of Catie for a month while we were getting through all the paperwork and legal issues that go along with an adoption. They had become really close with Catie and were all happy to see her.

Eileen was a doting mother, and I played the excited father to the hilt. "She's getting so big," admired one of the nurses.

"She's not missing any meals," Eileen said wryly, bringing a laugh. I left the ladies alone to adore the baby and took the opportunity to go to the washroom.

On the way back I heard a voice come from one of the patient rooms. "Sir?"

I wasn't sure she was referring to me, so I kept walking slowly. "Sir!" she shouted with more emphasis. She got my attention, and I turned around to see a young African-American girl about 14 or 15 years old. She was in a hospital gown and the front of the gown was soaked with blood.

"Oh my God," I said. "You need help! I'll get one of the nurses! Sit down here while I call for help."

The girl looked at me as if I was confused. She said, "I feel fine. There's no problem with me. I just want to talk to you." She moved back into her room, and I followed her from the hallway. The room was filled with mist. I realized my gift was extending into another environment.

She said, "Something's wrong, no one will talk to me! I can't get them to even give me a new gown! I haven't seen my baby yet. Do you know where my baby is?"

Now I realized something bad must have happened to her. The amount of blood on her gown and on her bed was far too much for a normal delivery. Something had gone terribly wrong in this room. As I entered further into the room, I got closer to the bed and felt the shocking feeling. On the edge of the bed sat Darnell. I hadn't seen him at first and I wondered if he had just appeared.

The girl looked at him, frightened, and said, "Dad what are you doing here? You're dead and it's scaring me that I can see you."

"Don't be afraid, little pumpkin," Darnell said, looking at her with love. "This is my friend Scott, and he helps people like you and me. He's good guy." Darnell stood up and hugged his daughter. "Little darling, I've got something to tell you and you're not going to like it. Do you remember delivering the baby? How you were pushing so hard and then the doctors and the nurses started running around a lot?"

Darnell's daughter looked up at him and said, "They kept calling my name they kept saying 'Chantel can you hear us?' I could hear them, but I couldn't talk to them. It was like I was invisible. They started running around trying to get as many people in the room as possible. They put a tube down my throat and started pounding in my chest. They brought in machine after machine hooking me up and trying to pull some life out of me. They had to cut my belly open and pull out the baby. Then I was out of my body. I was bleeding, I was bleeding bad. All I could see was my baby and all the nurses trying to revive her. They got her breathing again. I walked with my baby to the nursery, but I couldn't see my baby's face. There was a mist around the nursery, and I could see the nurses working on the baby, but I couldn't see her. I started to cry and then walked back here to my room. I saw them cover my head with a sheet."

Darnell looked at Chantel and said, "Little pumpkin, you know passed away during the delivery of your baby, don't you? You bled to death. You're stuck here between earth and heaven. That's why my friend Scott is here. Actually, he's here for two reasons. You know that no-good boyfriend of yours?"

Chantel looked down to the floor, very embarrassed by the question.

Darnell continued. "That son of a bitch didn't want the baby and he gave her up for adoption. He didn't even want to see the baby. In fact, he was happy to wash his hands of the whole situation. Your mother was not in the right emotional state to take on a baby after you and I passed away. So I helped get someone to adopt your baby." Darnell's eyes slowly moved over to me. It just dawned on me where he was going with this story. Catie was Chantel's baby and Darnell's granddaughter!

"You got my baby?" Chantel asked, her eyes wide with surprise.

"Well, I didn't know it until this minute, but according to your father we did. My wife and I. We wanted to adopt a baby and my wife is a nurse here. She doesn't work on this floor but the nurses knew she had talked about adopting a baby. We thought you just gave the baby up for adoption. They didn't tell us you died. All we know is that you gave us a beautiful baby and she's become part of our family. We love her very much."

"Why would a white family want a black baby?" demanded Chantel, genuinely confused.

I looked at Chantel, her hands on her hips with the kind of attitude only a 15-year-old girl can muster and answered her as honestly as I could. "We just wanted a baby, we didn't care what color it was. We want to love this baby and take good care of her for you. We named her Catie."

Chantel laughed and said, "That's a white-girl name!"

I couldn't fault her for that statement because Catie was a white-girl name. I smiled. "I guess it is a pretty white name but it's the one we always wanted for another girl. I promise we'll take good care of her. She's already become such a big part of our family. We love her so much."

Chantel began to cry. She walked over to her father and hugged him while crying on his shoulder. Darnell held her tight and said, "Chantel you don't know how lucky you are. You have one of the best families to take care of your baby. I knew Scott when I was alive. He's going to be a great father for your baby. And your baby will grow up with a father. Besides, you were way too young to have a baby and you know that! Scott and his wife can take care of your baby better than you could have. Now let Scott help you come with me, and we'll all go to see heaven."

Darnell looked at me and nodded his head in the direction of the light. To Chantel, I said, "Don't be afraid of the light. We're going to the most wonderful place you'll ever see."

Darnell and I put our arms around Chantel and walked into the light. We were thrust through the light with such speed that I think it shocked Chantel. When we stopped at the end of the tunnel Grandpa was there waiting for us. He looked up at all three of us and with a smile on his face and a huge laugh he said, "Three for one! It's like a big party up here! We've been waiting for you Chantel. There are so many people up here who want to see you, including your baby girl."

I explained to Chantel that loved ones, even though not dead, could appear in heaven with the deceased. Darnell turned to his right to receive the baby from an older black woman. "Thank you, mama," Darnell said, and he handed the baby to Chantel, who began to cry.

The baby was the spitting image of Catie. Grandpa patted me on the shoulder as if to say it was okay. I'd had a fear that our baby would be taken away because Chantel had the baby up here in heaven, but Grandpa's reassurance helped me realize that this wouldn't happen.

Darnell said "Well it's time for us to move along. I know you'll take good care of the baby down there on earth. Remember she is my granddaughter, Scott! Make me proud." Chantel and her father walked away slowly to meet up with the family that had already crossed over. Darnell's mom had taken the baby back and was singing to her.

"That little girl went through a lot being pregnant at 15, and then dying on the delivery room table," grandpa said. "Do you see why I pointed you in the direction I did?"

"Well, I sure do now! If I'd had any idea that this baby was related to Darnell, it would've made me even more excited to have her! We really love her, Grandpa. Have you seen her? She's so cute! Everybody loves her."

Grandpa smiled and said, "Sometimes us old guys know what we're talking about, don't you think?"

I couldn't question grandpa's intuition; he was spot on. I just had one more question for him. "I'm just curious about something. What happens when my Catie gets old and passes away? Would she still be a part of our family, or will she become one with the baby Darnell's family has? I thought when you go to heaven you get to be with your family."

"The Catie up here in heaven is her own soul now," Grandpa answered. "The Catie you have down on earth is also her own soul. It's like splitting atoms. They both become separate life energies. So, your Catie will always be a part of your family. And the Catie up here will always be a part of Darnell's family. Almost like twins, they will coincide in both heaven and earth. When little Catie's soul crosses over, you as a family will be waiting for her."

Grandpa's explanation satisfied my fears and made me feel better about the situation. I liked the idea of splitting souls in cases such as this. As I watched Darnell and Chantel fade into the mist with Grandma and their baby in her arms, I knew that both their family and ours would forever be touched by this baby. Grandpa gave me the look that always accompanied the start of my trip back to earth and said, "Are you ready to head back? We've done great work again. Or should I say you've done great work again? You're really getting the hang of this. I must warn you your challenges may get harder. So be ready for them."

Being thrust through the tunnel backwards had become almost a routine for me. I found myself back at the hospital. I came out of the room Chantel had been in when she summoned me over. Eileen was at the front desk doting over the baby and showing her to every possible person that passed by.

I walked up to the desk slowly, still recovering from my trip back. I had only been gone for a couple of minutes, but she still wondered what happened to me. I just told her I had a little encounter back in one of the rooms and I would tell her about it on the way home.

After Eileen had said all her goodbyes, we took the elevator down to the main lobby and she spotted one more person she wanted to show the baby to. I think he worked in housekeeping on the same floor with Eileen. He was very excited to see the baby. He was a large black man that looked like he was in his early 60s. "She's got a tan just like me!" he joked. As we all laughed, he continued, "I'm proud of you both that you didn't let her race get in the way of adopting a beautiful child. And I know she'll grow up in a good home because you two are good people."

We both thanked him for his kind words. I slowly walked toward the front door with Eileen by my side and our little bundle of joy in her arms. We put her in her car seat, which was something we had to learn to use all over again. Car seats had become much more complicated than we remembered. I never thought I'd have to read the directions for a car seat, but in this case it was a necessity.

We arrived home to be greeted by John, Casey, and Dana who all quickly scooped up the baby and started with the challenge of making her laugh. They had taken to her so well and we were very proud of all of them. John would even change a diaper. Casey and Dana wanted no part of that.

The nights were sometimes long, and it was hard for us to get back into the swing of having a little baby around. She woke us at about six o'clock in the morning, which was also hard to get used to. But before we knew it we developed a routine and were managing just fine. Eileen reduced her hours at the hospital to one or two days a week so she could spend more time with Catie. It was nice to have her home.

We put Catie in Dana's room, which was spacious enough for the crib and another dresser. Dana never woke up when Catie cried at night, but she would sometimes wake up with her at six o'clock in the morning and play with her until she started crying for her bottle. We called her Mama's Little Helper.

Casey just loved to hold the baby. That was his thing. He would sit in the big recliner and just hold her. Sometimes she would fall asleep in his arms, which made him feel really good. He would always say how cute she was and that he loved being a big brother again.

John still did everything he could to make baby Catie smile or even laugh if he could. I'd never seen so many funny faces come out of one child in my life.

CHAPTER 25

Several weeks passed without any encounters or new souls appearing in my field of view. All that changed on a Sunday night when we heard sirens and the sounds of many fire trucks passing our house and continuing down the road. I knew it was something big because I saw fire trucks from neighboring communities. I decided to get in the car and see if I could figure out what was happening. Something was calling me to the area where the fire trucks had stopped. It was an apartment building with about eight units in it, totally engulfed in flames. I was unable to stop and the police made me make a U-turn and head back home, but something told me I would be back.

The next day the headline in the paper read "Five people killed in apartment fire." This was huge news in a small community like ours. The apartment building was on the outskirts of town and was set up for lower income residents. A lot of them were elderly. I figured that the people on the top floor were probably the victims because of the intensity of the fire. The fact that they may have been older and unable to get out of the building fast would've sealed their fate.

I waited two or three days to wander back into the area, figuring it would take at least that long to investigate the fire. I was able to pull into a parking lot just adjacent to the apartment building. There were several buildings that had all been constructed at the same time by the government to house these low-income elderly people. I walked toward the building that was now just a charred shell.

As I walked closer to the front door, a fire inspector came out and asked me what I was doing there. I realized at that point I had jumped the gun. "I might be interested in rebuilding this apartment complex if it's salvageable," I said, thinking quickly.

"No, I'm afraid this place will have to come down," the fire inspector said. "There's just too much damage to the structural integrity of the building. Even the firewalls were weakened by the intensity of the flames. Plus, you'll never get the smell out of all the remaining units and the water damage is extensive."

I figured this was a good way to keep his interest while I looked around to see if I could find any lost souls. The fire inspector said, "I don't want you walking through the building but if you want to go around back that's the part that's least damaged."

I pushed past the damaged boards that come off the side of the house during the fire and squeezed between a fence and the mulberry bush and was able to enter the backyard area. I saw a familiar face sitting on the back porch. During my early years of working for the county I had a supervisor named Dan Smithson. He was a rugged old man when I worked with him. Back then, he was probably only in his early 60s, but when you're in your early 20's everybody over 35 looks old. He was in a wheelchair and partially obscured by the mist around him.

Dan looked very old now. He was obviously confined to the wheelchair and was probably in his early 80s. I approached the mist slowly and entered Dan's world with the usual shocking feeling.

Dan looked up at me from his wheelchair and said, "Is that you Scott?"

"Yeah Dan, it's me," I answered.

Dan looked a shell of himself, withered and worn down to a skinny old man with a weathered face. He'd worked outside all his life, and it showed. It was obvious to me that his body was giving out since he was forced to get around in a wheelchair.

"Dan, do you remember what happened here?" I asked, wondering if he had any clue of the tragedy that he was a part of.

"What's all this fog around me? And how did I get here on the back porch? I haven't been downstairs in ages. My son brings my groceries, and my daughter takes care of the apartment. I don't even remember seeing this back porch when I moved in. So can you tell me Scott, how the hell did I get back here?'

I realized Dan was more than confused about the situation. "Dan there was a big fire here," I told him. "Your apartment building is a total loss. The front units are completely gone, and your apartment was engulfed in flames. That leads me to tell you why I'm here. A while back I was given a gift, a gift that allows me to see souls who haven't crossed over to heaven yet. I've got something to tell you that you may not believe. You have passed away. You were killed in the fire here. Did you know the building was even on fire when you were in it?"

Dan looked very confused about the situation. His wheelchair looked old and barely had any rubber left on the tires. I could imagine the carpeting in his apartment must've been worn through from the constant movement of the wheelchair back and forth from room to room. "All I remember is going to bed last night and the next thing I know I'm back here on this damn porch. This part of the building looks fine. Can't you just get me upstairs to my apartment, Scott?"

I shook my head slowly. "You don't understand Dan. You have no apartment. It's completely gone. They're not sure where the fire started but it may have been in the apartment below yours. It looks like it went up through the floorboards and started your apartment on fire. You probably died of smoke inhalation and never woke up. That's why you don't remember the fire."

Dan still looked confused, maybe realizing that all of this confusion was justified because he had passed on. "So that's it. Just go to sleep one night and not wake up the next morning. Now that I think about it it's not a bad way to go at all. Mr. 'I got a gift' Man, tell me what's next? Am I supposed to sit here for the rest of eternity on this back porch looking out over all the weeds?" Dan always had a sense of humor when he wasn't complaining about something. He must've figured an eternity of looking over the weeds in the backyard was God's way of making a joke.

I told him, "Dan it's time for you to move on to a different place. That's what I'm here for, to help you get there. That's what I do now."

"I heard you were in a bad accident and that they didn't think you were going to make it," Dan said, looking up at me from his wheelchair. "I wish I could've come to see you in the hospital. But I've been stuck in that damn apartment for five years now. The only time I get to leave is for fricken' doctors' appointments. My son has to practically carry me down the stairs because I really can't support my own weight very well. That's why I've got the wheelchair. If I could've been there I would've. I'm just glad you made it out alive. Some of the old-timers that I worked with were amazed that you fought your way through it. Way to kick death's ass!"

I laughed. "Thanks Dan. It was a long road back but well worth it. Now I get to help people like you, an old friend, cross over into the light and see what your heaven looks like. What do you say we take a little trip Dan?"

"Why not?" Dan said. "It beats the hell out of looking at these weeds! What do I do next?"

"When you first got here on the porch, did you see a bright light?" I asked.

Dan pointed to the corner near an old rocking chair that looked like it hadn't been sat in for over 20 years. "The lights over there," he said. "It's been here since I found myself on the porch. I thought about wheeling over there, but just couldn't figure out what it was so I figured I'd better stay away from it. I'm not much of an adventurer anymore Scott. I used to like to take a risk every once in a while, but the older I got the less risk I wanted to take. I bet you're going to tell me the light is good?"

"Well Dan, let me give you a little hint. Go ahead and stand up. You can do it on your own because the light's here. So put those feet on the ground and push yourself up."

Looking apprehensive, Dan grabbed the sides of his wheelchair and slowly tried standing up. Then he suddenly shot out of the chair like he was 21. He flexed his knees a couple of times and was overwhelmed that they didn't hurt. He looked at me with amazement. "I haven't felt this good since I was a kid!"

I gave Dan a big smile and said, "Where we're going, you're going to feel that way all the time. No aches and pains. And you won't need that wheelchair anymore. What do you say we get our act together and start walking towards the light?"

Dan stepped over the leg rests on the wheelchair while turning to look at me. I took a step forward so that I was next to him, and we proceeded into the light. As we accelerated through the tunnel Dan's eyes widened and he looked over at me with a childlike wonder. We slowed, approaching the end of the tunnel, and the light became more intense. I could see the outline of my grandfather and a young woman standing next to him.

We came through the light and Grandpa welcomed both of us with open arms. "Dan, this is my grandfather," I said. "He helps me cross over people like you, people who are stuck between two worlds."

Dan reached out and shook Grandpa's hand but was fixated on the young woman standing next to him.

"I have longed for this day," he said. "The day Evelyn and I would be together again. And here she stands waiting for me. Evelyn, I've missed you. Why did you have to leave so soon?"

Grandpa pulled me to the side to let Dan and Evelyn talk. Grandpa said, "Evelyn died at 42 years old of breast cancer. Dan never got over it. He spent the rest of his life angry at God for taking his love away. He finished raising the children in his own and never remarried. There was only one love for Dan, and it was Evelyn. Evelyn has been waiting for him since she came to heaven. She has been dressed in that fine red dress since the day she crossed over. To her, only hours have passed.

To Dan that was a lifetime. As he grew older, he would look over the pictures of his broken family and try to remember the good times. But it was always hard for him to forgive God for taking Evelyn away. Now you know Dan's story."

"Dan didn't talk much about his personal life when we worked together. He was kind of quiet and only got loud when we would have a drink after work. He was kind of a mean drunk. There were a few times I remember pulling him out of bars because he was trying to pick a fight someone. Mind you he was in his late 50s or early 60s when this happened. He always seemed to have something eating away at him. Now I know what it was. It was his anger towards God. How do you change that kind of deep anger, Grandpa?"

Grandpa gave me a sheepish smile and said, "That's what Evelyn is doing right now. She's explaining to him that it was her time, that there was nothing Dan could have done to stop what happened. Anger doesn't transfer to heaven very well, especially pent-up aggression. The anger you saw earlier between Tom and Darnell was related to the taking of a life before its time. In this case, Evelyn lived her life until it was time for her to come over to the other side and so did Dan. So the anger he felt on earth has already been lifted here in heaven. Dan understands that things happen for a reason. The reason isn't always easily seen. Evelyn just explained it to him."

Dan turned to look at me and his face looked like it had lost 40 years. He looked younger than when I had worked with him. It was obvious Dan's body had reverted back to an earlier time, a time when he and Evelyn were in love. Dan waved goodbye to me and slowly walked hand-in-hand with Evelyn. They wandered through a beautiful meadow toward the mountains to a small cabin with flowers planted all around.

"Evelyn was quite the gardener when she was alive," Grandpa said. "And what gives you pleasure when you're alive is continued up here in heaven. She has the best garden she could possibly imagine and can't wait to show Dan. Their kids will be in the cabin as youngsters. They'll go back to a time when they were a young family."

Grandpa's descriptive powers were second to none, and he had drawn a beautiful picture of a life in heaven. He turned to me and said, "Well my son, how about if we take a little walk? I've got something I need to show you that will have to do with your next assignment."

As Grandpa and I walked along, a row of houses started to appear on the left-hand side of the path. When we got about halfway down the block, I recognized the house with the number 13 on the front of it. "Do you remember this place, Scott?"

As I looked at the house a flood of memories came back to me. This was my grandma and grandpa's house when I was a kid. We came over here to visit on holidays and sometimes just for fun. Grandpa used to build dollhouses in the basement and give them away to little girls. I was always much closer to my grandfather than my grandmother.

My grandmother had been kind of mean-spirited throughout her life. She had eight children and should have had none. She had her moments of softness and love, but they were few and far between. Now mind you, when I was a kid, she was a larger-than-life figure. She had also outlived my grandfather by some 30 years. She was in a nursing home now and was suffering from dementia. I hadn't spent much time visiting her because she no longer recognized me and would often get scared when a stranger entered the room. My mother spent as much time as she could with her, trying to get her to remember her life, but with little success. The last time I saw her she was curled up in the fetal position and was having some trouble breathing.

Grandpa looked at me and said "I know you weren't very fond of your grandma. She was a hard woman and was raised in a hard family. She unfortunately transferred those traits to her own family. But she wasn't always this way. When I met her I fell instantly in love with her and knew that she was the woman for me. We laughed a lot and had eight wonderful children. We also fought a lot and probably would have been divorced if they allowed that sort of thing back when we were married. But I still love her Scott, and she's almost ready to come up here. Sometimes people with dementia get caught between the worlds. I need you to be there when she dies so you can help her move along through the light. She will recognize you, but she may be confused as to what happened. After being in a subconscious state for so long she may not recognize the fact that she has passed away. I will give you the exact date and time that she will be leaving your world. If you could be there to help her, I would be in your debt. I'm looking so forward to seeing her the way I saw her the first time I met her. Can you do this for me, Scott?"

How was I supposed to say no to this wonderful man? He'd taught me so much in such a short period of time about how important the time you get on earth is. "Of course I'll help her. I know you think I wasn't fond of her, but the truth is I never felt like I got to know her. She was distant to me. I would've liked to know her when she was younger and more full of life, not after she had raised eight children and been beaten down by everything. But for you Grandpa, I would do anything. So what time and date do I need to be there?"

Grandpa pulled out a small piece of paper and put it in my left pants pocket, a note from heaven. He said, "It's time for you to go back now." and I found myself rushing through the tunnel and landing in a pile of leaves behind Dan's apartment. I walked through the side yard, noticing the inspector had left. I got in my car and started on my way home. When I'd pulled into the garage and turned the car off, I pulled the note out of my pocket. The paper had a slight glow to it and the writing on it was perfect. The penmanship would've made my second-grade teacher proud. The date he wrote was June 6 at 10:42 PM. I looked down at my watch and realized that was only two days away.

CHAPTER 26

I called my mother the next day and asked her if she had seen grandma in the past couple of weeks. She said she had just been there yesterday, and grandma had been having trouble breathing. She was un-responsive but my mother sat with her and read to her from one of her favorite books. My grandmother was an avid reader and basically had her own library. She installed her belief of the importance of reading in all her children.

Mom didn't know if Grandma could even hear the words, but figured if there was any life left in her she would enjoy hearing one of her favorite stories. I asked, "When do you think you'll get back there?"

"Maybe Sunday after church," she answered. It was Tuesday today and I knew that I needed to visit her on Thursday to keep my promise to Grandpa.

After getting home that evening I realized Grandpa had given me a task that may not be very easy. Grandma had dementia and was confused almost all the time. She didn't recognize me and unfortunately, she rarely even recognized my mother.

The time Grandpa had given me for her passing was after the customary visiting hours at the nursing home. I would have to figure out a way around this. Maybe I could justify my visit by telling them that I had a feeling she wasn't going to be around much longer. I'm sure they'd had times before where people stayed late when they thought a loved one was dying. Anyway, I would work it out. I debated whether or not to try to get my mom over there one more time before Grandma died. I then thought that they'd had a pretty good visit on Sunday, and she might be better off if she didn't see the death of her own mother.

I had to mention this one to Eileen because I was going to be out late on Thursday night, and I didn't want to catch any crap if you know what I mean. However, I thought due to all the things that had happened since the accident, she'd realize what I was doing.

Wednesday morning, I got up a little early so I could explain to Eileen what was going to happen the following night. I thought it was a beautiful thing that I was going to be there for my grandma when the time came to cross her over. Eileen expressed an interest in coming with, just to be part of the process. Even though this was something that I didn't clear with Grandpa, I've always wanted to know what happens to me during one of these more intense trips. Do I stay still and not move or am I in some sort of meditative state? My curiosity was getting the best of me, and I felt like it might be a good idea to bring Eileen so that she could tell me more about what I did while I was helping these souls. Though she'd seen me once when I'd helped her brother cross over, I was still very curious about what exactly happened to me when I was in the other dimension.

Again, I wasn't sure if this was something that would upset Grandpa but I guess I just wanted to know what my body was doing when I was having an out of body experience with such a close loved one. I asked Eileen if she would take notes in case, I said anything during the time I was involved in the process. I didn't know what was going to happen or whether or not she would be able to interpret what I was going through, but she was curious enough to want to watch, and I was curious enough to want her to.

Thursday night came and Eileen and I headed off to the nursing home. I felt strange going to see my grandma because I was never fond of her and wasn't that close to her. I kept thinking about what Grandpa had said about the early days when they met. I was excited to see her in a happy and loving state. Obviously, I didn't know her when she was young and he'd first met her. The pictures I had seen of both of them together were from an era when people rarely smiled for a picture. Those old photos made everyone look like they were having a bad day.

There was one photo that was taken kind of casually during a party at their house where they were both smiling and looking very much in love. This was obviously long before my time and I did not remember this grandma. She seemed to let the lights go out on herself and settle for an existence that she was not happy with. Don't get me wrong, she wasn't a mean person all the time, she just never seemed happy. I tried to think of that photo while we were on our way to the nursing home and hoped to see this young vibrant face with a big smile and her whole world in front of her.

We arrived at the nursing home at about seven o'clock. Visiting hours ended at 9:00, but I knew Grandma would start to have diffi-culty breathing or at least the process of dying would be starting at that point. I was afraid that my mother would show up at the nursing home. I called her just to see what she was doing, kind of as a cover for what I was doing. She said she was going to bed early because she didn't feel well. She said she had a little bit of a cold and figured the extra sleep would do her well. I said goodnight to her and knew that I was in the clear.

Grandma had a private room in the nursing home. Because she was confined to bed and physically could not get up anymore, there was no to keep the door locked. There were two high back chairs on either side of her bed. One of them reclined back and the other did not. Eileen took the recliner, and I took the other high back chair. I said hi to grandma, and as expected, got no reply. Her breathing was very labored. Her respiratory rate was kind of high and it seemed each breath was becoming more of a chore. She was lying on her side facing me. I ran my fingers through her gray hair and thought that in a matter of an hour or so she would be with Grandpa again.

Eileen and I talked about the kids and other things in our life for the first hour. I noticed a book on one of the shelves in grandma's room that I had remembered being in their house when I was a kid. The book had looked old then and now looked ancient. It was a novel by an unknown author, or least one I was unfamiliar with. The book was called Love United. It didn't seem like the kind of story I would pick up to read by any means, just based on the title. It seemed like a precursor to the Harlequin romances. But I guess Grandma liked it because she'd kept it for so many years.

I went over to the bookcase and snatched the book off the high shelf. Eileen knew my mother read to my grandmother on a regular basis and knew what I was going to do. For about an hour I read the first four chapters of this book. Love United was exactly what you'd think it would be. It was based on a soldier going off to war and the life he left behind. I'm sure Grandma related to it because she'd had the same thing happen to her when Grandpa went to war.

The first four chapters went a little slow, but I was actually starting to get into the story. Eileen seemed to be enjoying it too. I wasn't much of a reader and stumbled across many a word, but I managed to get through it. At about 9:30 one of the nurse's aides came by to mention to us that visiting hours were ending. I went out into the hallway with her and explained that I had a bad feeling. Grandma was breathing heavier than she ever had and was unresponsive. I told her, "I think she may go tonight, maybe sooner than later."

The nurse's aide understood what I was saying and mentioned that she had been getting progressively worse during the last 24 hours. She asked if we wanted to call anybody to be there with us in case she passed. I said I didn't think it would be a good idea. My mom wasn't feeling well, and this would just upset her even more to watch her own mother die. It would be better if she found out in the morning. The nurse's aide said she would have the doctor check in before he left. She said, "He usually isn't out of here till around 10 o'clock. I'll have him stop in and check on her and see how she's progressing."

As 10 o'clock approached I could see that grandma was starting to fade. I took her pulse, and it was pretty rapid. Her breathing had slowed down and she would have long pauses of about 30 seconds in between breaths. At 10:30 I turned her so she was lying on her back. I also switched seats with Eileen so I could recline back. I handed Eileen the paper that was given to me by grandpa, and she was amazed at the glow of the letters on the paper.

"That's the note Grandpa handed me in heaven," I said to her. "That's why the letters are glowing. You're looking at writing from heaven."

Eileen was shocked and almost dropped the note. "Why didn't you tell me this was written in heaven? I would've liked to have known that before you handed it to me!" We both kind of laughed about it and I looked at my watch.

"It's almost time," I said. "I should get ready." I wasn't sure what ready was because most of the people I had crossed over were already gone.

This was the first time I would be waiting for one. I reclined in the chair and looked one more time at my watch. Grandma's breathing had stopped, and her pulse was erratic. Within seconds her pulse was gone. It was exactly 10:42. I felt myself standing up but doing it without moving the chair from its reclining position. I stood at the foot of her bed and watched her spirit sit up and swing her legs over the side of the bed. She stood up on the floor, slowly putting on her slippers which had been under her bed for some time.

She turned towards me and seemed startled. "Scotty, what are you doing here? I haven't seen you in so long. How are the kids?"

"They're fine Grandma," I said. "But I'm here for a special reason. It may come as a shock to you but Grandpa asked me to help you. Grandma, turn around and look in the bed."

Grandma turned towards the bed and saw the shell of her old body lying there, lifeless. Her hand came up to her mouth in a surprised sort of look. She looked back over toward me and then back again at the bed.

"If I'm dead," she said in a shocked tone, "how can you see me? You're not dead, are you Scotty?"

I tried to explain. "Grandma, I've been given a special gift. After you went into the nursing home I had a real bad accident. I don't know if you remember any of it because you were already starting to suffer with Alzheimer's disease. I died several times on the table during surgery and since then I've been given the gift of helping people move from this life to the next."

Grandma looked kind of confused as to what she was hearing. "I could hear you reading my favorite book," she said, trancelike. It's been so long since I read it."

I turned to look at the book resting on the nightstand and caught a glimpse of Eileen still sitting in the chair looking at me in the re-cliner. She was writing furiously on her pad of paper. I assumed she was writing down everything I was saying.

I moved closer to grandma and asked her, "Do you see a bright light anywhere in the room Grandma?"

"Do you mean that light?" she said as she pointed to the corner of the room.

"Yes," I replied. "It's very important that we go into that light." Again, I got a glance of myself leaning back in the recliner and Eileen writing as quickly as she could. The colors and light in Grandma's room seemed to be fading into more of a gray than the original colors that were there when we walked in. I had never noticed that before in any of the other cases.

"The light is getting brighter," grandma said. "Do you see it there in the corner where my curio cabinet used to be?" The curio cabinet was still there but the bright light was obscuring it, at least in Grandma's eyes.

We walked over towards the light, but grandma hesitated. She turned back to look at her room and her frail body on the bed.

She glanced at Eileen and said to me, "You know she's the best thing that ever happened to you, right?"

"I know she is Grandma," I replied. "I don't know what I would have done without her during my recovery from my accident."

Grandma looked over at her books on the shelf and asked, "Can I take my books?

"Any book you want will be available to you in heaven, Grandma. Now it's time for us to go. There's a very special man waiting for you up there and he's very anxious to see you. He gave me the time and the place where you would pass on so that I could personally bring you back up to him."

Grandma looked at me with a smile, realizing that she was about to see the man that had left her in death some 30 years ago. Her eyes lit up and she said, "Can I have some time to get ready? I'd like to fix my hair and get my make up just right to see him."

I laughed and told her, "Grandma, by the time we go through the light, you will be taken back to a time when you felt most comfortable in your body and most in love with grandpa. It may be when you first met or just after you got married, we won't know until we get there. I don't think you need to worry about your hair or makeup."

She seemed to trust me at this point, and we walked toward the light. I looked back at Eileen who had stopped writing and now was looking at me in the recliner. It seemed like she was straining to hear what I was saying.

I turned back toward the light and grandma, and I stepped into it. The rush and intensity of going through the light seemed more intense than any of the previous times. I assumed it was because I was bringing up a very special loved one, or maybe because it was so soon after her actual death. As we got near the end of the tunnel, the light was brilliant. I could see Grandpa's outline just to the right of the light.

We burst through the light and Grandma was transformed. She looked about 22 years old, and her hair and clothing were perfect. Grandpa looked like he was in his mid-20s, wearing a suit and tie, with a smile on his face that was indescribable.

"Bill, I missed you so much! You've been gone so long! It seems like an eternity since I've looked upon your face," Grandma said excitedly.

Grandpa opened his arms, and she ran to him. Their hug was gentle but very genuine. They kissed ever so softly, and I saw a tear come down Grandpa's cheek.

Grandma took him by the hands and said, "What's next Bill? Do we get to see God?"

"All in good time my dear," Grandpa answered, "but Jesus is waiting to see us right now. We have to walk a little way and go through some times in your life. You will be enlightened and I'm ready to receive all the wisdom and answers we all get when we enter heaven. I have to tell you that some of the things you will see may be disheartening.

"We all have to be reminded that we were not perfect souls on earth. I'll be there with you the whole time to comfort you and get you through it. You may even see Scott in some of these memories. Scott had some issues with you and you need to know what they were and how you could've fixed them."

Grandma turned to look at me with tears in her eyes. "I know I wasn't the best Grandma," she said. "I wasn't really there for you when you were a child. I guess I had just given up on raising or being around children. I'm sorry for that, Scott. My anger overtook me and became a part of my life and for that I am regretful."

I offered her a big hug. She took it and whispered how sorry she was in my ear. "It's okay Grandma, I forgive you. I knew it just had to be something like you said, that you were tired of being around children.

But I am glad that you get to spend the rest of your time with Grandpa because that's when you seem the happiest."

Grandpa looked at me and said, "I'll take it from here Scott. We have a lot to see and even more to talk about. I can't thank you enough for making her transition easy. Sometimes the transition for Alzheimer's patients is difficult. Even though their faculties are restored, they sometimes don't recognize their environment because it has changed. They've usually been moved to a nursing home like your grandma was and can awaken in an environment that is so foreign to them that it sometimes takes days for them to recognize the light and go into it. You made the transition easy for her and I appreciate it. Now it's time for you to go back. Eileen is waiting for you. You've only been gone a short time, so you'll be able to handle the actual death of Grandma without too much grief. She will have just died when you return. You'll have to alert the nurses and make sure that they don't try to resuscitate her. She has a do not resuscitate sticker on her chart. Make sure they know about that. Now go back to Eileen and I'll see you the next time you come up."

The same cycle that I've gone through so many times started again. I was thrust into reverse, flying backwards through the tunnel and landed on the recliner. I turned to Eileen who was watching Grandma.

"She took her last breath about three or four minutes ago. I think we should go tell the nursing staff."

"What were you writing down so furiously?" I asked her.

"I'll show you later after we tell the nursing staff that she's passed away," she told me.

She shoved the notebook and her pen in her purse. We walked out together to the nursing station to find one nursing assistant on-duty for our area. I went to her and said, "I'm Mrs. Woodall's grandson and I'm afraid she's passed away. I know she was a DNR, so we don't want her resuscitated, but I don't know what we do next."

The nursing assistant got up came around the desk and gave Eileen and I a big loving hug. She had obviously dealt with this before and knew exactly what steps to take. She said, "Let me go in and check on her and make sure she is going to see Jesus."

This was obviously a woman who had a strong faith. We followed her into the room, and she gently put her stethoscope on grandma's heart. After listening for what seemed like at least two or three minutes, she wrapped her stethoscope around her neck, looked at us and said, "You're right, she's gone. The next step is getting the doctor back here to pronounce her dead and then we'll call the funeral home and have them come pick her up. You should be thinking about who you want to call and starting to make those calls now."

The first person I thought of was my mother and how she said she hadn't been feeling good. I really didn't want to bother her, but I felt obligated to. I picked up the phone and dialed her number. She answered with a groggy voice that sounded raspy.

"Mom," I said. "I'm at the nursing home with Grandma and I'm afraid she's passed away."

There was a pause on the other end of the line, and I could hear my mother starting to whimper ever so slightly. "Oh Scott," she sighed. "It makes me sad that she's gone but I'm glad she's no longer in pain or so confused. It's a blessing."

"At least she's with Grandpa now," I said. "And she's not confused anymore. She went very peacefully, mom. She was breathing rather slowly and then the breaths became further and further apart until they finally just stopped."

Grandma had eight children and I knew my mom had quite a few calls to make. I asked Mom which funeral home she wanted to use, then called them and said as soon as the doctor pronounced her dead, we would be ready for them to pick her up. All this occurred before midnight. They had obviously dealt with this many times before.

I said goodbye to Grandma, knowing where she was and how happy she was. As I watched the funeral director enter the room with the stretcher I decided it was time for us to leave. I briefly spoke to the funeral director saying I would be in tomorrow to sign whatever papers we needed and to set up the wake and funeral.

Eileen and I left the nursing home and started our ride back home. Eileen started the conversation by saying, "Scott, that experience was so different from when you helped Stephen cross over. I was closer this time, and it was the most amazing thing I've ever seen! You sat in that recliner and talked out loud to her spirit like she was standing right next to you. Your voice seemed to wander around the room as if you were walking with her but the whole time you were in the recliner. I heard you explain to her that she had passed away and I wrote down everything that you said. I can't believe how amazing that was!"

"When did I stop talking?" I asked, anxious to know. "What was the last thing I said?"

"The last thing I wrote down was you saying, 'It's time to go into the light.' Then you grabbed the arms of the recliner with what seemed like a death grip. You held on tightly for about 10 seconds and then you were silent and very relaxed. You didn't say anything until you looked at me after I had realized that she was gone."

This was enlightening to me. It appeared that as soon as I entered the tunnel, I became silent, which means that was where the worlds separated. This also made me think of all the people I have talked to on the side of the road for what seemed like 10 or 15 minutes before we crossed through the tunnel. I must look pretty funny standing there talking to myself. I guess I'm pretty lucky that no one has ever stopped, thinking I was off my rocker.

When we got home at Eileen showed me everything she had written down and it was almost verbatim, including the mention of Grandma's books. Eileen could not hear Grandma's voice, only mine; but could ascertain some of the questions I was being asked.

"You seemed to be leading her very gently and with great care to wherever you were going." Eileen said.

I began to give my description of the event. "She came out of her body the way I remember her before her confusion started. She was a little bit taken aback by what was happening but seemed to understand that she had passed on. I talked her through her concern about her books by telling her that the library in heaven would be immense and would have every book she ever wanted. She was also excited about seeing Grandpa. It'd been a long time since they had actually looked upon each other. Grandma appeared younger to him and Grandpa was genuinely moved by her presence."

Eileen was astonished by what I was telling her and seemed to be amazed to be in the presence of another one of these events.

CHAPTER 27

The next day I went to the funeral home and arranged for Grandma's wake and funeral. She had been sick for so long that it was no surprise to the family. My parents who were in their late 60s were still saddened by her death. They knew the old Grandma, the one that hadn't been beaten down by raising eight children and had experienced the early death of her husband. They also realized it was the best thing for her.

We held the wake in the late afternoon and evening and planned the funeral Mass for the following morning. As cousins, aunts and uncles, and many of Grandma's old friends filed past the casket at the wake, I realized that Grandma was the last of her group to pass away. All her brothers and sisters were gone, as were most of her friends. Still, our family was overwhelmed by the number of people who attended the wake.

The morning of the funeral was cold and damp. We gathered at the church that she attended most of her life and celebrated a Mass by one of her favorite priests. Her grandchildren participated in the Mass by performing the readings and bringing up the gifts. My mom and her brother each gave a short eulogy about what a wonderful mother she was and how they would miss her. After the Mass we all piled into our respective cars and proceeded to the cemetery.

As you can imagine, I was a little leery about a trip to the cemetery. I was afraid of what I might see and I didn't look around much. We laid Grandma to rest and had a small prayer session led by the priest. The finality of the cemetery service was very sad, but I knew in my heart that she was in a much better place. The luncheon after the funeral went off without a hitch and I got to visit with cousins I hadn't seen in quite some time. My mother gave the toast to my grandma and finished it with a "Rest in peace Mom, you deserve it."

On the way home from the luncheon I realized that there were so many ways to die. I felt like I had seen most of them with my new -- or should I say not so new -- gift. The deaths of young people are the toughest to deal with because it feels like they are dying without living a full life. These somehow seem to be the easiest ones to cross over. I assume it's because they realize their life was meant to be short and that when it was their time, they had somehow known about it. Sudden death in the more mature middle-aged group was a little more difficult. There was a feeling that they had been ripped off and weren't ready to go. They would miss out on grandchildren and other things you get to see in the golden years of your life. My grandma had made it way past the golden years into her late 80s and had very few friends left. She had lost a couple of her friends during her time of confusion and was unable to say goodbye. I'm sure they were waiting there for her in heaven, and she would be surprised to see them. After her reunion with Grandpa, I'm sure she was able to be with her friends and go back in time to a much happier, loving point in her life. I have truly forgiven her for not being the best grandma in the world. I guess I grasped an understanding of her personality and how it had changed over the years. Now she was free to live in the time of her choice and enjoy eternity in whatever way she pleased.

As I reflected on this special cross over, I wondered if this might be my last journey to the other side. But it soon became evident that I wasn't going to be the last trip I made.

I had paid for the headstone for Grandma and wanted to make sure that it had been installed properly and was what I wanted. I got up early a couple weeks after her funeral to go view the headstone and make sure everything was in its place. As I walked through the gate of the enormous St. Mary's Cemetery, I made a beeline for Grandma's plot. I could see the headstone had been installed but I wasn't close enough yet to it to make sure that the writing inscription had been properly done.

As I approached the headstone, I could see that they had gotten the name properly spelled and the dates were correct. The inscription read, "To the gates of heaven I commit my soul." It was all there, just the way Grandma had wanted it. I noticed that some of the grass seed they had put over the hole was starting to sprout and soon it would look like any other grave in the cemetery.

As I turned to leave, a small boy was standing directly behind me. He said, "Come and see my headstone, it's really pretty."

I knew immediately my work was not done and followed him over to his headstone. It was very old. It was a statue of a child-like angel with the inscription below that said, "God loves his children, and so he shall love ours."

The name on the gravestone was William Smith. He was born in 1931 and died in 1941. "I died a long time ago! I read your grandma's headstone and she died in 2011. That means I've been dead for a long, long, long time. I fell off the roof, you know."

I looked the boy I assumed was Billy and said, "How did you fall off the roof? You're too young to be on the roof, what were you doing up there?"

"It snowed a lot!" Billy exclaimed. "It was up to my chest! Me and my friends climbed onto the roof of the garage, and we were jumping off into the snow. I was standing on the top of the roof, and I slipped. I rolled down the roof and fell headfirst onto the driveway. I couldn't move my arms or legs and then my breathing was really hard. Then I went to sleep. When I woke up, I was in the cemetery standing next to my headstone. I looked around the cemetery and found all the new headstones to see how long I had been asleep. The latest one I saw was 1956. I had been sleeping for 15 years. I've been awake ever since." Billy paused for a second, seeming to think about what he'd say next. "I know I'm dead, but I don't know what to do. Do you think you can help me? There's no one to play with in the cemetery anymore they all went into their own bright light. My bright light is over there by my headstone. It scares me. so I don't want to go into it."

It dawned on me that Billy had been dead for some 71 years and had not been able to cross over due to his own fear of the light. "I saw my mom once," Billy said. "She looked very old. She came to put flowers next to my headstone and was crying. I tried to tell her I was okay, but she couldn't hear me. By the way, Mister, how come you can hear me and see me? No one else can."

I had to tell Billy the truth, so he'd be less scared of the light. "Billy, God has given me a special gift. He allows me to help people like you to go see him. That's what the light is for. That's how you go see him. We have to go into that light so you can see all your friends and your mom and dad who have probably crossed over to see God already."

"But I've always been afraid of the light," Billy said. "It just scares me and I don't know why. Sometimes I can hear pretty sounds coming from the light like birds, and wind. I almost went in once but got scared at the last minute and turned around."

Billy had obviously tried to get over his fear at least once but was still having trouble fully understanding what was on the other side of the light. I couldn't blame him; everything seems confusing when you're ten, especially going to heaven.

I suddenly thought of something Billy might like about the light. I was surprised I hadn't thought of this before.

"Listen, Billy, did you ever go really, really fast? Like on a roller coaster or in a car?"

Billy's face lit up." My dad took me to Riverview once and we went on the Bobs. I'll never forget how fast we went! It felt like we were flying!" he answered. He was talking about a famous amusement park in the Chicago area called Riverview. The Bobs was the biggest, fastest roller coaster there. The place was demolished in 1967, but it had been open when Billy was a boy.

"Well, Billy, when we go into the light, we'll go just as fast, if not faster than the Bobs. I'll hold your hand so you don't have to be afraid. I will help you get over to the other side to see all your friends and your mom and dad. Did you have any brothers or sisters?"

"I had two brothers and one sister," Billy said. "My sister was much older than me, she was like 17. My brothers were twins, and they were 14." I figured it was pretty safe to say that most of them had crossed over too. The chances of a reunion were pretty high, and I couldn't wait to see the look on Billy's face when he finally got to see his family and friends after all these years.

I said to Billy, "Let's head over there towards your tombstone and we'll see if I can help you get through the light to see everyone waiting for you on the other side."

"It won't hurt or scare me, will it?" he asked, still apprehensive.

"No Billy, I promise it won't. It will be like riding really fast in a roller coaster going through a tunnel."

"You're sure it won't hurt me? Because I don't like to get hurt. It hurt real bad when I fell off the garage and I've been very careful not to get hurt ever since."

Billy's fear was evident in his eyes. I said, "I promise you, it won't hurt one bit!"

H reached up with his hand and put it gently in mine. We walked toward his gravestone where he'd said the light was shining. It had started to rain, and I was pretty much soaked to the bone by now. Billy was soaked too.

He looked up at me just as we were about to enter what must have been the spot where the light was and said, "Don't forget, you promised it won't hurt."

"And I still promise," I said. Billy stepped forward and we were flying through the tunnel at the usual high rate of speed. Billy turned to look at me and had a big smile on his face with the excitement of a kid on his first rollercoaster ride. We stuck our arms out as if we were flying. The light at the end of the tunnel continued its brilliant intensity and as we entered it we slowed to a stop. Grandpa was on one knee as we passed through the light so he could be at eye level with Billy.

"Welcome to heaven, Billy! There are so many people waiting for you up here, you won't believe it!" Billy looked around and we noticed some 1930's style homes and cars parked on what appeared to be a street. He saw his bike leaning against the garage.

It was not a winter day, but a beautiful spring day. He stared at his bike and looked up at the roof of the garage, remembering what happened to him. The place look liked a Norman Rockwell painting with pansies growing along the side of the house, what seemed like a victory garden growing just off the side of the garage, and several pots with beautiful flowers growing in them. There was a 1930s era Buick in the driveway with oil stains spotting certain areas of the driveway where it had been parked. The windows in the house were open and I could smell a delicious dinner cooking.

"It smells like your mom's a great cook," I said to Billy. "I'm getting hungry just standing here!"

Billy laughed, seeming to know that things were as they had been in the past. He walked me up the back stairs of a house and opened the old-fashioned wooden screen door. I noticed Grandpa off in the distance enjoying the situation unfolding before him.

Billy and I went through the doorway to see a beautiful young woman standing by the stove cooking dinner. Billy ran up to her and laid a hug on her that resembled a linebacker tackling a running back. She hugged him and cried.

Billy's mom said, "We've waited so long for you to come see us again, Billy! But we knew someday someone would bring you to us. Everyone is here. Your brother and sisters, and of course dad is here too. We're going to the park to have a big picnic to celebrate you coming up here to heaven. You're going to love it here Billy, we get to do anything we want and be the family we always were."

I wasn't sure if Billy's mom could see me, so I stood back near the door and let her unveil the facts to Billy. Billy's mom asked him to get the picnic basket from underneath the cabinet. Billy practically ran over to the cabinet, snatched the basket out from underneath a stack of pots and pans, and quickly put it on the table.

"Your dad already took your brother and sisters down to the park while I finished cooking. You and I will walk down to the park with all the food and have a great feast to celebrate you coming up here to heaven!" she told him. Billy wandered around the kitchen looking for the essentials for a picnic. He asked his mom what blanket he should get. His mother told him that dad had already brought the blanket down to the park.

"I need you to carry all the utensils and the napkins in this basket Billy."

Billy loaded up the basket with the utensils and napkins and asked his mom, "Should I bring some glasses to for drinks?"

Billy's mom said "Well, I almost forgot! It sure is a good thing you showed up. We need something to drink down there too. Looks like you're going to have your hands full, Billy!"

As Billy climbed on the little step stool and reached up and to the cabinet, he retrieved five glasses. It was at this point that Billy's mom's eyes made contact with mine. She whispered under her breath, "Thank you."

Billy picked up the glasses and the picnic basket and said, "All set to go mom!" Mom was finishing loading up her basket with what looked like toasted cheese sandwiches and some sort of noodle dish. They headed toward the front door, not bothering to lock the back door or close any of the windows. It must've been great to live in a time where you never had to worry about these things.

Billy turned and looked at me and said, "Are you coming with Mister?"

"No Billy, I have to get back," I told him. I realized I hadn't told him my name. "By the way, I'm Scott. And I want you to have a great time up here in heaven!"

"Thanks, Scott," Billy cried as he and his mom left through the front door. Billy held the picnic basket in one hand and held hands with his mom with the other. Billy's mom had a lift in her step as if there could be no happier person in the world.

I watched as they turned the corner and disappeared from sight. I wandered through the house and out the back door to find Grandpa standing at the bottom of the stairway. I looked at him and said, "Is this really what it was like back when you were a kid?"

He smiled and said, "Much simpler times, don't you think? We didn't have all the worries you have. We also spent much more quality time with our families. No computers or cell phones to screw things up. We came home when the streetlights came on and everyone had dinner together. During the school year you did your homework and were in bed by nine o'clock. My mom was always there to greet us at the door when I got home from school and my dad would toss us up in the air when he got home from work. Like I said, much simpler times."

I shook my head. "Makes me wish I had lived back then. I think I would've enjoyed the quietness and less stressful atmosphere. But who knows, I've grown kind of attached to my cell phone."

"You would've gotten along just fine without it," Grandpa said. "Your generation doesn't have time to do anything other than run your mouths. I know some of that is necessary, but most of that is just crap."

I couldn't argue with him because he was 100% right. Seeing his generation had opened my eyes and exposed me to a much simpler side of life. I vowed that when I got back, I would use my cell phone less and communicate more on a face-to-face basis.

All too soon, the inevitable time came. "Come on Scott it's time for you to go. I know you want to spend more time here, but you've got other things to do."

Grandpa and I walked back towards the area where the light had been. It started to brighten as I got closer and Grandpa said," Something is about to happen to you that will shake you to the core. You must be strong during this time. You know I'll be here for you and will always be in your heart."

As I started to question what Grandpa had meant, I found myself flying backwards through the tunnel and landing back in the cemetery. It had stopped raining, and the sun was out. The ground was still wet, and I could see the drops of water running down Billy's gravestone. I slowly turned away and walked toward my car. I had no idea what Grandpa meant but his words haunted me. "Shake you to the core" kept rattling around in my head. I wondered about my own health and whether I was heading for another setback. I didn't know if I could make it through another health issue. I had been through so much that I felt that one more major ordeal would put me over the edge.

CHAPTER 28

I got home to find everyone getting ready for dinner. My beautiful bride was standing by the stove cooking her world-famous chicken casserole and all the kids were excited about it. I had grown to love it too. It was one of those special meals that no one complained about and everyone ate. A gallon of milk was hoisted onto the table, and everybody dug in.

Eileen asked me how it went at the cemetery. I didn't even know she knew where I was going. "I saw you looking around and staring at that one headstone during your grandma's funeral. I assumed you saw something or someone, so I figured you were going back today to see if you could make things right for them. So how did it go?" She said all this in a whisper so the kids couldn't hear what was going on. Not that they would notice, they all looked like sharks during a feeding frenzy.

"Tell you later," I whispered back.

Before we knew it the casserole dish was empty, and everybody was sitting back in their chairs like they had just been stuffed to the gills. We all talked for a while about how they'd spent their day.

The days were getting hotter and since we had replaced our old pool with an in-ground model, the kids were spending most of their days jumping in and out of it. John was like a fish. Getting him out of that pool was almost impossible. We'd spent quite a bit of money to have them put in an in-ground pool, but it also was good therapy for me. In the pool I could work my muscles without gravity interfering. I did a lot of water walking and stretching my damaged muscles trying to get as much range of motion back as I could. I had a hot tub installed next to the pool that was very therapeutic for my broken body. There was enough room in the hot tub for all of us and sometimes we'd even go out there at night just to relax before bed. It was one of the few things I'd splurged on with the money we received from the settlement.

As the summer days got hotter the pool became the neighborhood's hotspot. I acted as unofficial lifeguard watching that the roughhousing was kept to a minimum. That wasn't easy with a bunch of 14-year-old boys jumping in and out of an in-ground pool. There was always some sort of game going on and I was the official ball retriever for when the ball flew out of the pool. It was good exercise for me, so I didn't mind.

Casey and Dana also enjoyed the pool and sometimes had a hard time navigating around all of John's friends. When the pool was empty I took little baby Catie in there and let her splash around as much as she wanted. She was smiling all the time and was getting so big. We had a little blowup seat for her and would push her around the pool. She loved it.

Casey and Dana would also have their friends over and sometimes we would have a whole pool full of kids. Eventually I had to limit the number of friends they could invite over.

Eileen enjoyed lying out and working on her tan on her favorite raft floating around the pool. She would sometimes even fall asleep while lying out in the sun. I loved to float on my back and just enjoy the serenity of having the water surrounding me without the effects of gravity on my body. I'd say it was a great investment to get the pool. Or at least that's what I thought.

It turns out that a pool is a lot of work. It felt like I had to be a chemist to figure out the pH and all the other levels that needed to be precise to keep the pool water looking clear instead of like pond scum. There was the constant on and off of the solar cover. Somehow I managed to keep on top of the balancing act.

John had planned a pool party for a bunch of his friends before they went back to school. We were getting hamburgers and hot dogs ready, along with every other snack food known to man. John even helped get everything ready by making sure all his friends knew what time and date the party was so we didn't have to send out invitations.

Boys are great when it comes to sending out invitations, you don't really need to do it. They just tell their friends and they all show up.

August 15 came and by mid-afternoon we had a pool full of kids. John let Casey invite his friends so they could have even basketball and volleyball teams in the pool.

Things were going pretty well. All the boys had just finished eating and were ready to get back in the pool. Of course when I say getting back in the pool I don't mean walking down the ladder and slowly walking into the pool. I mean 15 cannonballs at once. I was lucky we had any water left in the pool. The roughhousing began and before I knew it a full basketball game had broken out. The only problem with basketball in the pool is that the basketball doesn't stay in the pool. Someone always had to get out of the pool and get the ball. If you were the last one to touch it you were the one who had a go get it.

I moved my chair over to the side of the hoop in hopes of kicking the ball back into the pool every once in a while. It worked a few times, and I did get up and get the ball several times, but after a while it got to be a little much for me. I decided to go in for a little bit and cool off. I issued the standard dad warning about roughhousing in the pool and getting hurt. I'm sure none of them heard me that they all waved to pacify me. I went inside to the cool air conditioning and sat back in my recliner with my feet up. Eileen was downstairs working on the endless supply of laundry and volunteered to go out and sit with the boys as soon as she finished folding the last load.

I was just starting to doze off in my recliner when the door flung open and Casey was yelling that John got hurt. I quickly got out of my recliner and hobbled to the door but Eileen had beaten me to it.

John was laying face down in the pool with blood around his head! Two of his friends were trying to turn him over and hold his head up. I jumped in the water and got him over to the shallow side of the pool, determining he was unconscious. I lifted him up on the side of the pool and realized he wasn't breathing.

Eileen, being a nurse, sprang into action and immediately started trying to get John to breathe with mouth-to-mouth resuscitation. I quickly went inside and dialed 911. I told them we were doing CPR on John and they said they would have someone there within minutes. I hung up the phone and ran back out to the pool.

Eileen had laid John on his side where he had thrown up all over the side of the pool and seemed to be breathing on his own. He was still unconscious though. We tried to wake him to no avail.

The ambulance showed up in what seemed like only minutes. They quickly strapped John to a backboard and stabilized his neck. He was still bleeding quite a bit from the back of his head. They put gauze on the wound and wrapped his head to stop the bleeding. I heard one of the paramedics radio in that there was a skull depression on the back of the head.

Eileen shot a panicked look at me and said, "That's not good. He probably has a skull fracture!"

They loaded him into the ambulance and helped him breathe with one of those bags that is put over the mouth and nose. They told us what hospital they were going to and we quickly got in the car to follow them. Our neighbor helped called kids' parents to come pick them up.

We blew through every red light that the ambulance did and made it to the hospital just as the ambulance was backing into the emergency room stall. They unloaded John and were rushing around him at a great pace. We knew our boy was hurt bad. We followed them into the ER and were stopped by one of the nurses at the front desk asking us to wait until they got him settled before we went in.

We gave them the necessary information for our insurance while we were waiting for the approval to see him. The action around John's room was intense and there were machines and physicians flying in and out of the room so fast it was nearly a blur. We were ushered to a small waiting room and asked to sit down and wait for one of the doctors to come talk to us.

This is the most painful part I think of having a severely hurt child. The time we spent waiting seemed like an eternity. Finally, a young doctor came out of the room and headed toward us. He didn't look much older than John. He introduced himself and said he was the chief resident of the ER staff and was sent out to give Eileen and me an update.

"It appears he has a skull fracture with the possibility of some significant bleeding in the brain," he said. "We're taking him to CAT scan right now to get a better idea of what's going on. It should only take us about half an hour but this is very important, so we know how to proceed. I can't promise you anything right now, it's too soon to tell, but a few prayers wouldn't hurt."

Eileen rested her face in my shoulder and began to cry. I felt the tears streaming down my face too. How could this happen? I was only gone for five minutes. He must've slipped when he was jumping in the pool and slammed his head against the side of the wall. I guess it would've happened whether I was there or not, but the guilt was still overwhelming.

They brought him back from CAT scan and were still hovering around him doing all sorts of things I didn't understand. Eileen had some idea of what was going on and how serious things were, even though the emergency room wasn't her area. The same doctor came out to talk to us about the CAT scan.

"Okay, folks, a skull fracture was confirmed by the CAT scan and there is some bleeding in the brain. His neck and back are fine, which is great news. A lot of these kids come in with broken necks. The skull fracture and the bleeding are pretty significant, though. We've already put a call in to the neurosurgeon, who is on his way to the hospital right now. We're going to get him prepped to go down to surgery. But I must be honest with you, there is a chance he won't make it through the surgery. I have to tell you this even though I think and pray he'll do just fine. It already looks like they're ready for you guys to go in and see him."

We practically ran to the room where they were still removing equipment and putting IVs in John's arms. They had wrapped a new bandage around his head and the blood was still coming through it. We were able to get to the head of the bed. A nurse told us they had to get him down there fast.

"Give him a kiss and tell him you love him," she said briskly, as if she did this every day. We did what we were told, but I couldn't help thinking how fragile his body looked at this moment. We watched as they wheeled him out and ran down the hallway with him toward the elevator.

Eileen was almost inconsolable by this time, and I wasn't far behind her. A chaplain from the hospital took us up to the surgical waiting room and offered to get us coffee. I know he was trying to be nice but the last thing I could think about was coffee. He sat with us for a while and even though I wasn't much of a praying man, I sat with him and Eileen and we all prayed together. He asked us if we wanted anything else and gave us his pager number and told us to call him at any time if we needed him.

A nurse came out of the operating room and called our names in the waiting area. She said, "I just want to let you know this is going to be a long operation. He could be in there for as long as eight hours. We hope it'll be less, but we want you to know ahead of time that this is going to be a long haul." We thanked her for the information and sat back down with our hands covering our faces.

Eileen called home to check on the kids who were being watched by her sister Mary. She told Mary that John was in surgery and his head injury was pretty bad. I heard her start to cry and try to explain that it could be up to eight hours before they would know anything. Mary was obviously consoling her on the phone, although it wasn't working very well. Eileen hung up with her and came over to me to say the children were okay and that Mary would take care of them as long as we needed.

Nothing slows time more than waiting for a loved one to get out of surgery. The clock seemed to crawl along at a slow, painful pace. About two hours into the surgery a nurse came out to give us an update. She told us that the bleeding in John's brain was not as bad as they thought it would be. The skull fracture was severe and would require them to wire the pieces of the fracture together. She said that the procedure might last a couple of more hours and then he would be placed in the intensive care unit after surgery.

After 2 ½ hours the neurosurgeon came out of the room slowly taking off his surgical cap. I noticed that he was covered in sweat. He called our names and walked over to him quickly. The doctor said, "Are you John's parents?" We both nodded our heads, almost afraid to answer. He said, "We got the bleeding under control and fixed a skull fracture with some wires. I also must tell you that his heart stopped once during the procedure. We were able to get him back with one shock and he did fine for the rest of the surgery. It must've been the overall trauma to the brain that caused this to happen. I'm not worried about it because he wasn't down that long. It's not unusual for something like this to happen after a head trauma. He'll be unconscious for a few days because we want to keep him in a coma to help reduce the brain swelling and keep him as stable as possible. He'll be in intensive care for about three or four days and then we'll try to get him to a regular room after we wake him up. Don't stop praying either; he's not out of the woods yet." The surgeon shook both of our hands and went on to his next case. Eileen and I hugged for a while knowing that there was at least a chance now that John would be okay.

It was hard to look at him in intensive care. He had a huge bandage around his head and his eyes were swollen shut. His facial features were distorted by all the swelling. We knew this would go down with time, but it was still hard to look at our little baby in this way. They monitored his heart, had a pressure gauge on his head to monitor the brain's internal pressure and had him on a ventilator. I sat there for hours at a time watching his chest go up and down. Eileen and I would take shifts spending three or four hours each at his bedside.

One day turned into two and two into three. On the third day they decided to start weaning him out of the induced coma. He started to move his limbs and became a little restless. The swelling around his eyes had reduced significantly but he still looked swollen overall. We held his hands and talked to him telling him he'd be okay and that he'd had surgery on his head. He was still so weak from the surgery. They slowly started to wean him off of the ventilator and it soon became obvious he could breathe on his own. This was a huge relief to us because the one thing that he was fighting the most was the ventilator. They took the tube out of his throat on the fourth day. When he finally woke up, he first thing out of his mouth was, "What happened?"

We told him he had been running by the pool slipped and fell and whacked his head on the way into the pool. His friends got him out of the pool as quickly as they could, but he wasn't breathing and obviously had hurt his head pretty badly.

John nodded with a wince and said, "Will I be okay?"

With tears in our eyes, we told him we were lucky to have him back and that he would be fine. He smiled through his swollen face and faded back to sleep.

As the days went by John perked up even more and began eating slowly. He loved milk shakes and soft foods because they were easy on his throat, which was sore from the breathing tube. They moved him out of intensive care after the fifth day to a regular room. They took the bandages off his head to change them, and John was amazed at his new haircut. He'd had a full head of hair and was now down to a buzz cut. The scar on the back of his head was very large. But we knew the hair on his head would cover it up.

John started physical therapy on the sixth day. They brought him a walker and got him up out of the bed and walked him out into the hallway. He walked only a short distance and asked to turn around and go back. He got back in the bed and looked exhausted. I told him that this was normal because he had been immobile for so long and reminded him of how tired I was after my accident.

The physical therapist came up twice a day and John progressed, eventually getting down to the end of the hallway and back. He complained of a little bit of dizziness. By the eighth day John was itching to go home. The neurosurgeon said it would be a day or two before he could go. This made John a little depressed, but I told him it was necessary to make sure he was ready to go home.

He was now taking regular meals and walking without the walker. The physical therapist put a belt around his waist just to hold onto him while he was walking. With time he wouldn't even need that.

John was counting down the days until he could go home and was determined to hold his doctor accountable for his promise of one to two more days. The neurosurgeon came in on the tenth day and told John he could go home that afternoon. John immediately gathered all his stuff, everything from his clothes to his video games, and had it all packed in about a half an hour. We had to pretty much tie him to the bed to keep him there for the couple more hours that they need to discharge him.

The nurses came in with instructions from the doctor about changing the dressing and keeping an eye out for certain signs that might indicate he was having trouble. They told us to watch for slurring his speech or sleeping a lot. Now as you know, most 14-year-olds sleep till about noon in the summer so I didn't know how we would gauge this. They said check on him and just wake him up every couple hours to make sure he was okay. We also had an appointment to see the neurosurgeon three days after John's discharge. We signed all the papers for the discharge and John was dressed and ready to go in a flash. It'd been the longest ten days in my life. This was by far much more painful to watch and be a part of than my own accident.

I went out to the parking lot to retrieve the car to pick up John and Eileen at the front of the hospital. On my way out there I couldn't help but think that Grandpa had a hand in this. I didn't know when I would get to see him again but I definitely was going to thank him for pulling John through this mess.

I pulled up to the front of the hospital and several of the ICU nurses and some of the floor nurses were there to applaud John for making it through what had to be a near-death experience. John got up and waved at the crowd like he was a rock star. I slowly helped him into the car and closed the door behind him. I walked up to the staff that had gathered and thanked them for everything they did. Tears were rolling down my face because without these people I knew I wouldn't have my son John anymore. Eileen did the same, hugging every nurse and doctor she could find. John sat in the car with this look on his face like. "Come on let's get going!" Eventually, Eileen and I both made our way to the car. We slowly pulled away from the hospital and were on our way home.

We set up everything that John would need in his room at home. I brought up the old TV from downstairs and hooked up his Xbox 360 to it. We put a tray table by the side of his bed, and of course the first thing he wanted was another milkshake. I had never seen a kid consume so many milkshakes in a 10 day period as I had seen John do. He would play Xbox for a while but I think focusing on the TV still hurt his eyes a little bit. So he could play for about an hour and then would have to rest for a while.

He would come downstairs for meals and sit at the kitchen table with all of us. Casey and Dana had been pretty shaken up by the whole ordeal and pretty much acted like his personal waitress and waiter during the meals. We didn't let them visit him in the hospital until after he was off the ventilator because he was just too sick for them to see. It'd still shaken them up quite a bit so now that he was home, they made their best effort to make sure he was comfortable. They were just happy to have their big brother back.

John had a steady stream of friends coming in and out of the house to visit him. Some of them were girls, which gave me reason to give him a hard time about it. He always said they were just friends but that didn't stop me from teasing them about it. I just wanted to see him laugh, that's all I cared about.

Three days passed rather quickly, and it was time for John to go back and see the neurosurgeon. His office was in the professional building next to the hospital, so at least John didn't have a long ride to endure. We got in the office and signed him in and the receptionist said "We heard all about his story! We sure are glad to see you here John. Dr. Johnson was pretty worried about you."

"I feel pretty good right now," John said. "I'm just a little dizzy every once in a while."

"If that's the only symptom you're having, that's pretty good," the receptionist encouraged him.

We waited about a half an hour to see Dr. Johnson. I'd had a fear that we'd sit there for two hours and John would get weak, but we were called into the exam room and Dr. Johnson came in within a couple of minutes. He had John's chart in his hand and it looked like a small book.

"So how's our little miracle patient doing?" he asked.

John said, "I feel pretty good except I get a little dizzy every once in while. Sometimes my head hurts near the incision. Can we take these staples out?"

Dr. Johnson said, "Yes we'll take them out today but it might hurt a little bit." John waited patiently as Dr. Johnson went to get the staple remover. Of course I was picturing the one that sat on my desk at home thinking how that was going to work.

The doctor came in with a kit that looked completely different from what I'd pictured. It took him a while to remove all of John's staples, but John was a real trooper and even though his eyes got a little misty he never really cried. Dr. Johnson told John that the dizziness would go away probably within a week.

We made an appointment at the front desk to see Dr. Johnson in another week. John and I walked to the car and started to make our way out of the parking lot.

In a thoughtful voice, John said, "Dad can I tell you something? It might sound kind of goofy but I just want to see if you had the same thing happen to you when you got hurt."

I had no idea where this was leading but I figured I needed to listen because it sounded kind of important to him. John said, "I could see myself in surgery! I was floating above the doctors and nurses and could see Dr. Johnson pushing on my chest. Then in the corner of the room I saw a bright light. I didn't know what it was but I felt myself going towards it. When I went into the light I was rushed through a tunnel really, really fast. The light kept getting brighter and brighter. When I came through the light on the other side of the tunnel there was an older man waiting for me."

At this point my heart was racing and about 140 beats a minute knowing what he was going to say next. "He said he was your grandpa. I remember seeing his picture on the wall in our hallway and I told him we had a picture of him in the house. He was smiling and I noticed that my head didn't hurt, and I felt really, really good. Then your grandpa asked me if I knew where I was."

By now I could hardly keep the car on the road, so I pulled over in the parking lot at the edge of the hospital. John continued. "He said I was in heaven! But it wasn't my time to be there. He said I had to go back and live the rest of my life before I could come back and see him. He gave me a hug and it felt so warm, and ...Dad, I have to tell you I didn't really want to leave. It was so nice up there and I knew beyond where Grandpa was there were so many nice things. I couldn't see them, but I could feel them. The only thing I could see was your grandma standing behind Grandpa smiling."

John knew my grandma before she started suffering from Alzheimer's disease and remembered her being kind to him. "She didn't say anything to me dad, she just stood there smiling. Then your grandpa said that I would see them again someday, but I needed to go back. It felt like I was being sucked back into the tunnel backwards and I was going just as fast as I was when I went into the tunnel. Then I could see the surgeons again and landed on the table and fell back asleep. The next thing I knew I was waking up and saw you and Mom."

We had been sitting in the parking lot for about ten minutes while John relayed the story to me. As the story unfolded I could see Grandpa hugging John and sending him back to me. I wanted one of those hugs.

I explained to John that what he had was a near death experience. People describe them all the time when their heart stops and the doctors have to revive them. Up until this point we had not told John that his heart had stopped during the surgery.

John said, "I was dead for a little while?"

It was hard for me to answer. "Yes John, only for a minute. The doctors were able to bring you back pretty quickly. I'm glad they got you back, I don't know what I would do without you."

John looked reflective and stared out the window finally realizing what had happened to him. We made our way home with very little verbal exchange. I asked John if he wanted to talk about it some more and he said not right now. I let it go at that and we made our way home.

That night lying in bed I relayed the story to Eileen. She sat there totally silent looking at me and wondering why her little boy had been put through this. I said, "Maybe because of my relationship with Grandpa. He got the chance to experience something very few people do. It really is a gift. He got to see heaven only for a brief moment, but at least now he knows it's there."

To say Eileen was taken aback by this would be an understatement. She asked me if she could talk to him about it.

"I don't see why not," I said. "He opened up to me and probably will open up to you to. I'm not sure if he's come to grips with the whole ordeal but it's definitely worth a shot."

A week went by and John's dizziness disappeared. He was anxious to get back to doing the things he had done before the accident but was on some pretty strict restrictions from the doctor. I kept telling him his skull had to take time to heal and reminding him of how severe his injury was.

John's appointment to see Dr. Johnson came up pretty quickly. We went to the doctor's pavilion next to the hospital just like before. Dr. Johnson looked at John and was very happy with his progress. He lightened up on the restrictions but told John that he still couldn't play any sports. He said his fractures were healing well and that he was glad that there were no more symptoms.

"You really dodged a bullet here, pal," Dr. Johnson said. "I hope you know that." John nodded his head in a typical 14-year-old response. He begged Dr. Johnson to let him go back to swimming. Dr. Johnson said "Let's wait a couple more weeks before we do that. You're just going to have to be a spectator until then."

John and I left the office and decided to get ice cream on our way home. It was a little out of the way but a fitting celebration for John's good news. As I turned onto Route 30, I noticed a roadside memorial just past the 50-mile marker on the right. I could see a man standing in the fog looking down at the memorial. At that moment I knew I'd have to come back later in the afternoon and see if I could help him cross over to the other side. Right at that moment John turned to me and said, "Hey, Dad, why is that guy standing there by that cross? And why is all that fog around him?"

The End

Copyright 2024 by Scott Moss